D0340336

THE
RISE OF
THE
OUTSIDERS

ABOUT THE AUTHOR

Steve Richards is an award-winning political commentator, writing columns for the *Guardian* and the *Independent*. He presents BBC Radio 4's *Week in Westminster* and is a regular guest on BBC1's *Sunday Politics*. He has also presented a series of unscripted BBC talks, *Leadership Reflections*, profiling modern prime ministers. He was formerly the political editor of the *New Statesman*, a BBC political correspondent and presenter of ITV's *Sunday Programme*.

STEVE RICHARDS

THE RISE OF THE OUTSIDERS

How Mainstream Politics Lost its Way

Atlantic Books
London

Published in hardback and trade paperback in Great Britain
in 2017 by Atlantic Books, an imprint of Atlantic Books Ltd.

10 9 8 7 6 5 4 3 2 1

A CIP catalogue record for this book is available from the British Library.

Hardback ISBN: 978 1 78649 201 2
Trade paperback ISBN: 978 1 78649 142 8
E-book ISBN: 978 1 78649 143 5

Printed and bound by CPI Group (UK) Ltd, Croydon, CR0 4YY

Atlantic Books
An Imprint of Atlantic Books Ltd
Ormond House
26–27 Boswell Street
London
WC1N 3JZ

www.atlantic-books.co.uk

CONTENTS

INTRODUCTION

A pattern forms. There are many jagged edges and there is no neat uniformity, but across much of the democratic world, outsiders trigger volcanic political explosions, in some cases by winning power or by forcing more mainstream governments to change direction, with historic consequences.

The outsiders are varied, but in an era of vague slogans and assertions they are easily defined. Some are from the right and some from the left, but they come from outside orthodox mainstream democratic politics. A lot of them are not elected to their national parliament. Most of those who are elected have not been close to government. That is what makes them 'outsiders', or allows them to claim to be from the outside. What is relatively new is that the outsiders have made waves in supposedly robust liberal democracies across the Western world. Their rise is explored in this book.

The pattern started to take vivid shape when UKIP (the UK Independence Party) secured more votes than any other UK party in the European elections in the summer of 2014. At the start of 2015 the left-wing party Syriza won the election in Greece. During the rest of 2015 support for far-right parties across the European Union (EU) start to increase significantly, a rise that had begun several years earlier. In Spain and Portugal left-wing parties appeared from nowhere and shook up the political landscape. In the UK general election in 2015 the SNP (Scottish National Party) won virtually every seat in Scotland, nearly wiping out the once-dominant Labour Party. And in its leadership contest in 2015 the UK's Labour Party elected the left-wing rebel, Jeremy Corbyn, to be its new leader. The veteran Corbyn won a landslide. In the same year Marine Le Pen's Front National made huge gains in local elections, coming first in six of France's thirteen regions. In 2016 the UK voted to leave the European Union, against the advice of the prime minister, all living former prime ministers, the leader of the Opposition and President Obama. A few months later Donald Trump was elected President of the US, as Obama's successor. Trump was a supporter of Brexit – the proposition that the UK should leave the EU – and had accurately proclaimed during his campaign that Brexit was a sign that he would win, too. The voters were in revolt against their traditional rulers.

The pattern of volcanic significance takes firmer shape when turning to the mainstream. Many mainstream parties have suffered a crisis of identity that partly explains the rise of the outsiders, and in turn boosts their ascendancy further. In the US, Democrats wonder how they failed to connect with once-reliable supporters in the presidential election in 2016. Republicans do not know whether to celebrate a presidential victory or distance themselves from it. The UK Labour Party has held two leadership contests since the 2015 election and has elected the same leader on both occasions – whacky behaviour that is a symptom of deep unease. The UK Conservative Party lost a prime minister a year after he unexpectedly won an election, and staged its own bizarre leadership contest that was over within days – as much a symptom of deeper unease as Labour's conduct. In Germany, Angela Merkel was forced to change her approach to the asylum crisis not because she believed she was wrong, but because her party panicked about the electoral consequences. In France, President Hollande did not dare to stand for a second term, fearing that he would be annihilated. And the former President Sarkozy failed in his attempt at a comeback – part of the recent past that is near-fatal terrain for mainstream leaders. In the US, Hillary Clinton was not helped by her surname and by her own vocation as a long-serving politician. In Greece, mainstream parties on the left and right agonize about their purpose, after ruling together. Many coalition partners across Europe suffer the same neuroses, as they look nervously to the left and right of their own vaguely defiant positions.

The jagged edges of the pattern are important, too. Outsiders across the democratic world are intimidatingly strong and yet transparently weak. They win power. They bring about historic change. They influence policy, even when still distant from securing national power. These are extraordinary achievements for political novices, like winning Wimbledon or the US Open, having played only a few games at the local park. Yet in most cases the outsiders are pathetic, fragile, inconsistent, inexperienced and often quite silly, the last quality being especially dangerous for those wishing to be taken seriously on the political stage. They espouse causes erratically and have no secure base on which to build. Their purpose is often unclear and the internal divisions are played out in public. As politicians, they are both mighty and hopeless.

Perhaps the ambiguity of their powerful and weak position explains why each time an outsider wins an election or secures a significant increase in support, nearly everyone appears to be taken aback: voters, the media and sometimes the bewildered outsiders themselves, responding to success they had not anticipated or prepared for. On one level, the fragilities are so deep that there is cause for astonishment each time an outsider rises from nowhere. On another level, the surprise is that any of us are still surprised. The pattern forms in front of our eyes.

Across much of the democratic world, large numbers of voters are turning away from mainstream politicians and looking to those who come from the 'outside' to rescue them from tumultuous change. Some outsiders soar from the left as well as from the populist right. A few of them rise fleetingly, only to decline just as fast when fatal flaws are exposed. On occasions, mainstream parties or individual liberal progressives get their act together and win elections with a confident flourish. The US elects Donald Trump. Canada elects Justin Trudeau. Austria nearly elected a far-right president, but in the end chose a progressive member of the Green Party in the 2016 election.

In March 2017 Holland's centre-right prime minister, Mark Rutte, was re-elected, defeating the far right's Geert Wilders by a relatively wide margin, and yet Wilders' party made gains. The result in Holland, and the reaction to it, showed how electoral assumptions had changed. Although performing less well than Wilders had hoped, his Party for Freedom came second in terms of the number of seats won. Wilders had set the agenda for much of the campaign. At times Rutte appeared to be racing to keep pace with the far-right leader and may have profited from the hard line that he drew in a diplomatic stand-off with Turkey towards the end of the contest.

For Rutte, the electorally convenient row erupted over his refusal to allow two Turkish ministers to address rallies in Rotterdam. The ministers had planned to speak about the referendum aimed at giving Turkey's President Erdogan greater powers. The controversy gave Rutte an opportunity to be perceived as a 'strong leader', in refusing to bow to foreign pressure. To some extent, he danced to Wilders' populist tunes as he headed towards his victory.

On the other side of the political spectrum, support for the mainstream Labour party collapsed, while backing for the Greens rose significantly. The Greens won several more seats than Labour, establishing them as the most formidable parliamentary and electoral force on the left. Such were the fearful expectations, in turbulent times, that mainstream leaders across the European Union expressed relief at the outcome of an election that had been shaped by Wilders' agenda and in which his party made some gains, while the Greens surpassed what had been the main centre-left party in Holland.

There is no denying the pattern. The policy changes that follow the rise of outsiders are momentous and transform the political landscape. A short time ago the proposition that the UK should leave the EU was advanced by a few seemingly eccentric figures and was not remotely part of the political agenda. In the late 1980s Margaret Thatcher raged against the EU, but signed every treaty. Never once, as prime minister, did she suggest the UK might leave. In the 1990s Tory Eurosceptic MPs fumed against the Maastricht Treaty and made the life of the prime minister, John Major, a unique form of political hell, but few called for the UK to leave. Instead, they put the case for a larger EU and an 'opt out' from the single currency. They secured both. When David Cameron became their leader in 2010 he urged his party to stop banging on about Europe. Six years later he held a referendum that led to Brexit – a revolution that would not have happened without the rise of UKIP. In Germany, Angela Merkel was forced to partially disown her own policy towards Syrian refugees, while her allies from other countries performed abrupt U-turns on the same issue, as support for far-right parties rose in the ubiquitous, intimidating opinion polls and local elections. In the US, President Trump announces travel bans, the building of a wall on the border with Mexico, and conducts his presidency as if it were a freakish TV show competing for high ratings: a revolutionary act in itself.

In spite of his mountainous flaws, the election of President Trump should not have been a shock. We should have recognized by then the space that was opening up on parts of the political stage. In the build-up to the election in November 2016 there was much comment in the US, the UK and elsewhere about the echoes with the referendum on Brexit, which had taken place a few months earlier. Yet when Trump claimed, in the aftermath of the UK plebiscite, that the victory for Brexit showed he was heading for a win too, his words were seen as mere hyperbole, the wishful thinking of a loser. On this, Trump read the trend accurately and looked towards its logical outcome in the US.

Many columnists wrote about the similar factors shaping the two contests. The parallels were precise. In the US presidential election the familiar and deadly juxtaposition was in place: an outsider versus the elite. During the UK referendum the same fatal divide – self-proclaimed outsiders taking on the insiders – was apparent. In both countries those who felt 'left behind' turned to those claiming to be on the 'outside', a part-fantasy made stronger by the imprecision of these two pervasive terms. Given that the build-up to the election in the US was so similar to the Brexit campaign, the result was always going to be the same, too: victory for those on the outside. Yet each time the pattern is confirmed, we are amazed once again.

Trump's victory was much the biggest contribution to the contours taking shape across large parts of the democratic world, but his triumph is the latest in a line of unorthodox developments.

In the US, Bernie Sanders gave Hillary Clinton an unexpected fright from the left, in the battle for the Democrats' nomination, a shock that stirred her into being a little less cautious. He partially forced her to break free of self-imposed chains, but not in a way that liberated her from a perception that she was part of an elite which had failed to deliver. Clinton's policy agenda was more radical than many left-of-centre proposed programmes, but few people chose to notice. They saw the figure framed by a different era – the one before the financial crash in 2008.

In Europe, the rise of UKIP from the right was the pivotal factor in persuading David Cameron to hold a referendum on the UK's membership of the EU. Without UKIP – a party with just one MP – the UK would still be in the European Union. Cameron's Conservative Party was already difficult to manage, but with a party rising to the right of his own and demanding a referendum on the EU, Cameron felt the need to respond. There were tumultuous consequences, which included his resignation one year after unexpectedly winning a general election. Cameron should have been prepared; his earlier referendum on independence in Scotland led to the remarkable rise of the Scottish National Party, now the dominant political force there. Its overwhelming triumph in the 2015 UK general election was again based on an argument about outsiders in Scotland taking on the mighty elite in London. In France, the centrist Emmanuel Macron rose from nearly nowhere and did so without being a member of an established party.

Elsewhere in Europe a far-right candidate made waves in the presidential election in Austria. A country that was once virtually conditioned to be wary of the extreme now almost hailed an extremist. And the far right in Germany increases its support. In Poland the parliament consists solely of parties on the right. France stages a presidential election between a Thatcherite candidate and one from the far right. The right asserts a seemingly mighty grip in Hungary. Even in northern Europe, once a model for vibrant self-confident social democracy, there are right-wing parties that worry the mainstream.

The left-wing outsiders are part of the pattern, too, although they struggle to make up much of the fabric. Syriza rules in Greece, and the Left Bloc is part of a coalition in Portugal. Jeremy Corbyn is leader of the UK's Labour Party – a left-wing rebel when Tony Blair was its determinedly centrist and timidly expedient leader. In Spain charismatic left-wing leaders, hailed like rock stars, move erratically a little closer to government and then further away again.

Support for once-mighty mainstream parties is fracturing and they are becoming less coherent. In the US election, senior Republican figures distanced themselves from Trump's candidacy. Their protestation made no difference, or might even have helped him. The Democrats chose the most respectable figure available to them, one with unmatched experience of government at the top. But their support for weighty credibility was misplaced. Experience of government is a disadvantage in the new topsy-turvy political era.

While having no experience of power – of being on the inside – is an advantage electorally, the challenges for governments from a globalized economy become impossibly intimidating. This is one of the bizarre ironies of the outsiders' ascendancy. The global economy requires leaders with titanic skills and experience. But there are electoral advantages in having no experience whatsoever.

Often out of all proportion to their ideological coherence, the outsiders terrify the insiders and influence major policy decisions, even when they do not gain power. Mainstream rulers read the opinion polls, tremble at the results in local elections and change their policies in an attempt to appease the supporters of outsiders. The threat that outsiders might win a national election has been enough for them to wield influence in relation to policy. But Trump is the biggest signal yet that the outsiders can do more than simply hold influence out of power. They can win elections. The outsiders are becoming the new insiders.

In March 2011, less than three years after the financial crash, the then Governor of the Bank of England, Mervyn King, noted candidly: 'I'm surprised the real anger has not been greater than it has... The people whose jobs were destroyed were in no way responsible for the excesses of the financial sector and the crisis that followed.'[1]

King was both insightful and premature in his analysis. He made a noteworthy observation. The global Occupy movement against social inequality came closest to an insurrectionary protest, but there were no riots related directly to the crash across Europe or the US. Instead of riots, the anger of electorates was channelled largely into support for parties and candidates away from the mainstream. Those who were victims of the crash, or felt they were, discovered a far more effective way of expressing their anger: they gave power or influence to an outsider on the left or right, through the ballot box. If there had been riots in the US, it is unlikely they would have had much impact on policy. Instead, the angry rebels elected a president who claims to speak for them; and in UK they voted to take the country out of the EU. These are protestations of immense proportions. They were democratic revolutions, although in some respects they pose at least as big a threat to democratic politics as a riot might have done.

The outsiders vary in origin and aspiration. As well as those on the far right and the far left, a few veer towards forms of populist nationalism that can easily lapse into overt racism. Most are subtler in public projection, deliberately seeking a wider audience with their claims to be compassionate patriots. Those on the left focus more on the need for an economic revolution as a counter to the ongoing revolution of globalization. Those on the right highlight immigration and security. There are tonal overlaps and some common ground. In different ways the outsiders on the right and left share a faith in the nation state, as they vow to protect their supporters from the consequences of the global economy. Trump is closer to Sanders in his ambition for huge increases in capital spending than he is to the small-state Washington Republicans. Marine Le Pen moves close at times to the politics of the late Tony Benn, the mesmerizing orator who propelled Labour to the left in the 1970s and early 1980s. In the French presidential contest she is the statist from the right taking on the Thatcherite on the right.

Some of the factors behind the rise of the outsiders are obvious. Globalization forms the background to their ascent – the sense of powerlessness and loss of national identity that accompanies sweeping change. The financial crash in 2008, as well as widening inequality, immigration and shapeless new work patterns, is the stormy consequence of globalization, ones that help to explain outsider electoral breakthroughs.

At the same time there are related but distinct technological revolutions. These are not incremental, but fast-moving sequences, a leap from relative security to insecurity on several fronts. Forms of communication change on an almost daily basis. Driverless cars are just around the corner and, with them, robotic machines and software that will apparently carry out the duties of those who once assumed they had a career for life. Coffee shops in towns are crammed with people who once had staff jobs and are now part of the fractured world of work. They are the lucky ones. In many places there are no coffee shops or much chance to join tentatively, laptop in hand, the alternative vocations. Amidst such shapeless fragility, simple and simplistic messages can resonate.

What is less obvious is why once-robust mainstream parties have struggled to adapt to change, giving space to the outsiders to make the incredible seem credible. Their messages about making their countries great again were not bound to propel them to electoral triumphs. Their political opponents gave them the opportunities to make hay.

———

The purpose of this book is to seek the answer – or answers – to these questions: Why have the mainstream parties on the right and left allowed the outsiders to thrive? Why have they shown such puny resistance to the populists within their ranks and from outside? There is no automatic reason why voters in the US should back a TV celebrity like Trump, or at least enough of them to make him president. There are more reasons for voters who felt 'left behind' not to have backed a billionaire who pledged to make tax cuts for the wealthy. The same applies in other countries where outsiders make epoch-changing impact. The UK's exit from the EU was not inevitable, and arguably some of those who voted for Brexit risk becoming victims of the UK's departure from the EU. The electorally strong performance of the far-right-wing presidential candidate in Austria, Norbert Hofer, was at odds with the banality of his campaign. In Italy the policies of the former comedian Beppe Grillo and his Five Star Movement are hard to discern, partly because he stands as an anti-politics candidate and can therefore argue that he is a different sort of potential leader, without the need for detailed policies. But while his pitch has an obvious superficial appeal, some of his supporters will be dependent on a coherent policy programme as Italy struggles, like Greece, with its membership of the eurozone and the demands of its own economy. In Germany the right-wing AfD (Alternative for Germany) party seeks wider appeal by adopting a more emollient tone, but then its leadership appears to make the case, in some circumstances, for shooting refugees. These are not formidable political movements. They have become formidable in spite of themselves.

So why are mainstream parties feeble rather than formidable, and their representatives not as strong as they might – or should – be? Not so long ago the Republican president was George Bush, Senior, a figure so removed from Trump in his largely pragmatic approach to power that the two of them could have come from different planets. In the UK the Conservative Party won landslides in the 1980s, and the Labour Party did the same from the late 1990s, an era when the social democrats were the dominant force in Germany and across much of the European Union. Now social democrats suffer a crisis of identity and purpose in much of Europe, and mainstream centre-right parties look nervously over their shoulders at forces to their right.

In seeking to find a solution to the mystery of their decline, and their deep (and in some cases potentially fatal) identity crises, I will focus largely on countries where mainstream parties have previously flourished in long-standing democracies and are now in a state of bewildered fragility. I will do so sympathetically. Governing has become even more nightmarishly complex, and it was never easy. Opposing a government, in the hope of winning an election, has become equally daunting as parties fracture and become less coherent. Seeking power from opposition was more straightforward in the mid-1990s than it is now. Globalization throws up many new dilemmas for those who rule, or seek to rule. Instead of seeking to appreciate the constraints of power, voters and much of the media choose the easier option, which is to view the democratically elected with disdain. This is a book partly about politics, and how the vocation is wilfully misunderstood. If democracy is in danger, we are all to blame.

Politics comes to life more vividly when we seek to understand how the world looks from inside the minds of the Clintons, Merkels, Blairs and Camerons: at their dashed hopes and fears quickly realized, their sense of what is possible and what is not, their outdated assumptions and, in some cases, their shallow philosophies. It does not get us very far to condemn them all as useless, stupid, mad or criminals, although such condemnation is fashionable.

I perform a live one-man show on politics. In the second half I ask the audience to become a specific leader and to get into his or her mind, to see the world as they see it. I then present the audience with a current dilemma faced by the leader. Quickly the evening changes from one in which we are laughing at the tragic absurdities of political characters, or getting angry at them, to an exploration of what it is like actually being one of them – and the risks they face as they contemplate making their moves. As columnists, we urge leaders to do this or do that, and express bewilderment when they are foolish enough not to follow our advice. But from their perspective, they must contemplate the dangers of making each move. As journalists, we file a column urging them to act and move on. For leaders, there are always consequences.

As one of Blair's senior advisers once said to me: 'Each day he faces decisions that come down to this – Do I cut my throat or slit my wrist?' There are few easy answers, or clear routes towards the resolution of dilemmas. This was in the late 1990s, when Blair was twenty points ahead in the polls and facing an Opposition in bewildered disarray.

But empathy with the struggle of mainstream politicians has its limits. They are culpable, too. For decades the mainstream on the left has been too timid, acting as if it was still adapting to the 1980s – the era of Thatcher and Reagan and the light regulatory touch. In contrast, the mainstream on the right has become too daringly ideological, especially in the US and the UK, as if it too was still in the 1980s, determinedly anti-government when voters cry out for government to do more. In both cases the consequence is the same: a lack of clarity about the role and purpose of the state. The mainstream left is too scared to frame arguments around the benevolent potential of the state, and the mainstream right is ideologically disinclined to do so. Outsiders fill the vacuum by pledging to pull a thousand levers – even if some of those levers no longer exist. They are statists, and sometimes fantasy statists, but they get away with it because the mainstream parties have given them the chance to do so.

The failures of the mainstream, and our reluctance to understand or seek to understand the vocation of democratic politics, combine to create an era of heightened danger. This is not because outsiders are bound to seize power across the democratic world. The dangers lie in the framing of the electoral battles – contests increasingly perceived to be between so-called outsiders and elected insiders. By implication, the elected insiders become the villains. The juxtaposition works on the basis that elected insiders in Washington, London, Paris, Berlin, Vienna and the rest are loftily cocooned, indifferent to the voters, compared with the noble, in-touch and yet-to-be-elected outsiders. There can be no more sinister dynamic in democratic politics. Those we elect become cut off, arrogant to the point of near-indifference to the electors.

The dynamic is not true. In reality, the supposedly powerful are nowhere near powerful or secure enough to make sense of the new global order. They are too weak to address daunting questions about how democratic states can flourish when the old levers of power are no longer reliably available. How to pay for increasing demands on healthcare and elderly care? How to compete with countries where wages for some workers are much lower and hours at work much longer? How to address climate change – a global phenomenon that no country can address alone? How to pay for a modern transport system? How to address the terrorist threat in the era of the suicide bomber?

In addition, elections, opinion polls, the media, constitutional checks and balances and the near-impossibility of managing a party's internal tensions mean that elected power is fragile and often fleeting. Most leaders or governments in democracies rule precariously, partly because they pay so much attention to the voters. Yet voters regard the democratically elected as out of touch, part of a lofty, arrogant elite. The opposite is closer to the truth. So how has an untruth reshaped electoral politics? How have the elected insiders allowed themselves to be seen in a fatal light, when that illumination is a false one?

In seeking answers to these questions, ubiquitous phrases recur: the 'left behind', the need to 'take back control', 'the end of liberalism', 'elections are won on the centre ground'. Their very ubiquity obscures a lack of clarity. Left behind from what? What institutions or individuals take back control, and in what form? As for liberalism, the writer Edmund Fawcett, author of *Liberalism: The Life of an Idea*, an elegantly readable survey of this evasive creed through the years, attempted a definition on the BBC at the end of 2016:

At the risk of sounding abstract as a set of ideals, it's all about improving people's lives. Treating them and their enterprises with equal respect... and ensuring protections against undue power... whether it's the power of the state, of wealth, or popular majorities. Liberals also have a picture of society... they take moral and material conflict as inevitable... For liberals they hope to contain conflict and make it fruitful if they can in argument, experiment and exchange.[2]

There will be no more impressive attempt to explain this vague term, but even this one leaves lots of gaps. How does it guide leaders or their followers to a decision about how to run a health service, or to intervene in a market that appears to be failing? How does it reconcile a country that votes against austerity, and yet is part of a single currency in which a non-elected Central Bank demands spending cuts on a scale never before imposed? There has been a lot of speculation about the 'death of liberalism', an epoch-ending drama. But the term 'liberal' acquires so many forms that it becomes almost meaningless. Can a meaningless term define an era that has died? On the right, or at least the mainstream right, most representatives would regard themselves as liberal. David Cameron described himself as a Tory liberal. On the left, there are social democrats who see themselves as liberals – believers in greater equality and a state that provides decent services free at the point of use. There are other liberals on the left who are more wary of a robust state, regarding the big division of the era as being that between 'open' and 'closed', with the liberals backing free trade and international institutions. The term is flexible.

The Independent newspaper in the UK declared itself to be 'liberal'. It was determinedly non-partisan and, in its early years, was a beautifully produced and authoritative alternative to other noisy, mainly Conservative-supporting UK newspapers. But the term 'liberal' proved to be such a poor guide to coherent identity that the newspaper, in its final phase, was left-wing one day and right-wing the next – and sometimes both on the same day. It was incoherence and lack of weighty credibility, rather than limited resources, that led to *The Independent*'s closure as a printed newspaper. Readers struggled to make sense of it. The same problem afflicted the Liberal Democrats, when they were faced with the choice of coalition with the Conservatives in 2010. They had pitched themselves to the left of New Labour in that particular election, and yet some of its leadership felt closer to the social and economic liberalism of David Cameron, or felt they did at the time.

There are common themes that link the disparate groups that speak for 'liberalism', and they are internationalism, tolerance, open-mindedness and a vaguely defined support for freedoms of various forms. This is not quite enough to sustain a political movement at times of sweeping change. What does it mean to be a 'liberal' today? Here is a question the mainstream parties across the world have avoided answering with precision – even those with the term in their title.

Lack of clarity can be an advantage in democratic politics, widening a party's appeal on the basis that different voters recognize entirely different attributes. But to what extent is this related to a deeper and disturbing question: How is it that we quickly loathe and mistrust those we elect?

Much of the investigation that follows seeks answers about the nature of power in the era of globalization. Who rules, and in what form? Answer that question and we start to get to the heart of the matter: the failure of the mainstream to reassure and inspire voters, as change erupts.

If the answer to the question 'Who rules?' is not clear, there are bound to be openings for those who appear to have no problems in offering clarity. 'I will rule' was the essence of Trump's message, and is the thrust of most outsiders' pitch. The simplicity of the assertion is powerful, but leads to silly pledges: building walls between countries, and the rest. Wielding power is more complex. Mainstream leaders are acutely aware of the constraints they face, to the point where some overestimate their powerlessness. Their assumptions, and our assumptions about them, help to explain the rise of the outsiders. The political brilliance of the outsiders cannot be an explanation for their ascent, because the outsiders are usually not politically brilliant.

But that is where we must begin, with the new (or newish) political forces that at the very least influence policy, and in some cases secure national power. Outsiders-versus-Insiders sounds like an innocent game. The juxtaposition has lost force, from overuse. But the game is deadly serious. When voters view the more orthodox elected politicians with indiscriminate disdain, the elected politicians are not the only ones who are vulnerable. Democracy is threatened, too.

1

THE OUTSIDERS ON THE RIGHT

Globalization is a consequence of revolutions in technology and transport. It is not a government policy. No party leader can say credibly, 'We will introduce globalization.' Globalization is happening. But the political consequences are inevitably huge. The challenge for governments, and those that aspire to govern, is to address many of the thorny questions that arise from tumultuous change.

Will a steelworks close, with lifelong jobs no longer lifelong, as it struggles to compete with cheap imports? Will immigrants distort a jobs market that is already changing and offering few of the old, familiar securities? Will the housing market make it impossible for voters, or their children, to buy – or even to rent in some areas? Is it safe to fall ill or become old, when health provision fails to meet demand? Will machines make human beings redundant in vocations that traditionally provided long-term security? The turmoil is bound to fuel the insecurity of voters – many voters, and not just those in the US Rust Belt and equivalent regions in other countries. How do politicians respond to such complex questions in ways that are both reassuring and candid? The right-wing outsiders appear to have the answers.

In one respect, they do. Compared with the timid mainstream left and the small government mainstream right, they are statists.

They are willing to intervene in markets, or at least pledge to do so. They will manage immigration. They will protect their industries against cheap imports. They will be tough on crime and security. Their nationalism propels them almost leftwards in their faith in government, at a point where those on the mainstream – guided by an attachment to imprecise liberalism – have become confused about the role of the state. The outsiders on the right prefer to talk of the nation state rather than 'the state', but it is their promises to be highly active in government that resonate.

The ideological pitch is combined with an erratic charisma – enough of a distinctive public personality to get noticed, even if the attention derives from their unpredictable eccentricity. Some voters like the eccentricity, as it stands out from the cautious, determined normality of the orthodox insider. The character details become irrelevant. The difference from a perceived robotic norm is what matters.

The far-right candidate in the 2016 Austrian presidential election, Norbert Hofer, was disabled in a paragliding accident. Although slim and youthful, he often walks with a stick. Hofer said he had been deeply hurt throughout the first presidential campaign by how often his disability had been used against him. 'They have repeatedly abused me, saying I'm a cripple,' he said. 'But I tell you, the stronger the pressure they put me under, the stronger I become.'[1] The vulnerability helped to humanize him, an important part of the right-wing outsider's allure: the tough leader who suffers, just as voters suffer. He was his party's spokesman for the disabled. At the same time he was a gun enthusiast and carried a Glock pistol, conveying an enigmatic machismo.

Geert Wilders, the founder of the Party for Freedom, is one of the more telegenic leaders in Holland, known mockingly – or admiringly

– as the 'blond bombshell', although the colour of his luxurious hair is closer to grey. Frauke Petry, the chairwoman of the Alternative for Germany party, with a pixie haircut and a trim, athletic build is also telegenic. Fluent in English, after studying at Reading University, she is a patient, gracious interviewee, even in the face of aggressive interviewers. But she is not a gifted orator. Her speeches tend to be dull, with ornate sentences and technocratic talking points. She is more comfortable citing economic studies than discussing the lives of ordinary people. Still she stands out as a figure who does not conform to the caricature of a far-right leader, if the stereotype is closer, say, to the undisciplined exuberance of Donald Trump.

Trump's candidacy was based largely on his own unpredictably wilful charisma. At the start of 2016 he declared, with a provocative flourish, that he 'would gladly accept the mantle of anger'.[2] Anger was the driving force of the candidate and of his followers. Voters were angry, and he was equally angry on their behalf. At the beginning of the presidential campaign *The New York Times* noted that Trump's supporters 'directed their wrath toward career politicians, unlawful immigrants, terrorists and people who they said were taking advantage of welfare'.[3] That was a lot of anger and a lot of targets. Trump promised single-handedly to protect them. He was the mighty business leader who could make the US great again. Crucially, Trump became the personification of the state. He did not make overt left-wing arguments about the benevolent potential of government. Instead, he framed an argument about the benevolent impact of himself. Here is a sequence from a typical Trump rally in the summer of 2016, shortly before he was confirmed as the Republicans' candidate – an address he had been making, with few variations, since announcing that he was standing for the candidacy on 16 June 2015:

TRUMP: Our country is in serious trouble. We don't have victories any more. We used to have victories, but we don't have them. When was the last time anybody saw us beating, let's say, China in a trade deal? They kill us. I beat China all the time. All the time.

[*APPLAUSE*]

AUDIENCE MEMBER: We want Trump. We want Trump.

TRUMP: When did we beat Japan at anything? They send their cars over by the millions, and what do we do? When was the last time you saw a Chevrolet in Tokyo? It doesn't exist, folks. They beat us all the time.

When do we beat Mexico at the border? They're laughing at us, at our stupidity. And now they are beating us economically. They are not our friend, believe me. But they're killing us economically. The US has become a dumping ground for everybody else's problems.

I would build a great wall, and nobody builds walls better than me, believe me, and I'll build them very inexpensively, I will build a great, great wall on our southern border. And I will have Mexico pay for that wall.

AUDIENCE MEMBER: Yes.

TRUMP: Mark my words.

[*APPLAUSE*]

TRUMP: Nobody would be tougher on ISIS than Donald Trump. Nobody.

[*APPLAUSE*]

TRUMP: I will find – within our military – I will find the General Patton or I will find General MacArthur, I will find the right guy. I will find the guy that's going to take that military and make it really work. Nobody, nobody will be pushing us around.

AUDIENCE MEMBER: Yes.

[*APPLAUSE*]

> TRUMP: I will stop Iran from getting nuclear weapons. And we won't be using a man like Secretary Kerry that has absolutely no concept of negotiation, who's making a horrible and laughable deal, who's just being tapped along as they make weapons right now, and then goes into a bicycle race at 72 years old, and falls and breaks his leg. I won't be doing that. And I promise I will never be in a bicycle race. That I can tell you.
>
> [*APPLAUSE*]
>
> TRUMP: I will immediately terminate President Obama's illegal executive order on immigration, immediately.

The crowd cheered the warrior Trump, as similar large gatherings hailed Shakespeare's Coriolanus. The euphoric crowd saw Trump as a figure who, like Coriolanus, could save them, as a solo warrior. Under Trump, with the wave of a wand, there would be no more immigration from Mexico. He would build barriers to make such movement of labour impossible. Later in the campaign he proposed banning all Muslims from entering the US, a solution even more drastic than his plans to block the Mexicans. He would defeat ISIS almost on his own. He would control any nuclear ambition in Iran. After winning in New Hampshire, he declared with intoxicating imprecision, 'Nobody is going to mess with this country any more.'[4] He meant that, when he was president, nobody was going to mess with him.

His fans did not shout in response: 'We want the government to act on our behalf.' That would not be one of the great rousing slogans of our time. But in proclaiming, 'We want Trump', that is what they were calling for. They wanted an elected figure to intervene to protect them from the harsher consequences of free trade; they wanted investment; they wanted protection from the terrorists' threat; they wanted job security. They wanted Trump.

They were succumbing to a message about the role of the state via the charisma of the TV celebrity.

But there was little or no explanation from Trump as to how these mighty ends would be achieved. Charisma only goes so far in politics. The outsiders proclaimed their ends without a clear route-map as to how they would be achieved. Much depended on an assumption that the charisma of the outsider would in itself deliver the specified ends.

Nonetheless they stand out in a noisy media environment with their swagger and self-confidence about what they can achieve on behalf of a nation state. Standing out is part of the electoral trick, as parties fracture and multiply. There is competition for attention, and right-wing outsiders are tabloid communicators. They can secure headlines. Indeed, Trump's policy programme was closer to a series of headlines.

As well as the wider background and their charisma as distinctive individuals, such outsiders have an issue to help them in their bid to be distinctive. For decades mainstream politicians have twitched nervously or opportunistically as they read polls suggesting that immigration tops the list of voters' concerns, or comes close to the top. One way or another they have made a series of misjudgements as to how best to address the issue. Sometimes they ignore it. When countries from Eastern Europe joined the EU there were few (or no) speeches or press conferences from prime ministers and presidents explaining the impact of free movement. In the UK, where no constraining transitional arrangements were deployed, the then prime minister Tony Blair made major speeches on just about every other topic, and held a monthly press conference to project on all matters, from public-service reform to Iraq. Free movement was never a chosen theme. Alternatively, prime ministers made big claims to cut immigration, which were never met – and could never be met – as they must have known. Long before Brexit was an issue, some Conservative leaders sought popularity by highlighting the issue in the UK. In the 2005 general election the Conservative leader, Michael Howard, opened his campaign on the issue by pledging an annual limit on immigration. He could not explain how this would be achieved, which was one reason why he later campaigned for the UK to leave the EU in the referendum. Before the 2015 election, David Cameron made impractical pledges to cut immigration, which were never met. He was in power, whereas Howard was not. He did not have the excuse of being in opposition. Over-promising on immigration was as bad as not saying anything very much at all. Some voters noted the gap between promises and reality, concluding that the reality had to change and that mainstream politicians were liars.

Immigration is a complex and highly charged policy area. Politicians are expected to take clear positions, as in 'immigration is good' or 'immigration is bad', as if they were talking about a single tangible object. Instead they are grappling with sensitive economic and social questions that can disrupt or improve an economy, cause social tensions or stimulate diversity, improve public services or increase demand on them and, above all, can lose them an election or divide their party, if they fail to be clear and yet nuanced. Immigration raises questions about economic security and national identity. For some voters, the issue serves as an explanation for wider worries, anxieties and anger about poor public services and insecure job prospects. Quite often there is no connection between the issues, but sometimes there is; and even when there is not, it is easy to see how the idea of immigrants moving into another country could be seen as the cause of disruption.

But this is not an era for nuance. In interviews, mainstream leaders are asked persistently whether they want immigration to come down in their country – and within the next twelve months. They are not asked whether they want food prices to fall, because interviewers recognize that prices are largely beyond the control of a leader. But immigration is framed as a simple good-or-bad question. If leaders qualify their answers – arguing wisely that the level of immigration will depend on demand for labour, and that in turn will be determined by the state of the economy and the ambitions of government – they are slaughtered: 'But what is your answer? If you were in power, would you reduce the numbers? Yes or no?' These were the binary questions posed constantly to UK politicians responding to the Brexit referendum, which was itself a binary question that allowed no room for nuance and qualifications.

The right-wing populists do not qualify their assertions. Without hesitation they cry, 'Yes – we will reduce the numbers' and appear strong as they make that unqualified promise. The pledge to 'take back control' became a defining one for the leading supporters of Brexit in the UK referendum. And Trump used the same phrase in his campaign.

Yet the vote-winning slogan also leads us towards a fundamental weakness of the outsiders. They do not know what they stand for. In a way that is almost childlike in its confusion, right-wing outsiders are supposedly anti-government and yet they pledge to utilize the levers of government like none of their mainstream equivalents.

While being an inadvertent statist on a grand scale, Trump can hardly bear the idea that he is even a politician, because he also loathes the state. 'I suppose that is what I am now, a politician,' he declared with revealing despair at his Washington press conference in February 2017, almost regretting becoming president, as that makes him a politician.[5] The slogan at a rally in Florida that Trump held a few days after the press conference was 'We are going to put People before Government' – a contortion of illuminating confusion.[6] Trump views politicians and government with disdain. Yet he has become a politician who has pledged to govern more actively than Democrat presidents. Other right-wing outsiders making waves in Western democracies despise the state, regarding it as a large, inefficient monster. Yet they are also statists, intervening not only in labour markets but also in the free trade of goods, and in proposing big spending increases. They pledge to take back control.

This gaping and transparent ideological contradiction should be an insurmountable problem for the far right. The source of their popularity is a pledge to intervene in the labour market and to do so on vast scale. Several leading outsiders, including Trump, plan to increase spending on capital projects in ways that make some on the left seem miserly. Yet on the whole they disapprove of government and politicians. They are anti-government and pro-government intervention simultaneously. Immigration – the policy issue that keeps on giving, as far as the right-wing outsiders are concerned – exposes their incoherent attitudes to the role of the state.

But there is a twist. Such a contradiction might have been exposed, mocked and torn apart, if mainstream insiders had the confidence to do so. In its lack of confidence, the mainstream has no coherent view of the state, either. Here is the key, once again, to the rise of puny politically unformed outsiders: the failure of the mainstream to take them on.

The mainstream leaders are caught in a catch-22. They are even more fragile than they were, when they had the political stage largely to themselves before the 2008 financial crash. While they become or feel precarious, they are not strong enough to expose the ideological inconsistencies of outsiders.

———

During various regional and local elections in Germany in 2016, support for the AfD grew largely at the expense of Angela Merkel's Christian Democratic Union (CDU). Each electoral setback was greeted with familiar comments from senior figures in the CDU, such as candidate Lorenz Caffier's comment: 'There was only one subject during the campaign, and that subject was the refugee policy. The refugee question was decisive.'[7]

After one significant defeat Peter Tauber, a leading member of the CDU, described the outcome as 'a bitter result, a new experience'. 'We are all responsible for this. It was noticeable that the refugee subject was very present. Of course many people are looking at Angela Merkel.'[8] Roughly translated, he meant that Merkel was uniquely responsible or culpable.

After more than a wearying decade as chancellor, Merkel became trapped by a crisis without resolution. That is what happens to long-serving leaders in power. Options narrow, as dilemmas deepen and voters become disillusioned. While hailed in much of the democratic world for her leadership skills, in Germany she was widely criticized for her lack of vision and for being exhausted. When she displayed energetic, courageous vision in the face of the refugee crisis, she was condemned for not showing more cautious expediency. Many of those leaders who paid homage to her negotiating prowess and leadership turned away, in the face of the refugee crisis.

Yet the far right has been allowed to get away with seizing the issue, without being able to explain fully what they could – or would – do about immigration and the separate issue of asylum-seekers escaping from the hell of their own countries.

The leader of the AfD, Frauke Petry, appeared to suggest in one interview that border police would have the right to shoot refugees, in certain circumstances. When her words caused a storm, she sought to play them down, asserting with some justification that she was stating the legal position and not issuing an 'order to shoot' – a reference to the order East German guards had to use firearms if necessary, to shoot anyone trying to escape illegally from the German Democratic Republic.

But her clarification was late in coming, perhaps because her words appeared to have some traction with a significant section of the electorate. Whatever she meant to say, the furore obscured the lack of meaty, credible policies in relation to immigration or asylum. Similarly, Trump's proposal to build a wall between the US and Mexico, claiming that those on the other side of the partition would pay for the construction, was obviously not practical, even though he presses ahead with his project from the White House. These are not solutions in a world where people are on the move to meet a demand for labour, in the case of most immigrants; or out of desperation, in respect of asylum-seekers.

In Germany the economic implications of the refugee crisis were inevitably more nuanced than the right-wing outsiders dared to acknowledge. The right could not afford to be nuanced because their cause would collapse. Nuance is a threat to the outsiders.

One argument from the far right is that immigrants would compete for work and drag down wages. Another is that they would make impossible demands on public spending. Yet when it comes to pay, Germans and neighbouring countries have little cause to feel alarmed. Evidence suggests that immigration and asylum have only a small impact on employment and wages. Unskilled workers and existing migrants are most vulnerable, as they are the closest substitutes for the new arrivals. But the effects are still measly. In 2016 *The Economist* magazine cited a paper by Stephen Nickell and Jumana Saleheen that found a 10 percentage-point rise in the share of migrants working in menial jobs, such as cleaning, depressed wages for such positions by just 2 per cent, and that this wage-dampening could even have positive side-effects.[9] Research in Denmark, on refugees arriving between 1991 and 2008, found that they did nudge low-educated natives out of lowly jobs. However, rather than sulking at their displacement, the natives switched to jobs that involved less manual labour, sometimes with higher salaries.[10]

In the very short run, the International Monetary Fund (IMF) estimated that refugees would add around 0.19 per cent of GDP (gross domestic product) to public expenditure in the European Union, and 0.35 per cent in Germany. This would increase public debt and, given the higher joblessness among refugees, unemployment would rise. But later on, as the new arrivals integrated into the workforce, they were expected to boost annual output by 0.1 per cent for the EU as a whole, and 0.3 per cent in Germany.[11] They should also help to reverse the upward creep of the cost of state pensions as a share of GDP, given their relative youth. Indeed, one of Merkel's calculations – beyond the resolution to act for humane reasons – was that the refugees would soon boost Germany's economy and the ageing labour market. She was not acting out of electorally fatal altruism.

Inevitably these figures were highly uncertain and depended on how many more refugees arrived, how quickly their asylum applications were processed and how soon they found jobs. Governments could make their impact more benign by accelerating all those steps. But there was an argument to be made on humanitarian grounds, and in terms of the positive impact the refugees would make on the countries they moved to, if EU countries all took a share of the responsibility.

There is no willingness to share. The positive arguments were rarely made. On the whole, the stage was left to the right-wing outsiders, changing the policies of supposedly mighty governments even when they are out of power.

During the UK's referendum on the country's membership of the EU in 2016, the evidence on immigration was incontestably clear. EU immigrants were net contributors to the UK's finances, and were less likely to claim benefits than the native British. The average immigrant was younger, better educated and healthier than the average British citizen. Overall they made a positive contribution to the economy and were not drug-addicted, boozy benefit claimants. They came for the work, and would not come if the work were not available.

For every immigrant the UK let in, the country was richer, more able to pay for its health, education and welfare needs, and less dependent on benefits. They were exactly the demographic the UK needed. As for the much-touted Australian 'points system', which was highlighted in the referendum as being one option outside the EU, the UK had nothing to learn from it: immigrants to the UK were better educated and more skilled than immigrants to Australia. In addition, most of the people who appeared as immigrants in the migration statistics were students, because the Home Office chose to count as migrants students who come for the duration of degree courses. Of the 330,000 net arrivals, in the numbers published by the UK Home Office in 2016, 169,000 were students.[12] Most students who study in the UK return home after their degree, and those who stay face strict conditions; in effect they must find a job or face deportation. They do not swamp the UK labour market. Given their skills and capacity for hard work, perhaps they should be encouraged to do so.

Is there an argument the mainstream could make, in ways that are accessible and at least counter some of the highly charged assertions from the populists? The question cannot be answered because, apart from a few exceptions, the mainstream makes no attempt to make a case. It has mishandled every complex element of the immigration saga. Voters' concerns are partly one of scale. In 2004 the UK government had legal powers to put limits on immigration from the new member states in the EU. It chose not to do so. It also underestimated by a huge margin the numbers that would move to the UK in the following years. The then prime minister, Tony Blair did not impose legal powers because there was a strong case not to do so. The immigrants came to the UK to work; they boosted economic growth. But the numbers arriving so speedily were disorientating, and while some immigrants came to work in the UK's creaking public services, they put a demand on them, too. There was little or no explanation as to what was happening and why. Bewildered voters, already struggling to adapt to change, felt disconnected because there were few connections with the state. Mediating agencies, local government, the NHS and schools were weak and fractured, with no clear lines of control. The Home Office took its line from Number Ten and was one of the institutions underestimating the numbers arriving, and overestimating those they thought would leave the UK.

The political fallout was still being played out in the UK's referendum in 2016. Similarly, there were many reasons for Merkel's generosity towards desperate asylum-seekers in 2015, but the scale triggered a political crisis from which she struggles to recover. Inadvertently she fuelled support for the far right.

Even so, the myths about immigration overwhelm the reality. Why is the contest between those who can see a case for immigration and those who are opposed not at least a little closer? It takes comedians to make accessible arguments in favour of immigration. In the UK, the stand-up comic Stewart Lee brilliantly highlighted the absurdity of the one-sided argument as part of his 2014 stand-up act:

> UKIP is warning we're about to be swamped by Bulgarians... they're warning it's even worse... they're skilled Bulgarians... here they are coming over here with their skills... ten years ago it was the same with the Poles... bloody Poles coming over here being all Polish and mending everything... coming over here and fixing things we've broken... mending things better than us.[13]

By the end of the sketch, Lee goes back in time beyond the Anglo-Saxons 'coming over here'. He mocks the anger at those 'coming over here', to improve the lives of those who fume against them. Confident politicians could do the same. Although elected politicians are not allowed to mock voters, they could use humour and context to make a case for immigration, even if they argue for some constraints on free movement. Lee's technique is not greatly different from that of great political communicators such as Tony Benn, who would link the miners' strike in the UK of the 1980s to Jesus Christ, the Levellers, the Chartists and the Suffragettes – partly for comic impact, but also to make a wider point. Benn was a communicator who knew how to make sense of what appeared to have no sense at all, even if his arguments became nonsensical at times. Lee shows how the case for immigration could be made in a way that makes the outsiders seem silly. And a political cause is doomed when it appears to be silly. In the UK a comedian can do it, but no currently elected mainstream politician could effectively expose the weakness of the populists' argument. Tony Blair came closest when he pointed out, during a speech on Brexit in February 2017, 'A job in the North-East of England is not going to be saved by stopping someone from Eastern Europe working in a coffee shop in London.'[14] But former prime ministers, like comedians, have limited sway.

———

On the whole, comedians do not stand for election, although the outsiders are testing even that proposition. Beppe Grillo, who started the Five Star Movement in Italy, was a comedian and blogger. Trump had a comedic streak, his tongue in his cheek as he starred in the US version of *The Apprentice*.

Those leading the populist right have their issues, in the form of immigration/asylum, their eccentric charisma and the context of globalization with all its destabilizing consequences. But their confident swagger disguises fragility. The ammunition should not have been enough to propel one of them to the White House, to force the UK out of the EU, and to alarm the mainstream across the democratic world.

Partly their frailty is inevitable and derives from what they claim to be a defining strength – they are untainted by political power. Mastering the art of politics is the equivalent of learning a language. Experience and practice are required in order to learn the rhythms. Politics is closer to an art form than a science. Successful leaders must be great communicators; their public words must relate to policies, and the policies must connect to a series of values. The values and policies must make sense of the changing world in which politicians seek to make their mark. They must lead their parties, and yet make a wider appeal at an election. Smart leaders, or aspiring leaders, are like the composers of a beguiling symphony. The ingredients must come together to form a coherent whole.

Most of the right-wing outsiders are embryonic composers, being fairly new to politics. They make a virtue of their inexperience in the anti-politics era, but on the whole they are buskers rather than virtuosos. They are not as sure of themselves as they seem. As relative newcomers, they cannot be sure of themselves. No one would confidently seek to become a successful chief executive without some experience of business. A successful newspaper editor will have been tested at some point by journalistic challenges. Arriving at Wimbledon with a tennis racket is not the same as playing a final on the Centre Court.

But it seems that a candidate who seeks to rule a country can thrive electorally, precisely because he or she has no experience of democratic politics at the highest levels. Trump had not served in any public office before becoming President of the US. He did not even have a racket before appearing in a Centre Court final. Such inexperience should have made him more vulnerable in the election. Instead it became a fleeting qualification.

There is one obvious but important reason for the potency of inexperience. Untested by power, the right-wing outsiders have not been around long enough for voters to feel disillusioned with them, or betrayed when their simple populism comes up against the constraints of politics on 'the inside' – an unavoidably challenging space where elected politicians and informed advisers gather to battle it out and, in some lucky or unlucky cases, get the chance to implement policies.

After Trump was elected president he became unavoidably the ultimate insider, rather than the unconstrained, yet-to-be-fully-politicized outsider. In his triumph he inadvertently exposed the vacuous basis of the deadly juxtaposition. In the end, an outsider is a figure who has not been elected. Once elected, the outsider becomes an insider. Inevitably Trump started to struggle. His struggle is with the unavoidable demands of politics. Immediately, as the victor, he faced complex decisions about who to appoint to his team and the policies to adopt. Within days he seemed to drop some of his campaign pledges as if he had never made them. Members of his newly appointed Cabinet took different positions from him, not on trivial matters but on fundamental ones, such as the future of NATO, attitudes to Russia and the intelligence agencies. In response to the divergence, Trump became fleetingly an orthodox politician. He pretended to be relaxed at this early act of insurrection – the only course available to him. 'All of my Cabinet nominees are looking good and doing a great job. I want them to be themselves and express their own thoughts, not mine!' he tweeted on 13 January 2017. He could hardly say the opposite: that he was *not* relaxed and was ready to sack those he had just appointed. Instead he dissembled a little: the fate of the insider.

Like most insiders, Trump is doomed to disappoint as he comes up against the constraints of leadership. The outsider on the inside is an even more vulnerable political species than those who seem to have been on the inside most of their lives. He or she has claimed distinctiveness, only to discover that it was not being part of the political establishment that made them distinctive in the first place.

Most right-wing populists have not been unfortunate enough to win national power yet. Those who have achieved victory recognize within a nanosecond that they face mountainous challenges, when they made their visions seem so easy to realize during the preceding campaign. The reaction of outsiders who unexpectedly win is almost comic. Trump appeared as a penitent, naughty schoolboy when he visited the White House and the outgoing President Obama for the first time, in the aftermath of his victory, as if he had been found out for telling outlandish stories. He was hesitantly polite – a new character trait, but a real one. Trump is a performer but not an actor. He is transparent. For all his bravado, he showed he had not expected to win. He had assumed he would remain an outsider from power, in a comfort zone where the art of politics is limited to the utterance of words without the dilemmas of decision-making and policy implementation.

Trump's fleetingly modest demeanour was an echo of the reaction of the UK's two leading Conservative Brexiteers. In the immediate aftermath of the referendum that they thought they would lose, the Conservative politicians Boris Johnson and Michael Gove seemed pale with fearful apprehension. Suddenly they had to make sense of the words uttered with vague defiance during the campaign. They were not euphoric. They had had an easy time of it on the outside; now there were deep and complex consequences as they became the insiders they always were. The leader of UKIP, Nigel Farage, *was* euphoric, but he did not stay on to face the consequences. He took the easy route by announcing his resignation. Of the leading campaigners in the 'Out' campaign, only Boris Johnson plays a role, as Foreign Secretary, in what form Brexit will take. Even his role is limited. The rest do not have to face the consequences of their campaigning swagger.

Early in 2017 one of the architects of the victory in the Brexit referendum, Dominic Cummings, formerly an adviser to Gove, wrote a wittily provocative account of why his side had won.

Cummings insisted, as part of his compelling exposition, that contrary to mythology, Gove and Johnson were relaxed and delighted on the day after the referendum. Perhaps the close ally and behind-the-scenes witness is best placed to make the definitive judgement. But those of us that watched their victory press conference saw a suddenly more burdened duo, with their tentative assertions of what should follow and their lack of exuberance. No doubt they had other matters on their minds, such as who should replace David Cameron as prime minister, since he had resigned earlier that morning. As it happened, neither of them would be the successor, although both tried, as one turned on the other. Whether or not they were contemplating leadership as well as a transformation of the UK's place in the world, we were witnessing two politicians who had campaigned from the 'outside' creeping back to the inside, with all its mountainous dilemmas.

The juxtaposition in play all over the world is so obviously false-outsiders versus insiders, which allows right-wingers to escape ideological incarceration. They are not on the far right; they are on the outside. Serious, probing debate becomes almost impossible when such a framing takes hold. When presented with evidence on the economy, or any other issue that challenges their claims, the populists can retort that they reject the claims because they originate from elite insiders. There is no obvious winning retort, as they have moved the debate on from substance to a circuitous exchange about the legitimacy of those who have served from the inside.

As part of this absurd but dangerous exchange, the right-wing outsiders claim to speak for 'the people' – the vacuous slogan that has fuelled so many campaigns. If this were a pantomime, some of 'the people' could shout back, 'Oh no, you don't', except that this is not theatre. Instead, in the deadly-serious battle for power, the outsiders deploy a cheap device that should be easily exposed by mainstream opponents, who are more used to standing for elections than their new opponents; campaigns in which they are persistently and unavoidably held to account by 'the people'.

Stand back from the populists' familiar trick, and the outsiders cannot speak for the people and do not do so. There is no such political entity as 'the people'. Democratic debate has not died yet. The views and hopes of the electorate still vary considerably. They always have done and always will do. The right-wing outsiders are on the march, but they do not have the support of 100 per cent of the electorate. Quite a lot of 'the people' still look elsewhere. Even in the US, where Donald Trump persistently claimed to be the voice of the people, Hillary Clinton won the popular vote.

As Jan-Werner Müller points out in his illuminating book *What Is Populism?*, the assertion helps to define the populists' pitch. The right-wing candidate for the Freedom Party of Austria, Norbert Hofer, tormented his rival, Alexander Van der Bellen, an economics professor and now President of Austria, with the deadly claim, 'You have the high society behind you; I have the people with me.' Even at the peak of Hofer's electoral pomp, half the people were not with him.[15]

The term 'high society' is another way of portraying Hofer's opponent as an insider, a specialist in economic policy who mixes with other experts, who base their judgements and public proclamations on the forensic use of evidence. Hofer implies that such lofty types ignore the people. The claim is so sweeping that some voters, who feel unrepresented or ignored, choose to accept it. But what about the half of the electorate that voted for the elitist professor who does not speak for the people? They collude with the elite; they are not the people. The trick is a simple one. When some voters hear that a candidate speaks for them, and the opponent represents an elite, the claim of representation is enough for a connection between 'outsider' and voter to be made.

With good cause, many voters across the democratic world feel disconnected from the state – that increasingly distant and bewildered force in their lives. They respond when a candidate who is unused to power claims to speak for them. Again the reasons for the appeal are obvious, but not inevitable or unavoidable. The act of claiming to speak for the people should not be enough in itself to propel the outsiders towards heady influence and power.

The claim is not in itself sinister. The assertion is vacuous but not a threat. The Labour Party ran its 1964 campaign on the slogan 'People Matter', as if their opponents were arguing that people did not matter. There are many other examples of empty claims to speak for the people amongst mainstream parties. It is the juxtaposition of 'the people' against the elected insiders that is chilling. Roughly translated, it conjures up a bizarre contortion in which the people elect representatives who, irrationally, betray them. The people then turn to outsiders to save them from the consequences of the democratic process. Or outsiders encourage them to think along these dangerous lines.

Such populist swagger partly explains the appeal of those who led the referendum campaign in 2016, on the question of whether the UK should leave the European Union. The advocates of coming 'Out' unexpectedly won by 52 to 48 per cent – a substantial victory, but not a landslide. In the immediate aftermath of the result, the leader of UKIP, Nigel Farage, declared the outcome as 'a victory for real people'. Did he mean that the 48 per cent who voted to remain in the EU were unreal people? Like Hofer, Farage was speaking nonsense. Even so, the claim that the real people had prevailed partly explains why Farage was the victor, rather than the existing or former prime ministers who supported the losing 'Remain' campaign. As democratically elected rulers and former rulers, they were perceived as loftily out of touch, and in it for themselves. They were speaking for the *un*real. In contrast, Farage spoke for the people against the might of Brussels and the self-interested elites who are elected to the House of Commons or had ruled in the recent past.

We know what he means: that 'people' previously ignored by the insiders now have a voice. But even this assertion is not true. Voters are not wilfully and perversely ignored by those who seek to be elected. Outsiders do not necessarily represent them. But that elevation of a minority of electorates to 'the people' is a dangerous one, when placed against the elected representatives who are supposedly cocooned in a bubble.

In his claim that the referendum was a victory for real people, Farage implies that a strange and sinister sequence took place. The voters elect MPs to Westminster. The voters then loathe the MPs they have elected, a form of weird self-loathing worthy of a psychiatrist's enquiry. The whacky theory only works if MPs ignore the voters, even though they are dependent on their support to be re-elected. MPs do not, and cannot, ignore voters, even if parts of the electorate are defiantly convinced that is the case. The combination of self-loathing from voters and electoral immolation from the masochists they elect would be perverse, if it were true. Democratic politics is undermined by the false, but strongly held assumption that outsiders speak for the people and elected insiders speak only for themselves.

In different circumstances the 'Remain' campaign might have regarded the support of all living former prime ministers, and the serving one, as an advantage. When the UK held a similar referendum in 1975, that was certainly the case. One of the most prominent campaigners for staying in Europe was Edward Heath, even though he had lost two elections the previous year. But as a former prime minister who took the UK into what was then the Common Market, he had authority. In 2016 backing from such a tainted elite as former prime ministers was, rightly, seen as a potential vote-loser.

The recent past is a dangerous place in modern democracies. On this terrain former elected rulers face intense accusations of betrayal. They are perceived to have let their voters down almost intentionally and wilfully. Again the perception is irrational. No prime minister would go out of his or her way to betray voters. They might, and do, make terrible misjudgements, but that is a different matter. As we shall explore later, the breakdown in trust is a key factor in the rise of insubstantial outsiders.

If a former prime minister makes a case based on his or her experience, some voters are likely to scorn and turn with greater enthusiasm to the likes of Farage, untarnished by the dilemmas of power in a democracy. At one stage of the UK referendum the 'Remain' campaign contemplated a major event in which the former living prime ministers and the current one would proclaim together, on the basis of their experience, that the UK would be better off in the EU. The campaign decided to drop the event, on the basis that it would be counter-productive. The closest it came was a relatively subdued gathering in Northern Ireland, where John Major and Tony Blair – agents of the peace process – spoke together. The voices of those that had once won elections, governed in the UK and worked with EU leaders had to be muffled. Too many voters would regard their contributions as acts of provocation.

In contrast, the voices of the outsiders are loud and deceptively confident. There is no muffling. In Germany, Frauke Petry seeks to widen her party's remit with an engaging style. After being founded to oppose the euro in 2013, the AfD is now a significant political force that ranges well beyond the single currency.

Hailing regional election victories, Petry describes each result as a blow to Angela Merkel and declares: 'Now it is our responsibility to make politics for the people. The people no longer trust the old establishment parties to do so.'[16] The sentiment is almost precisely the same as that of the nearly victorious presidential candidate in Austria and of Farage in the UK. Petry speaks of the old establishment being against the people. She will make a politics for the people – as if other leaders seeking to win elections are indifferent to the electorate and are busy making politics for everyone *but* the people.

In Denmark the right-wing nationalists make the same claim as Petry. The Danish People's Party attributes much of its popularity to staying close to the concerns of real people, rather than being sucked into the game at 'Borgen', the Copenhagen complex that houses the Danish parliament and is also the title of a popular television drama. 'It is very important to be a part of the people, not be such high-ranking politicians that don't know what is going on in the population,' says Pia Kjærsgaard, who founded the party twenty years ago.[17]

Do Danish politicians, burdened by the demands of coalition politics, not know the concerns of 'the people'? When they contemplate elections, are they indifferent to the voters? Kjærsgaard must know that they cannot be indifferent, or else they would be the most determinedly self-defeating politicians in the democratic world. Nor do they seek to be sucked up in Borgen-like negotiations – a form of hell for all politicians, who want to act rather than be locked in talks with other parties. They do not choose such impotence. The voters have produced outcomes that give them no choice but to negotiate. They contest elections with a voting system that will almost always produce close outcomes, in which at least one party must work with another in government. The claim that such a sequence ignores the people, when it is an unavoidable response to the 'people's verdict' in an election, is preposterous and yet potent.

Jan-Werner Müller uncovers in his book *What is Populism?* a glorious quote from Donald Trump, the most revealing contortion in relation to the populists' potent and meaningless message. At a rally in May 2016, during the build-up to the US presidential election, Trump declared: 'The only important thing is the unification of the people – because the other people don't mean anything.'[18]

This statement is a form of genius. There is almost candour in Trump's attempt at a unifying theme. He does not even bother to dismiss his critics as the 'old establishment' or members of 'the high society'. Those who toil in Washington as elected politicians or advisers to elected politicians, or as policy specialists who challenge Trump's assertions on the basis of the evidence, are the 'other people that don't mean anything' – an alternative species. Those who cheer Trump rapturously are 'the people'. After Trump's victory, he joins the 'other people': an outsider on the inside.

Quite a lot of the outsiders are still in some way on the inside from the beginning. Marine Le Pen comes from a highly political family and is a successful lawyer. She has not yet had the misfortune to be elected, but she is still part of the political elite. UKIP's Nigel Farage was a wealthy stockbroker from Surrey and a member of the European Parliament. The leading figure for the 'Out' campaign Boris Johnson was educated at Eton and Oxford, was a former editor of the weekly *Spectator* magazine and a former Mayor of London. The leader of the Dutch far-right party, Geert Wilders, has been a member of the Dutch parliament for years. Trump has been a famous multimillionaire entrepreneur and celebrity for decades. He is part of a rarefied privileged elite that has enjoyed fame and wealth on a scale that is unimaginable for most of 'the people'. More to the point, he is transparently so, with his Trump Tower, his ostentatious flashy wealth and his ubiquity on TV.

Somehow they managed to become outsiders taking on the insiders. They were the noble amateurs taking on the experts. 'Britain has had enough of experts,' the leading 'Out' campaigner Michael Gove declared during the UK referendum. Gove was at the time Justice Secretary and had previously been Education Secretary. He was an insider who occasionally ignored the evidence as he pursued some of his policy ideas, but in those jobs he was too smart to dismiss expertise altogether. He was condemning experts rather than addressing their assertions: the trick of the outsider, or the insider on the outside.

———

Now on the inside, Trump faces the conundrums of government. The right-wing outsiders – those who have the luxury of distance from power – are not burdened by dilemmas. They are free to feel strong and appear to be mighty, partly because they declare themselves to be so. Self-deprecation was once a considerable political asset for electorally successful leaders, deployed for humanizing comic impact and to show that power had not gone to their heads. Now the use of self-deprecation risks being regarded as a sign of weakness, while comically self-aggrandizing proclamations of strength from the outsiders resonate, in an era when democratically elected rulers are so weak. In this phase of democratic fragility, an elected ruler's attempts at self-mockery are likely to be met with a nodding concurrence from voters: 'Even he or she admits he or she is stupid.' There is no danger of the outsiders on the right inviting voters to reach such a verdict. They all claim to be strong and do not go in for self-deprecation.

The assertion of strength cannot altogether hide the incoherent and contradictory arguments they espouse. Ultimately, coherence is an essential qualification in democratic politics. Perhaps consistency between values and policies that arise from such values does not matter much at first, when novelty tops all other forms of political ammunition. As outsiders project confidently, maybe some voters are not bothered by incoherence and contradictions or choose not to notice them. But if voters hear a set of arguments that leap from one premise to the contradictory opposite, it is patronizing to assume they will never take note. Even if at first they wilfully choose not to discern the shallowness of the pitch, over time they will do so – or should do so – if mainstream parties find ways of exposing the weakness of their new opponents rather than validating them.

The ideological incoherence of the outsiders is most vivid in the US. In the election Trump was supported by a significant section of the Tea Party, a movement that has three central tenets: fiscal responsibility, limited government and free markets. One of the Tea Party's defining characteristics is a recurring display of vociferous anger at Congress and the White House. Mistrust of politicians and government runs deep. The Tea Partiers were as disillusioned with George W. Bush's big-spending Republicans as they were with Barack Obama's Democrats. They were rebelling internally as much as they were railing against Obama himself.

But Trump is not a fiscal conservative. As the Republican candidate, he was a big spender. He might have claimed to be fiscally conservative when he was in the mood, but the proposed infrastructure plan he put forward during the presidential campaign advocated a trillion-dollar government stimulus programme. In an appearance on the Fox Business network during the campaign, Trump claimed that Hillary Clinton's $275 billion-dollar infrastructure plan was only 'a fraction' of what was needed. He was not only a big spender, but sought to make his plans a winner over the more frugal Clinton. On this basis, Clinton should have been the Tea Party's candidate.

Trump was openly hostile to free trade, a sacrosanct principle among right-wing small-state free-market conservatives. Yet some small-state free-market conservatives have cheered Trump on. Sometimes Trump described himself as anti-government and small-state. Meanwhile he cheered himself on as he put forward government spending programmes on an unprecedented scale, and supported government-imposed tariffs to protect US industry. The right-wing outsiders have prejudices, but no coherent ideology or policies. In his ambition, and again when he was in the mood, Trump was more statist than any of the left-wing outsiders on the march. The Tea Party is being inconsistent in supporting Trump. Trump is being inconsistent as the anti-government president working the levers of the state with a speedy ferocity.

To varying degrees the same applies to the Freedom Party in Austria, Marie Le Pen's Front National in France, the Sweden Democrats, the Danish People's Party, the AfD in Germany, Hungary's Jobbik party and the Dutch Party for Freedom. Each of these parties has different values, but they are dependent on charismatic or distinct leaders, like Trump, who project a populist nationalism and are more vague about the means and consequences of policies than they are about their objectives.

Refugees, immigrants and terrorists are their enemies; they are going to 'sort them out'. They blame ruling 'insiders' – elected politicians – who have created the land of their nightmares.

Forming parties is not easy. All new parties face vivid crises. Such is the scale of the task that problems over identity, purpose and personnel are unavoidable. In the UK in the early 1980s a moderate centre-left party, the SDP (Social Democratic Party), was formed, with trumpets blazing. It did not survive the decade. Across Europe a lot of the parties on the far right are relatively new, still formalizing internal rules and often rowing loudly over what form they should take. Their novelty has advantages, when disillusionment soars in relation to the mainstream, but can also lead to spectacular implosions. Structural fragility combines with ideological incoherence to make them even more frail.

The extraordinary rise of the populist Five Star Movement (M5S) in Italy is emblematic. In barely seven years it has become Italy's biggest opposition group. At the last election in 2013, the M5S took a quarter of the vote. Since then, Silvio Berlusconi's Forza Italia party – once the principal rival of the Democratic Party (PD) – has imploded. Italy's other main right-wing party, the Northern League, has so far been unable to take its place; its appeal is constrained by its regional character and by familiar divisions at the top. Its most recent leader, Matteo Salvini, has formed close ties with Le Pen in France and with Wilders in Holland. In the ideological confusion that marks the far right, his political friendships have been criticized by other senior leaders, including one of his predecessors who argues for a more left-wing approach. Against this background, an M5S government is no longer unthinkable. In June 2016, its candidates for mayor won in Rome and, more surprisingly (and traumatically for the PD), in Turin, a left-wing stronghold.

Neither of the two men who founded the movement in 2009 was a politician at the time. One was Beppe Grillo, the exuberant comedian who has lent the M5S visibility and celebrity charisma. As other outsiders have discovered, not being an orthodox politician is a huge advantage, at least in the early phase of a new party. But it was his co-founder, Gianroberto Casaleggio, an IT executive, who gave it its distinctive character. Casaleggio persuaded the comedian – who was banished from television because of his attacks on the powerful – to start a blog. He then encouraged devotees of the blog to use the Meetup platform to form the local cells that laid the foundations for the M5S.

At the core of the movement's philosophy is the view that it is not a party, but an organization set up to get rid of parties, which many in Italy view as sources of patronage and graft. This idealistic, almost messianic vision explains some of the M5S's other distinguishing traits: its refusal to do deals with pre-existing parties, its cult-like nature (dissidents are regularly purged in online ballots) and its insistence that it is neither of the left nor the right (since it aims to embrace the entire electorate).

Though most of the M5S's leadership came from the left, it has picked up large numbers of votes on the right. Facing in both directions at once, it is a fearsome opponent, especially in two-round elections of the sort introduced by Italy's new electoral law: having eliminated, say, Forza Italia in the first round, the movement can then scoop up many of the eliminated party's voters in the second. But that very advantage makes it vulnerable: its left- and right-leaning members are increasingly clashing over policy and forming informal factions within the movement. The other big challenge it faces is to show that its elected officer-holders can overcome their inexperience to govern effectively. The new M5S Mayor of Rome has made a disastrous start. Virginia Raggi was elected Mayor of Rome in June 2016 – a major victory for Five Star. By February 2017 senior Cabinet members had resigned, and one of her aides was in jail on corruption charges. If the movement cannot run a city, voters may conclude, then it should not be given charge of a country. The M5S is a more extreme manifestation of the outsider and yet, in its attempt to seek a wider appeal and to benefit from an anti-politics culture, it is typical.

Its policies are as much about process as they are about a particular approach to the economy, or funding healthcare. The movement selects candidates through the Internet, with online voting, and regards this form of democracy as the modern equivalent of the outdated political parties. There is a strong emphasis on green issues, and yet they supported the election of Donald Trump, who does not believe in climate change. Not to have a set of rigid coherent policies is almost now a policy. M5S's star performers appear 'modern', but when they have to rule they discover that chaos can be a consequence of wilful and naïve evasiveness.

New parties that evolve without clarity from the top have an advantage. They are flexible enough to widen their appeal and change their pitch, whenever they feel the need to do so. The fatal disadvantage is that they very quickly cease to have a clear sense of purpose and direction.

In Germany the AfD was founded in 2013 as a protest party against the largely German-funded bailouts for indebted eurozone countries. In a short period of time the party has morphed into an ultra-conservative, anti-immigrant party that appeals to those on the right, as well as those wanting to rebel against the establishment. The party is fundamentally split. On one side there are relatively moderate members, for whom the AfD is basically a protest vote; and on the other, there are true believers who claim that what they call the 'reproductive strategies' of Africans are diluting the ethnic-German population. Its leader, Petry, has been a link between the two wings, but inevitably she is vulnerable, because the more overt extremists have succeeded in moving the AfD even further to the right than she would like it to be. Petry is partly with them, in developing and espousing silly and inflammatory ideas. But she is smart enough to realize that a wider appeal requires an appearance of fair-minded policy-making. She struggles to blend the two. In the end she gave up trying, announcing in April 2017 she would not be her party's candidate to become Chancellor in Germany's September general election.

AfD campaign events are attended by protesters holding up signs against the 'lying press' and the 'warmonger United States'. Some wear T-shirts emblazoned with the proclamation 'Großdeutschland', which describes Germany's pre-Second World War borders. Others complain about the 'step-by-step Islamization' of Germany. Some protest against 'gender mainstreaming', such as school children being taught about homosexuality. The only common denominator is their disapproval of the current government's refugee policy. The rest is an assortment of resentments and discontents that do not amount to a clear policy agenda.

AfD has a strong profile in the former communist east of Germany, but a growing following in western parts as well. In interviews, Petry calls the party 'liberal-conservative', rejecting labels such as right-wing populist, far right and anti-immigrant. Interestingly, the ubiquitous term 'liberal' is now being deployed as a weapon by the far right in Germany. She deploys the term because it is partly the case that the AfD adopts, at times, a small-state anti-government pitch that fits with one version of liberalism. But the AfD is also statist and authoritarian when it chooses to be.

During one interview in 2016 Petry noted, 'The idea of the party is embodied in its name, "Alternatives", a response to Merkel's repeated insistence that her policy on the euro was "alternativlos" ("without alternative"). Basically we are a very necessary corrective in German and European politics.' And she predicts that, like the far-right Freedom Party (FPÖ) in neighbouring Austria, the AfD will benefit from 'a breakdown of the big parties'.

Petry is right to note the crises engulfing the larger parties, but her interview highlighted the awkward contortions that she has to make, as the far-right leader seeking wider appeal. Most broadly, any attempts she makes to dismiss the far-right labels might seem hollow, after the party's recent announcement of a European alliance with the far-right FPÖ. 'True, our meeting with the FPÖ could be seen as moving the party to the right, but on the other hand the FPÖ is something you just cannot ignore from a German point of view because it's so near in terms of language and political structure – it would be stupid not to talk to each other. We found similar characteristics with other parties, whether the Danish People's party, the Swiss People's party, the Sweden Democrats, the True Finns, also the Front National,' she says. So does she accept it is a move to the right? She simply says that it could be seen in such a light.

'The migration crisis was the catalyst for our success,' Petry admits in one interview, although she is smart enough to reject the phrase used by Alexander Gauland, the party's leader in the Brandenburg state parliament, who called it 'a gift from heaven'. This is a typical problem for a leader of a newish far-right party. He or she cannot control what their more ardent supporters say. Petry also rejects the idea that her party is opposed to Germany having welcomed refugees. 'Not the real refugees,' she says, arguing that many of the arrivals are not genuinely in need. 'There is enough space for refugees in Germany but the problem is that we don't distinguish any more between migrants and asylum-seekers.' But it is Petry and other right-wing leaders who have conflated migrants and asylum-seekers into one troublemaking group.

Now that new arrivals have largely ceased – due to the closure of the Balkans route, the erection of fences and the sealing of borders around Europe – the AfD has markedly shifted its campaign agenda to one of stopping the 'Islamification' of Germany. Among Petry's concerns are separate swimming classes for boys and girls in schools; the rise of sexual harassment, which she puts down to migrants (she quotes a website that she follows daily, which collects new data from police reports); and the destruction of Christian prayer rooms in homes for asylum-seekers. Occasionally she is candid: 'Well, sometimes, I don't deny, we think we have to use provocative arguments in order to be heard.'[19]

Meanwhile, Petry complains, her party's other policies get little media attention. They want to see more balance between the state and the individual ('at the moment the state interferes in everything'). Yet she wants the state to intervene in order to control the labour market. AfD wants to improve state television ('a regimen of football, telenovellas and American movies with no sign of its legal obligation to inform and educate').[20] In itself, this act of improvement is very statist, for a leader that believes the state interferes too much.

Such issues have been buried, she says, while headlines are made by the party's frequent confrontations with religious, cultural and political figureheads and by its more 'colourful' controversial remarks. New parties on the right are partly shaped by 'colourful' incidents. They are young. They attract eccentrically inexperienced politicians. UKIP has played its part in the UK leaving the EU. At the same time, some of its leading figures have been involved in punch-ups, alleged racist remarks and publishing personal details full of untruths.

As the AfD becomes more popular, the tensions grow. But how does it become more popular? The same thorny question applies to slightly older parties on the right. In its early years, UKIP's leadership espoused a right-wing Thatcherism. At one point its party's ever-changing programme advocated the privatization of the NHS. At the last UK general election in 2015, knowing it was making inroads in traditional Labour areas, UKIP became passionate advocates of the NHS and of higher spending on welfare for the indigenous population. When asked about the party's change of direction, its long-serving leader Nigel Farage declared that past policies were irrelevant and that he could not remember many of them. He denied reading one of his party's more zany manifestos, let alone writing them.

He gets away with it by exuding charming, good-humoured accessibility. Farage is one of the best communicators in UK politics, but his own personal views on tax and public-service reforms are miles away from those of the Labour voters his party wants to attract. His latest successor, Paul Nuttall, aims to destroy Labour, on the basis that he comes from the north of England and from a working-class background. This should not be enough; the policies and the values should be more important. The contradictions widen as UKIP tries to seek wider appeal. In some respects, their growing electoral support makes them more fragile, as they seek to become something they are not.

The far-right Sweden Democrats party has appeared to disavow its roots in the white-supremacist movement. In Denmark, the leader of the Danish People's Party has tried to soften the party's image, making its message less about immigration and more about issues relating to levels of public spending and choices concerning how such spending should be allocated. At its core, the party promises to protect the generous Danish welfare state by restricting access to it. In essence, the party has captured some Social Democrat voters by casting itself as the best defender of the system that the Social Democrats built over decades.

'In Scandinavian countries there is a worry that we send too much welfare out of the country, that we need to think about taking care of our elderly people, our children, our sick people,' says Peter Skaarup, the Danish People's Party's parliamentary leader, in a clever but risky contortion in which he pledges to cut welfare spending, but increase it on the elderly, children and the sick – the main recipients of welfare spending under the current arrangements.[21] The risk is that the outsider becomes more incredible, rather than more popular. But incredibility relies on the insiders exposing the ideological leaps.

In Holland, Geert Wilders, founder and leader of the Party for Freedom, long refused to align himself with European far-right leaders such as Le Pen in France, and expressed concern at being 'linked with the wrong rightist fascist groups', viewing himself as a right-wing liberal.[22] At the end of 2016 Wilders was found guilty of inciting racial discrimination for leading a chant calling for 'fewer, fewer' Moroccans in Holland. He is often seen with other right-wing leaders, including Le Pen. He is the right-wing liberal who is opposed to liberalism.

———

The attempts to project a compassionate pragmatism are half-hearted and unconvincing. Parties cannot escape the essence of their appeal. To take one example, it is not just their roots that have put the Sweden Democrats at the radical end of the spectrum of far-right Nordic populism. Echoes of its past can be heard in its political statements even now, as they attempt to move on from it. One party ideologue wrote about 'the great decisive battle for our civilization, our culture and our nation's survival'. A theme of the party leader's election speech in August 2016 was that Islamism was 'the Nazism and Communism of our time'.[23]

Niclas Nilsson, the Sweden Democrats' group leader on Kristianstad council, rails against 'the huge number of immigrants' and says the country has 'the most irresponsible immigration policy in western Europe… Swedish people don't feel at home any more… The problem we have is basically with the Muslims. They have difficulty assimilating, so much of their culture is based on Islam.'[24] Nilsson acknowledges – but has no explanation for – the fact that the vote for his party is higher in isolated, rural areas where there are fewer immigrants.

In France the leader of the Front National, Marine Le Pen, strikes a more reasonable tone than her father (a previous presidential candidate), but her social vision is of a mythical, homogeneous France that never existed. At a convention of right-wing, populist parties in Milan in January 2015 she argued that Europe's ongoing migrant crisis was set to 'impoverish' the continent. Around a thousand people attended the convention, which also hosted Italy's Lega Nord (Northern League), the party overtly rooted on the right, compared to Five Star's convenient apolitical flexibility; the Dutch Party for Freedom; the Austrian Freedom Party; and other right-wing parties from across Europe.

In her opening remarks, Le Pen said the influx of migrants arriving on the continent would 'kill their civility forever'. Heinz-Christian

Strache from the Austrian Freedom Party declared at the gathering: 'We all agree that Europe and European culture and freedom are under threat today because of irresponsible mass immigration.'

'The European Union and leaders of national governments have failed in a dramatic fashion. We are here to say that we want a Europe as normal, that another Europe is possible,' said the secretary of the Lega Nord, Matteo Salvini. He added that we must 'recover sovereignty as a matter of urgency'.[25]

What is a 'normal' Europe? What precisely does he mean by 'sovereignty'? What does Le Pen mean when she warns of impoverishment and the end of civility?

Like other right-wing outsiders, Le Pen is a statist. She speaks at a time of heightened fears in France of terrorism, and of unemployment at a much higher level than in Germany and the UK. Like Trump in the US, she sees government as a more benevolent force than many on the centre left. Like Trump, she proclaims ends without being sure of the means towards those ends: shielding voters from globalization, promoting protectionism, leaving the eurozone, imposing taxes on imports and on the job contracts of foreigners, lowering the retirement age, increasing welfare benefits and boosting defence spending. Only the mainstream's reluctance to make the case for the state as a benevolent force gives the outsiders the space to pledge to pull a thousand levers.

The outsiders make their claims with only fragile structures below them. Under Marine's father, the Front National was closer to a neo-liberal club for churlish business owners. Jean-Marie Le Pen was a convicted Holocaust-denier, who showed more interest in rabble-rousing. Marine Le Pen is subtler and more sophisticated, but beneath her are some of those unreliable eccentrics who followed her father's leadership. The internal machinations of some parties on the outside are darkly comical, and perhaps inevitably so. Forming new parties is a difficult task, and many do not last very long.

UKIP struggled to find a successor to Nigel Farage to lead it, after the Brexit referendum. One candidate, in one of several leadership contests that took place within months of the referendum, ended up in hospital. Steven Woolfe was involved in what was described as an 'altercation' with another UKIP MEP. Based on the photographs of Woolfe recovering in hospital, it was quite an altercation. The injured Woolfe withdrew from the contest and soon afterwards left UKIP. After many twists and turns, UKIP elected Paul Nuttall as its leader. He was the one with embellished claims on his website and LinkedIn about his academic qualifications and his footballing prowess. He later maintained on British television that he was not directly responsible for the claims in question. The amateurish shapelessness is not surprising, when most of the parties on the far right are fairly new. Like their inexperience, this is not their fault. Parties take a long time to take on definitive shape and become robust. As they do so, there is no guarantee they will survive.

Without clear definition, the egos of leading figures within the parties can be more of a driving force than ideas and policies are. But dependence on a single ego is a precarious starting point for a political force. Egos are erratic and unpredictable. They come and go. Parties are meant to be for the long term. It is Trump who leads the outsiders' revolution in the US, and not the rest of the Republican Party. Farage was the driving force behind the rise of UKIP. Without him, there would be no UKIP, but with Farage leading, a party grew up under him without many binding principles beyond the overwhelming cause that it met: the UK leaving the EU.

These are not incidental problems in democratic politics. Coherent ideas and values are the starting point to sustained popularity. A strong party structure is the essential mechanism that binds in support. Party unity is a precondition to sustained electoral success. Ultimately big, ill-disciplined egos are a distraction and are not the solution to a party's appeal. The outsiders are dependent on outsized egos in order to make a mark, and egos can quickly reduce a new party to rubble. Again, the seeds of the outsiders' success are also the cause of their precarious existence.

Even presidential candidates stand for a party – or are supposed to do so. In the US election, Trump was the Republican candidate without the support of many senior Republicans. He was a symptom of a crisis in the Republican Party, and not part of a substantial revival on the right in the US. Some of Trump's rivals for the presidential candidacy were at least as right-wing as he is. Their campaigns were more confused ideologically and were tinged with a simplistic moral verve that made even Trump seem expedient and sophisticated. Yet others among his rivals were so horrified by the rise of Trump that they felt compelled to disown him.

Trump speaks for himself and not the Republican Party. The 'people' turned to him because he was Trump, and not because he was a Republican. 'We want Trump,' his audience cried. They got him, but his party is still in the doldrums. The figures around him on the whole have as little experience as Trump himself. Senior Republicans working with him do so warily and reluctantly. Trump relies mostly on friends and family, rather than a party infrastructure in Washington that in the past was capable of providing a president with substantial political figures, who were experienced and from different parts of the party. Even the then-reviled President Bush was able to appoint Colin Powell and Condoleezza Rice, along with Dick Cheney and Donald Rumsfeld. The Bush administration was too wide to be coherent and disciplined, but at least its width reflected a still semi-buoyant Republican Party. Trump has no such party to turn to because, in its current ideological bewilderment, the party of the recent past no longer exists.

UKIP makes the Republican Party, with its whacky array of potential presidential candidates and wider confusion, seem wholly sensible. Months after it secured an historic victory in the EU referendum, UKIP's newly elected leader, Diane James, resigned after being in the post for just eighteen days. There was then the added farce of Farage stepping back in to become the party's leader for the third time, albeit this time as acting leader. Farage had resigned after the 2015 general election, only to announce that he was ready to lead again. He resigned again after the referendum, but returned as acting leader. Like the leadership candidate who ended up in hospital, James left the party. This was a period when UKIP should have been flourishing. Having won the referendum, its supporters believed that it would play a leading part in defining what form Brexit would eventually take. Instead, UKIP behaved as if it was taking part in a revival of *Monty Python's Flying Circus* – the silly party breaking all records for silliness. The post-referendum rowdiness reflects a wider pattern. In recent years prominent councillors and candidates have frequently been expelled and, in a small number of cases, arrested.

Such parties and individuals are weak. Yet they are strong. Liberal democracies in northern Europe change their policies on immigration and asylum. Leaders who supported Merkel's sympathetic response to asylum-seekers from Syria conduct panic-stricken U-turns. The UK makes plans to leave the European Union. Trump is the most powerful elected leader in the world.

How to explain the strength of the politically weak? A fashionable theory suggests that we are living in a post-truth era, in which lying and lack of knowledge become electoral assets. For reasons that are understandable, the voters who were victims of inequality, economic and social insecurities – or who felt they were – hear or see what they want to hear and see.

There is something in this. Uncontaminated by the complexities of power, the outsiders' propositions are untested. They utter words to euphoric audiences, and do not implement policies that can fuel intense disillusionment and cries of betrayal. Yet the concept of the post-truth era is also dangerously untruthful, in its implicit evocation of a recent past that was a glorious age of candour. The implication is untrue partly because it cannot be true. Truth in politics is always partly subjective, and rightly so. One person's noble public-spending commitment is another's reckless waste of taxpayers' money. More importantly, the concept of the post-truth era obscures the main reason why mainstream parties have become so fragile.

In the new, traumatically constraining context of the globalized economy, mainstream parties on the left and right have failed calamitously to find ways of telling the truth about what they can do, what they want to do and what they believe, with conviction, they should do. Their failure to frame arguments based on an essence of truth gives space for the outsiders to flourish mendaciously.

In 2015 the general election in Britain was contested on an untruth. George Osborne framed the election around his plans to wipe out the deficit in the following parliament – a framing that had only a very limited relationship with the truth.

In the drama of post-Brexit events, the then chancellor announced almost casually that he had dropped the target, which he was never conceivably going to meet. Yet twelve months earlier, the election was dominated by the deficit mistruth. The UK Labour leader, Ed

Miliband, was forced – or felt he was forced – to make arguments that he did not believe, in order to appear 'responsible' on spending. Miliband had to propose Osborne-like cuts or face accusations that he was planning to trigger tax bombshells. In order to appear even more 'responsible' than Osborne, in relation to the untruthful deficit target, Labour refused to commit even to the modest increases in NHS spending that the Conservatives had proposed. Privately, Labour's leaders knew they would have to spend much more, but they could not speak openly because they would be accused of spending recklessly, rather than focusing on the deficit.

When Miliband did speak the truth, on BBC's pre-election *Question Time*, insisting that he did not accept that the spending of the last Labour government had caused the financial crash, his honesty was widely viewed as a fatal gaffe. He should have lied and played the untruthful game, in which the profligacy of the past would be replaced by an Osborne-like stringency, even though Osborne had no idea how he would be so stringent without wrecking lives and the economy – and the Conservatives would later drop the whole facade. The entire election was based on a fantasy.

Trump might have taken fantasy politics several steps further, but the fantasies have always been in play during campaigns. It is the task of opponents to expose them and persuade the voters to listen to them, as they are doing so. This is not happening, and that is why the right-wing outsiders go unchallenged. The insiders are not sure any longer *how* to challenge.

The right-wing outsiders are deeply flawed in terms of experience, organization and coherence. But they declare loudly and confidently that they will come to the rescue of those in their countries who feel ignored. They have a view of the state – their state – and its potential to bring security and stability. That is their strength, in the era of globalization. For different reasons, mainstream parties on the left and right have chosen to be self-effacing about their purpose in government. In contrast to the right-wing outsiders, and indeed the left-wing outsiders, the mainstream leaders on the centre left and centre right have partly chosen to be weak.

2

THE RISE OF THE LEFT-WING OUTSIDERS

In some respects the outsiders on the left are incomparably different from their right-wing equivalents. Fewer of them rise as prominently as their counterparts, but not quite as few as fashionable orthodoxy insists. A popular theme in political columns since the 2008 crash is that, counter-intuitively, the right has benefited and the left has been plunged into crisis. Yet the swing to the right is not uniform. Since 2008 the US has elected a Democrat president twice and New York has opted for a radical-left mayor; Canada has elected an ambitiously liberal prime minister; and France has voted for a socialist president, even if that particular winner only managed to serve a single term. Even in the UK, where the Conservative Party won landslides with their eyes closed in the 1980s, its leader at the time of the financial crash, David Cameron, failed to win an overall majority in 2010. After the 2015 election, UKIP had a single MP – one who did not talk to the leader at the time, Nigel Farage. As for the left that rose from the outside, it came to power in Greece; brought to life the battle for the Democrats' presidential nomination; and changed the political dynamics of several EU countries. It is a myth that disillusioned voters have turned instinctively to the right. Some have tiptoed leftwards. And a few have made a leap.

The differences with their right-wing counterparts are stark and important. The left-wing outsiders do not use the 'threat' of foreigners as a populist theme, as some on the right do. Their view of the state is more coherent than the 'small-state and big-government' right-wing outsiders. They do not spend half their time arguing against the state and the other half telling us what they would do with the levers of government. They spend *all* their time telling us what they would do with the levers. Some propose economic policies that are rooted in an analysis framed by the 2008 financial crisis. Respected economists are often part of their entourages. Quite often, in their radical distinctiveness, they bring the cautious mainstream left to a semblance of political life. Hillary Clinton might have lost the US presidential campaign more decisively, if Bernie Sanders had not forced her to become a little more daring. And the UK's Labour Party risked dying of boredom, before Jeremy Corbyn's candidacy in 2015 brought a soporific leadership contest to life. In Greece and Spain mainstream left parties were languishing, before movements to the left of them forced a rethink of sorts.

While they spark distinctively, the left-wing outsiders have one significant connection with the right-wing alternative: not only do they speak of the levers they will pull to transform the lives of voters, but they imply a power to act unilaterally that does not exist any more. While highlighting forcefully the iniquitous consequences of globalization, they are reluctant to recognize the constraints on individual governments arising from the same phenomenon. They imply that they can act as if a single country can determine its course on its own, and do not explore too expansively the potential damage of acting with such parochial resolution. In this respect, they dance with the right.

The delusion of parochial resolution closes when power is secured. At the start of 2015 the left-wing Syriza party won a general election in Greece, an early sign of the much wider political explosion that was to follow. The pattern has become familiar, but was relatively fresh then. Few predicted such an outcome when the campaign began, including the leader of the victorious party, Alexis Tsipras. But as the contest got under way, Tsipras discovered that he was tapping into an appetite for defiant change amongst a significant proportion of the electorate. On the whole, the left-wing outsiders in Greece have been treated closer to celebrities than their right-wing equivalent. Even the older left-wingers were hailed as if they were Mick Jagger on another mesmerizing tour, although most were a little younger than him.

In January 2015 the BBC reported that Tspiras was 'welcomed like a rock star' when he came to cast his vote in his local polling station.[1] By polling day the adulatory hope of the campaign was turning into a far more intoxicating collective sensation. Voters were using the apparent power of the ballot box not to protest, but to make Tsipras their new prime minister.

A few hours later, as the votes were counted, it became clear that Tsipras and his party had won by a wider margin than most analysts had expected, even in the final days of the campaign. As the scale of the victory became obvious, Tsipras made an emblematic declaration to doting crowds in the centre of Athens – one that should be framed, for its deceptive sense of direction: 'Our future is not austerity… Are we to stick to the rules on monetary union even if those rules are wrong? The new government will stand for justice and equality… We have a compass to change direction.'[2]

The declaration was as disingenuous as the claims of the right-wing populists to represent 'the people'. In one form or another, the

Greeks' future was doomed to be austere, even if the term 'austerity' joins the lexicon of overused and imprecise terms deployed in the era of the outsiders. This dismissal of 'austerity' was followed by one of the defining questions of the time.

Were Greeks to stick to the rules on monetary union, even if those rules were wrong? The question implied a defiant 'No'. Or was Tsipras suggesting that, without question, they would change the rules? The ambiguity, dressed up as a new policy, was a form of genius, but one that would land him in trouble. This seemingly assertive posing of a dilemma raised many others. Who decides whether the rules are wrong? How were Greeks to remain part of the euro, if they were not going to stick to the rules that were already being applied with a degree of flexibility?

Who rules? This was the fundamental question at the heart of the Greek election and, more broadly, is one that lies at the heart of the rise of other outsiders, too. The outsiders insist that they will rule as they wish, if elected. They have a point. Winners in a democratic election have earned the right to govern as they choose. And countries have self-interested obligations to work with others, at least in areas of common concern. Yet what form does self-interest take, and what are the areas of common concern? The question is more complex for a relatively poor country that is part of the single currency, contorting to the pretence that an interest rate that suits the German economy will suit theirs, too.

Crowds in Athens celebrated through the night in January 2015, chanting Tsipras' name. They were hailing their stunning and provocative act of electoral upheaval – a revolution at the ballot box. The newly elected Greek government would decide the future of their country's economic policies: how much they would cut spending and raise taxes, and the degree to which they would stimulate the struggling economy. That was the plan. The leaders of other, more powerful countries in the eurozone, and non-elected figures who ran the European Central Bank, would no longer be able to tell them what to do.

In the heady excitement in Athens, the contradictions in Tsipras' beguiling message were easily, and perhaps wilfully, overlooked. But the act of defiance was not as resolute as it seemed. In effect, Tsipras was proclaiming: 'The rules are wrong. We want to remain part of the project where the wrong rules apply.'

Like Trump in the US, Tsipras had the fortune, and misfortune, to win. His words were tested by power. Inevitably and very quickly they were shown to make only limited practical sense. He and most Greek voters wanted to remain in the euro, and therefore they could not defy the rules governing the single currency. He could negotiate with his eurozone partners, but from a weak bargaining position: they knew he did not want to leave. Tspiras was in the opposite position from the UK, in relation to the EU. The UK was in an equally weak position after the 2016 referendum, because it had decided to leave as its government began what was misleadingly billed as a 'negotiation'. Its best hand would have been a threat to leave; now that hand could no longer be played as a threat.

The election of Syriza raised some fundamental questions relating to democracy and accountability. Who or what institutions decided the economic policies of Greece? Was it the Greek voters, who had supported with a desperate enthusiasm a party pledge to end austerity? Was it the European Central Bank, which sought to police the rules governing membership of the eurozone? Was it the German government, under pressure from its own electorate to show it was being tough on Greece and not subsidizing the perceived profligacy of previous Greek administrations (Angela Merkel was already being punished electorally for being soft on Greece, even though that was not how it seemed from the Greek perspective)? Was it the newly elected Greek government, which had put the Keynesian case for an end to ruthless spending cuts, to replace them with investment that would boost the economy?

The early answer was that it was largely the hard-line views of the German government, EU foreign ministers and other EU institutions that prevailed. Given that the Greek government wanted to be part of the euro, Tsipras was very quickly forced to face the reality of pooled sovereignty. He and the voters who put him in power could not decide alone what rules were right and wrong. Those being hard-line in other parts of the EU were doing so partly because they were accountable to their electorates. In the eurozone, accountability is a thorny issue that threatens to become a fatal one.

Faced with insoluble dilemmas of power, one outsider on the inside discovered a solution. He resigned. Very quickly the charismatic Greek finance minister, Yanis Varoufakis, left the new government. The sequence was inevitable and the script could have been written on the night of Syriza's victory. On 25 June 2015, six months after the election, Varoufakis was presented with an ultimatum – the conditions for staying part of the euro. It comprised a fiscal proposal, a reform agenda and a funding formula that Varoufakis considered, with some justification, to be a form of economic tyranny that could not be implemented by any government, let alone one elected to pursue an anti-austerity programme. The next day Tsipras called for a referendum, so that the Greek people could in theory decide for themselves whether to accept the programme.

On 5 July 2015 the referendum took place, after a short campaign. Tspiras and Varoufakis had campaigned vigorously in favour of a 'No' vote, against the united support for a 'Yes' of Greece's media and of Europe's leadership. To make his position clear, Varoufakis declared on television that he would resign as finance minister if the Greeks voted 'Yes'. The outcome of the vote was a resounding 61.5 per cent vote in favour of 'No'. Varoufakis went on television, soon after the result was announced, to celebrate the Greeks' outstanding courage and to declare that the government was determined to honour this new mandate for what he described as a more sensible, honourable agreement with its creditors. This was one of the more short-lived statements in recent times.

A few hours later, far into the night, Varoufakis resigned, after discussions with Tsipras. Varoufakis concluded that Tsipras was ready to concede what, in his view, would be too much ground on spending cuts. Perhaps Varoufakis could not see a way through because there was no clear route to follow. He no longer had to face the dilemmas of power – in his case, an acute dilemma. Who was in control? Who decides? In his resignation statement the following morning Varoufakis said that 'other European participants' had expressed a wish for his absence. Later he explained that he decided to resign during a meeting with Tsipras on the night of the referendum, during which he discovered that the prime minister, instead of being energized by the 'No' vote, declared his intention to accept some of the proposed austerity measures. Unwilling to sign such a 'surrender' document, Varoufakis chose to stand down.

Tspiras had no choice. The referendum gave him a mandate, but a meaningless one. Merkel and other EU leaders could not declare to their own voters that, in the light of the verdict of the Greek electorate, they were giving in. Again the referendum raised questions about who ruled over whom. Could the Greek electorate impose its view on the electorate of Germany? The answer was that it could not. Tsipras made a misjudgement in calling the referendum.

His victory in the plebiscite gave him no fresh ammunition and a lot of trouble. Leaders are nearly always mistaken in calling referendums. They appear to offer a way through nightmarishly blocked paths, only to block them altogether.

Subsequently Varoufakis was cheered by packed audiences at book festivals around the world. The cheers are deserved. He is a vivid speaker with some powerful arguments, which combine continued support for the euro – and, indeed, the wider European Union – with ambitious arguments about what governments can achieve in the era of the global economy. Nonetheless, in choosing to resign, Varoufakis took the easy route. He no longer had to navigate the contradictory contours of Syriza's victory in an election and a referendum.

Tsipras remained in power, armed with a referendum victory against the EU-imposed cuts. But over time he did concede far more ground than he had ever suggested he would, in his various triumphant campaigns, because the alternative option of leaving the euro would have been even worse.

By the summer of 2016 he had agreed to automatic spending cuts, if stringent fiscal targets were not met. The automatic trigger had been imposed by the European Stability Mechanism as a condition of continuing aid from a third bailout of €86 billion. Once again, the thorny democratic question is raised. Who is running Greece? Is it the bodies responsible for the European Stability Mechanism, or a Greek prime minister who won a referendum by seemingly refusing to accept economic discipline, but knowing that an economic implosion would follow, if Greece were forced out of the euro with chronic debts?

That mechanism, as well as a raft of new taxes that Tsipras had also vowed he would never impose, went to the parliament in Athens for approval. The only way to escape the dilemmas of government was to lose power or resign and go on a book tour.

———

The leader of the Labour Party in the UK, Jeremy Corbyn, never sought to explain how he would address different but related dilemmas, if he were elected as prime minister. Unused to the disciplines of government or indeed Opposition, Corbyn was indiscriminate in his policy pronouncements. His programme, as far as he formed one, was coherent in its faith in the state, and to some extent did offer hope to those left behind by the increasingly fractured agencies of government. But the lack of interest in how policies were paid for – a defining theme in UK elections – and in the detail of particular proposals that came and went meant that Corbyn has struggled for a wider appeal. In relation to his confused approach to Brexit, did Corbyn support the free movement of people as a matter of unyielding principle? Sometimes he did and sometimes he did not. How would he pay for the renationalization of the railways? He was opposed to 'austerity' and pledged to reverse 'the cuts'. Did that mean he was opposed to all cuts? Where would he find the money to reverse them all? There were strong arguments to do so in certain cases, but he made a more sweeping pledge in some speeches, without explaining where the money would come from. Corbyn showed little interest in policy detail or how to frame an argument with broad appeal.

His failure to do so followed one of the most sensational ascents in the history of modern British politics. Once again we were taken aback – even though Tsipras had already shocked us with a bigger triumph. Most of the left-wing outsiders rose from distinct far-left parties, but the rise of Jeremy Corbyn was unusual because he became the leader of a mainstream party in the UK. The Labour Party had ruled the country for thirteen successive years, from 1997 to 2010. Tony Blair had been its leader from 1994 to 2007. By the end of his tenure as prime minister, Blair had moved so far towards the right that the then leader of the Conservative Party, David Cameron, agreed with most of what Blair was seeking to do as a leader. Cameron described himself sincerely, and with justification, as the 'heir to Blair'.

Corbyn was not the heir to Cameron or Blair, which is partly why he became leader. The virtually interchangeable Cameron and Blair eras were products of different times, and the chickens were now coming home to roost, as chickens always do. In contrast to Blair's view that there was no longer a left/right divide in politics, Corbyn had been a defiantly left-wing Labour MP since 1983 – the same year Blair was elected to the Commons. In contrast to Blair, Corbyn had never served on his party's frontbench, either in government or in opposition. His rise was unprecedented in UK politics. Corbyn had moved from left-wing rebel to party leader in the space of a single leadership contest – one that Corbyn himself had assumed at the beginning he could not win.

As with the right-wing outsiders, his lack of experience was an early asset. Corbyn had not been in the Labour government that supported the war in Iraq. He had opposed economic policies that played their part in the banking crash. His hands were clean – a cleanliness that arose partly because he had avoided the impurities of office. But the fundamental reason for his appeal also made him weak. Corbyn had never had to give a moment's thought as to what it took to lead a national party, which was the only alternative government to the Conservatives in the UK. Such thoughtlessness should have been a bar to leadership. As with some on the right, it became a qualification.

He was one of four candidates in the UK Labour Party's 2015 leadership contest, a political battle that took place in the summer, after the party's latest traumatic and unexpected general-election defeat. When Corbyn agreed to be the left's candidate, his close ally, the Labour MP John McDonnell, tried to be supportive about the tedious campaigning to come. McDonnell told Corbyn that the two of them would be like characters in the sitcom *Last of the Summer Wine*: two old men reflecting on life in near-empty rooms. After the ordeal, McDonnell told Corbyn, he could spend more time growing vegetables on his much-loved allotment. Neither of them could believe what happened next.

Early on in his campaign Corbyn addressed a rally in north London. The hall in Camden Town was so crammed with excited supporters that he was obliged to address three more overflow meetings, a sign of the seismic change that was about to take place. Like Tsipras, Corbyn was a rock star. In order to be seen and heard at one of the overflow rallies, Corbyn climbed to the top of a fire engine, to ecstatic cheers from a large crowd of admirers. Minutes earlier, when he spoke in the main hall, some of the younger fans, who had failed to get a seat, scaled the outside wall to peer hopefully through the open windows, taking up their precarious position so that they might get to see their new political hero. No political figure in British politics has generated such enthusiasm since a youthful Tony Blair managed to make the 'radical centre' sound simultaneously exciting and reassuring in the mid-1990s. Corbyn was seeking to lead the same party, but from so much further to the left than Blair that the duo might as well have come from different political planets.

The aspiring leader made the same speech to each of his audiences in Camden Town that evening in 2015, and to similar ecstatic rallies around the country for the rest of the summer. The sixty-six-year-old Labour MP told his audiences that Labour had a duty to 'offer something more than austerity'. With a flourish at the beginning of each speech, he proclaimed that the financial crisis of 2008 was not caused by 'firefighters, nurses, street cleaners, but by deregulation and sheer levels of greed'. This was a smart juxtaposition and an accurate one, too. In his own way he was echoing Sir Mervyn King's insights from 2011. Corbyn was not only highlighting the causes of the crash in the most general of terms, but pointing out that the victims of the post-crash policies were innocent, while those who were responsible had not been punished. This was the most potent of messages for left-wing outsiders and, indeed, even on the right across the Western world.

In Corbyn's assessment of the response to the crisis he pointed out that the banks taken over by the government, in the aftermath of the crash, were not kept in public ownership permanently, as they should have been, suggesting also that in opposition from 2010 the Labour Party had made the mistake of accepting 'more austerity and more cuts'. Instead it should have opposed 'the wage freeze, the lower wages in the public sector, the brutality of the welfare system', which were introduced by the Conservative government that came to power in 2010.

In contrast, Corbyn proclaimed his three major objectives to be 'the elimination of poverty, the promotion of an expanding economy and opportunity for all'. As a climactic he declared: 'I want a civilized society where everyone cares for everyone else. Enough of free-market economics! Enough of being told austerity works! We can create an economy where we invest in manufacturing industry, invest in green energies, invest in railways and invest in housing. And no more massive debts for students!'[3]

The crowds cheered but, like those attending Trump's rallies in the US and the Tsipras victory rally in Greece, they did not want to spoil the heady excitement by asking how Corbyn would achieve his objectives. The aspiring leader had no obligation, at such an early stage in his speedy political journey, to give precise details about how much he planned to borrow and how he would reassure the mighty markets that he would not be profligate. But he was implying, in his various statements, vast sums of additional spending: renationalizing the banks and railways; high spending on public-sector wages; higher welfare payments; free tuition fees for students; investment in manufacturing, transport, housing and green energy. No wonder the ecstatic audiences cheered. Separately and together, the prospect of such wonders sounded exciting. But there was no attempt, even in the broadest terms, to explain how this would happen. Explanation is a requirement of leadership, not least when a potential leader plans to take his party much further in one ideological direction.

In the short term, such realism was not a requirement of Corbyn's adulatory supporters. At the end of the speech audiences repeatedly chanted, 'Jez we can!', a play on their hero's first name, an echo of the 2008 Obama presidential campaign, and an assertion of their justified confidence that Corbyn could sensationally become the next leader of the Labour Party. The chant was also an expression of a wider hope – one that was less precise – that Corbyn could bring about radical change in the country.

Throughout August, Corbyn toured the UK, now the latest political idol. Everywhere the ecstatic reaction was the same. The following month he was elected leader of the Labour Party in a landslide victory. Two months earlier he had been a last-minute candidate in the contest, without any hope of winning. He had assumed he would put the left-wing case for a few weeks, before resuming his role as a backbench MP, part of a small band of similar-minded MPs who regularly rebelled against their leader.

During (and after) the contest Corbyn thought often of his hero, Tony Benn, the left-winger who loved taking part in leadership campaigns, regarding them as a platform to make a case, to 'teach' socialism to as wide an audience as possible. Benn was a more powerful orator, the most mesmerizing speaker in British politics during the 1970s and 1980s, and had been a long-serving Cabinet minister. Benn had written books and had thought deeply about democracy and accountability, based on his experiences as a minister. His views were widely derided when he first espoused them, but he repeatedly raised a question at the heart of the outsiders' ascendancy: Who rules, and how are they held to account? Partly as a result of their opposition to the EU, several senior Conservatives became in some respects ardent Bennites, sharing with Tony Benn a passion for the sovereignty of the UK parliament and narrowly defined forms of democratic accountability. When Benn died in 2014, it was the future Tory Brexit secretary, David Davis, who presented a gloriously counter-intuitive tribute on the BBC – the best political programme in the UK that year.[4] (When Davis stood down as shadow Home Secretary and MP to trigger a by-election in his constituency in July 2008, Benn was one of Davis' most enthusiastic supporters. Davis fought the by-election to secure a democratic endorsement, as he saw it, for his opposition to some anti-terrorist measures, along with his wider focus on civil liberties.) Davis and other senior Conservatives became gripped by arguments relating to democracy and accountability, just as Tony Benn had been in the

1970s and 1980s. Constantly they posed the question, especially in relation to the EU: Who is accountable to whom?

Benn never won a leadership contest. Corbyn won a landslide, twice. The difference was the context – a pattern forming across democratic politics – and not the quality of the candidates. Suddenly the rebellious backbencher was the UK leader of the Opposition. His elevation marked the most remarkable outcome of any leadership contest in the history of British politics. Yet he had got to the very top of his party without explaining how he would realize his dream. He had never had to explain 'how' in his long career as a backbencher. He had never been tested by policy implementation.

In the short term, such realism was not a requirement of Corbyn's adulatory supporters. For a BBC Radio 4 series, on Corbyn's first year as leader, one of those who attended a Corbyn rally declared, 'Jeremy is like a religious prophet. He has integrity. He represents something new and exciting'.[5] Such sincere observations show why no further explanations were required from Corbyn, at least in order to win the leadership contest. He would take his followers to the Promised Land because he was inherently decent, a sincere, principled radical who wanted a fairer country. That was enough. Corbyn did face three other candidates in that leadership contest, and one candidate when he was challenged again a year later. Yet none of them could get close to his support among Labour members, even though nearly all Labour MPs were opposed to Corbyn. None of the other candidates could highlight the inevitable weaknesses of a resolutely backbench MP who had accidentally become leader. Like Tsipras, Corbyn was a consequence of the post-financial crash politics and, unlike Tspiras, of the long rule of New Labour in the UK.

―――

A few months after Corbyn became the unexpected leader of the UK's Labour Party, a left-wing government was formed in Portugal. A key to making the government possible was the rise of a relatively new party, the Left Bloc, led by the former charismatic actor Catarina Martins. In the election in November 2015 her party secured 10 per cent of the vote, becoming the third-biggest party in Portugal. Martins' party agreed to back the socialist leader, António Costa, in the new parliament. The socialists, under Costa's leadership, were regarded as expedient, so much so that they had inadvertently created space for Martins to flourish to the left of them. Martins' message was the same every night during her campaign: 'The Portuguese want change and an end to austerity.' As with other left-wing outsiders, the assertion was not accompanied by much of an explanation: How? What precisely does 'an end to austerity' mean? Like other left-wing outsiders, Catarina Martins conveyed an impatience for change by looking different. She was much younger than Corbyn.

The forty-two-year-old actress with a penchant for jeans and red blouses shook up a Lisbon political scene that was dominated by men in suits. Corbyn had done the same in a different way, by *not* looking especially smart or bothered by his appearance. Syriza's leadership had done so by conveying a casual, cool look. In Portugal, as the only female leading a major party, Martins took the far-left to the brink of sharing power for the first time since the mid-1970s, when a revolution ended four decades of rightist dictatorship. 'They are mostly men with the same background and same way of thinking,' she said of Portugal's political class. 'Politicians need to speak about things that people understand, in a language they understand.'6

Her assertions were similar to those on the right. She spoke a language the people understood. Other elected politicians did not. On the whole, mainstream politicians have lost the art of communication, of explaining constantly what they are trying to do and why. The outsiders tend to be powerful communicators, or they are at least direct and accessible. There is little point in dense messages that are inaccessible.

But quite quickly Martins discovered the compromises required of leadership. While leading negotiations for her party with Portugal's centre-left socialists and old-school communists to give support to an 'anti-austerity government', the Left Bloc had to back away from some of its more radical demands, such as withdrawing from NATO and abandoning commitments to eurozone budget rules. Like Tsipras, the Left Bloc was part of a government that wanted to stay in the euro. They had to obey the rules.

Founded in 1999, the Left Bloc pre-dates Syriza, and Podemos in Spain, but is still relatively new. Like the new parties on the right, it suffers from splits and personality clashes as it tries to widen its appeal while agreeing on values and the policies that arise from them. Politics is difficult. Forming new parties that make it, beyond the novelty of the early phase, is almost impossibly difficult.

Martins took over as party spokeswoman in 2012. Her politics combined straight talking, in an attempt to woo centrist voters, with hard-edged rhetoric to rally activists. 'I was always political, even if I've little experience in party politics or public office,' she declared in one interview.

She runs the Left Bloc with a supporting cast of dynamic young women. 'I've always fought for greater visibility for women in public affairs, because I think it's the only way to get equality,' Martins says. 'I discovered that women are really affected by the fact that a woman was leading the campaign. That created a closeness that enabled us to discuss certain themes, to put more things onto the political agenda.'

She and other leading women make a tonal difference to politics. They are younger and more informal. They raise issues that are too casually overlooked by the mainstream. But they struggle, along with the government, to resolve the impossible dilemmas.

The government in Portugal struggles with the same question as the government in Greece: Who governs? It seeks to balance its 'anti-austerity' objectives with the demands from the EU for fiscal prudence. In some respects, it wrestles with the dilemmas of power imaginatively and innovatively. In 2016 the Portuguese government unveiled plans to raise pensions, reduce income tax and increase support for the poor, without running foul of EU deficit rules. The prime minister, António Costa, also has to reassure investors that Portugal is not at risk of needing another bailout. He walks a high wire, fearing downgrades of Lisbon's only investment-grade credit rating – downgrades that could lead to Portugal being excluded from the European Central Bank's bond-buying programme, removing a vital safety net from government financing.

Mário Centeno, his finance minister, describes the government's economic plans as a 'budget of the left' that would lift incomes and lower direct taxation, while at the same time ensuring 'good relations' with Brussels. This is the eternal balancing act of the left-wing outsiders in, or close to, power within the EU.

Although the EU decided in August 2016 against fining Portugal for repeatedly breaching deficit limits, the Commission warned that it would suspend EU structural funding if Lisbon continued to miss its budget targets. The government had no choice but to seek lower budget deficits through higher taxes and selected spending cuts.

The balancing act involved long negotiations between ministers, the radical Left Bloc and the hard-line communist party, the two groups on whose parliamentary votes the minority socialist government depended.

To help offset higher spending in some areas, the government made choices that were bold and fair, introducing a new 'fat tax' on sugary drinks, as well as a controversial 'luxury' charge on homes valued at more than €600,000. Tax on income from apartment lets to tourists, such as those rented through Airbnb, was to be increased from 15 to 35 per cent. Costa, who had vowed to 'turn the page on austerity', said the measures would help restore incomes after a punishing three-year EU-led bailout programme that had 'set the economy back 30 years'.

However, international forecasters, rating agencies and opposition parties expressed concern about low growth, high debt and a fragile banking sector. In September 2016 the IMF warned that the country's fragile economic recovery was 'running out of steam'.[7]

Martins might have claimed to speak the language of the people, but she was now involved in sustaining a government that must answer to the IMF and those that govern the eurozone, as well as its own voters, who had supported her leftish objectives. Who governs? The recurring question becomes a more intense nightmare for left-wing outsiders who move onto the inside. But it is becoming equally nightmarish for the European Union. In its attempt to enforce rules, it fuels support for the outsiders.

As a radical-left coalition took shape in the Portuguese parliament, with the smaller left parties backing the socialist government, a general election was being contested in Spain. Podemos has not yet been challenged by power, but is unavoidably tested by division over the most propitious route to government. Podemos made waves, before losing support in elections later in 2016. As with Tsipras, Corbyn and Martins, there were the familiar fragilities behind the compelling early campaigns. Once again they were the fragilities of a young party, not fully formed, as it made electoral headway. There were the ideological and strategic tensions that arise from early electoral success. Do we seek much wider support by moving more pragmatically? Can we continue to make progress as a left-wing people's movement? Early electoral success for the outsiders can raise the most fundamental question: Who are we, as party, and what is our purpose? The mainstream parties ask the same agonized question without noting that the intimidating outsiders are posing it of themselves, too.

The star of the 2015 campaign in Spain was Pablo Iglesias Turrión, the leader of Podemos ('We can' in English, another nod to Obama in 2008). Two years previously Podemos had not existed. But under its distinctive ponytailed leader, it was now making a powerful impact. A correspondent for *The Independent* newspaper in the UK reported from a rally in Madrid that Iglesias, as he is known, 'received a welcome usually reserved for rock stars'.[8] In advance of his appearance onstage, the theme music from the film *Ghostbusters* was played, whipping up the advance excitement. The political rock star followed the upbeat musical introduction with an anti-austerity message, delivered with unyielding confidence. After he spoke the crowd shouted, 'Yes, we can' – the increasingly deployed assertion that celebrates a new sense of empowerment and possibility, rather than precise policy objectives. Podemos came third in the election, securing more than 20 per cent of the vote – a stunning achievement for a party that did not even exist when the previous general election in Spain had been held.

But after the heady days of 2015, support for Podemos declined. Why did the blisteringly successful force that erupted from popular discontent over austerity and corruption in Spain, to threaten four decades of two-party rule, suddenly fall short? This was not meant to happen, its early momentum going into reverse. But the decline is yet another sign of a wider vulnerability for the outsiders.

Perhaps the UK's Brexit vote in 2016 had sent voters scurrying back into the familiar arms of the Spanish Socialist Workers' Party (PSOE) and the conservative People's Party (PP); perhaps the inevitable strategic divisions at the top of the party were the cause. Should they reach out more to the centre ground and, if so, how? Should the regional branches of the party be virtually autonomous and, if so, how to handle differences between the regions and within them? What should be the balance of power between the national leadership and the regional branches? These are the familiar dilemmas of democratic politics, and it takes experienced politicians to navigate them successfully. Few outsiders are experienced politicians, or else they would be on the inside. Such differences are inevitable because new parties do not arrive fully formed. There will be unavoidable division about how a party should evolve. Such tensions can lead to a party developing towards a more stable position, or it can destroy a party. The more common pattern is for unresolved differences to lead to near-terminal destructiveness.

Whatever the reason, Podemos' poor performance led to a period of introspection that has further revealed the ideological tensions at its core. For a political party, introspective debate can be constructive and dangerous. For a young party, the danger is heightened. Some senior figures pushed for a more pragmatic approach to the mainstream centre-left PSOE, with a view to sharing power. In contrast, Iglesias – although seeking to widen the party's electoral support – had gone out of his way to antagonize the mainstream socialists; he is less interested in wooing them, hoping instead to replace them as the major force on the left.

Iglesias has forged an alliance with non-party-based anti-capitalist movements in Spain, in the hope of forming a formidable march towards power under the Podemos banner. Some of his colleagues are more focused on short-term routes to power; the party's policy chief, Íñigo Errejón, has argued: 'First you deliver and do things for the people, then you create dominance.'[9]

Antonio Barroso, an analyst at the political risk-advisory firm Teneo Intelligence, sees the internal divisions as a sign that Podemos is coming of age politically. 'It was like a virgin party when it emerged, formed of *círculos* [working groups] to represent the people. At the end of the day it's just becoming a classic party with its internal quarrels.'[10] In other words, the outsiders are facing the unavoidable dilemmas of politics, just as the insiders do.

In one way, observes Barroso, Podemos is now little different from the PSOE. The former socialist leader, Pedro Sánchez, faced dilemmas arising from close election results, where no party can govern alone. Should he form a government with the centre right or remain pure in opposition? But suddenly Podemos faces similar questions. They are the outsiders facing the insiders' dilemmas. Inevitably some of the romanticism fades, as they argue over whether or not to do deals with another party in parliament. In Europe proportional representation provides both an opportunity and a challenge for the outsiders. It gives them parliamentary representation, but forces them to consider working with other parties, compromising in ways that mainstream parties are often compelled to do. The outsiders appear strong in their early days because they can assert, and offer visions, without the hell of negotiated compromises. Once they are elected to parliaments where no single party commands a majority, the hard, unglamorous grind begins, in which parties have to talk to each other and weakly concede ground.

———

In the United States, presidential candidates or aspiring candidates are less bound by the internal divisions of their parties. Although they are not free to be wholly authentic, their calculations are different, as they seek to climb the mountainous hurdles towards the White House. How do I win the party's nomination? How do I win the presidential election? They are towering questions, but are less bound by the disciplines of holding together a party in non-presidential democracies.

In 2016 the US staged its first presidential election campaign that was shaped by outsiders. One of the candidates for the Democrats' nomination, Bernie Sanders, opened the year with a series of TV interviews in which he outlined a programme that was well to the left of any Democrat candidate since John McGovern in 1972 and, in terms of economic policy, more radical than even McGovern's progressive proposals. Echoing Corbyn, Tsipras and the Podemos leadership, Sanders' overwhelming theme was that since the financial crash there had been a huge bailout for Wall Street. In contrast, the middle classes and the poor had suffered a drop in living standards.

Sanders argued that the way to transform US society for the better was to demand that the wealthy and big corporations 'pay their fair share of tax'. Having raised additional cash, partly from what he called 'fair taxes', he pledged to 'guarantee' free healthcare for all. In seeking definition against the Democrats' front-runner, Hillary

Clinton, Sanders stressed that he was not part of the Washington establishment and, unlike her, was an opponent of the 'disastrous' war in Iraq.[11] Outside the TV studios Sanders continued to address vast rallies, attracting bigger crowds than Clinton. He was the veteran rock star and, like Corbyn, brought a soporific contest to life.

Echoing her husband in the past, Hillary Clinton was used to pitching a cautious, technocratic, centrist message. Unlike her husband, she was not a political artist with the skill to make cautious expediency seem exciting. With the rise of Sanders, Clinton had no choice but to move leftwards for the first time in her campaigning career. Sanders was the anti-establishment politician arguing that neither markets nor global climate were unbuckable forces of nature. Here was Sanders at his most politically potent, combining idealism with an apparent humdrum realism. 'The problems we face did not come down from the heavens. They are made. They are made by bad human decisions. And good human decisions can change them.'[12] Sanders was a good communicator, a politician teacher making sense of his arguments – or trying to do so – with accessible language.

In doing so, he did Clinton a favour. By frightening her in the battle to win the Democrats' nomination, she became slightly less cautious and dull. Clinton still lost to Trump, but she fought a livelier campaign than she intended to.

Sanders was part of the pattern.

In the case of each outsider from the left, the audiences that gathered in vast numbers to hear their political heroes ached to be excited. None of the leaders on the left who became popular expected such adulation. They were as surprised as everyone else at their sudden rise to a wider prominence. As their popularity grew, they projected two themes: they were the anti-establishment candidates, and their arguments were rooted in a precise economic context, one that had generated such angry yet hopeful energy among their audiences.

The impact of the 2008 financial crash can be measured very precisely. Each of the suddenly potent figures on the left framed their arguments with reference to the banking crisis and what followed. A constant refrain in their speeches was that the bankers caused the emergency, and yet the middle classes and the poor were taking the punishment. As Sanders declared, after his triumphant victory in New Hampshire: 'The people bailed out Wall Street. Now it is time for Wall Street to bail out the people.' As with the other left-wing outsiders, his fervent supporters did not probe too deeply as to how this would come about.

The financial crash, and its consequences, gave the left outsiders the space to make accessible and powerful arguments around the theme of 'fairness'. Few would disagree that it was unfair for those who triggered the crash to continue receiving mind-boggling salaries and bonuses, while the majority of voters struggled with the consequences of their recklessness and, arguably, their criminal behaviour. Before the crash, the left struggled to find populist ways of addressing issues relating to fairness. Calls for a fairer society could easily be interpreted by voters as a demand to hand over their hard-earned cash in order to redistribute it to those had not worked as hard as they had. Fairness is not a theme that is automatically popular. After 2008, however, the left had a new canvas on which to make its case.

The response of the mainstream to the crash gave the left more ammunition. The outsiders opposed the 'austerity', public spending cuts and tax increases that followed a financial crisis. They noted that the bankers still got their bonuses, while the cuts descended on the electorate. In the gloomy darkness, the left's rock stars seemed to light up the skies with visions of what could be achieved with a different set of policies and approaches.

In Greece, Portugal and Spain the level of political energy was heightened because of those countries' membership of the eurozone. And voters had other targets beyond the financial sector. They had the European Central Bank in their sights, and other non-elected institutions that bound the eurozone together. But that additional layer of complexity did not detract from the common origin and message from the left across both the EU and the US. In effect, each leader asserted their country's right to determine economic policy, irrespective of the supposed constraints of the euro or membership of a global market where capital moves around close to the speed of sound. Each of them argued for an 'end to austerity' and increases in public spending. All sought higher taxes from the wealthy and called for big business to fund the increases in public spending that they sought. Each was relaxed about more borrowing, rather than following the obsession with wiping out deficits, although all argued too that by spending more – especially on capital projects – the economy would grow faster than if governments imposed sweeping cuts. They would cut deficits faster on this basis than those who cut ardently.

The chant 'Yes, we can' was much more significant than it seemed. Those words, which greeted some of the left-wing leaders at their rock-style rallies, were an assertion of autonomy – emphasizing the right of countries to decide their own policies and to challenge a global economy that rewarded the undeserving with unimaginable levels of wealth, while failing to help the rest. Their impotent anger took the form of a cry that implied they would put up with impotence no longer.

In the US battle for the Democrats' nomination, Sanders pointed out that at the start of the campaign he had no budget or infrastructure, compared with the wealthy Hillary Clinton machine. He was the solo artist taking on the establishment. In response, Clinton had to argue that she was the candidate who threatened the Washington establishment. In their first televised debate in January 2016 Clinton turned to Sanders and proclaimed, 'How can I be part of the establishment when I am standing to be the first woman President of the United States?'[13] For once it was Sanders who had no available riposte. There was no getting away from the fact that he was a white middle-class man.

At times such exchanges represented the shallow level of the anti-establishment debate, and yet it provided much armoury for the left. In her previous battle for the nomination eight years earlier, Clinton had played up her experience in the White House against the less-tested Barack Obama. Now, wanting to win in the era of the outsider, she played down her experience of the establishment. For the Republican hopeful Jeb Bush, his surname was fatal, as Trump and Ted Cruz strode in from 'the outside'. Similarly, Hillary's surname was a mixed blessing.

In the UK, Jeremy Corbyn was boosted in the Labour contest by his rebellious record as an MP, when in previous contests his record of disloyalty would have been a problem. Although an MP from 1983, Corbyn was not seen as part of the 'Westminster' establishment. In Greece, Syriza was taking on not only the Athens establishment, but Brussels, too. In Portugal and Spain the soaring parties of the left were relatively new, implicitly posing a challenge to the way politics had been conducted. Their leaders were young and casually dressed. They looked good. Even much older leaders, Corbyn and Sanders, attracted younger audiences as they proclaimed their wish to challenge the establishment.

In retrospect, it is obvious why Syriza flourished in the Greek election. Tsipras appeared to offer an escape from the hell of austerity, while retaining the protective barrier of eurozone membership. He did not explain how these incompatible objectives would be met. He made some powerful arguments about how the Greek economy was being damaged by the scale of the austerity, but was vague when explaining how his vision would come together.

And Corbyn transformed the Labour Party in a single summer. His speeches were a series of wishes: punishment for the bankers, public spending cuts restored, an end to austerity, the renationalization of the railways. Again, these were perfectly valid aims, but they were unaccompanied by an explanation as to how they would be achieved. In the US, Sanders highlighted vividly the iniquities of a booming financial market while lower- and middle-income earners were struggling. How the rebalance would be addressed was less precise.

The very circumstances that created the rise of the left make it almost impossible for the left to deliver its promises, to pull the levers that no longer exist in the way they once did. The insecurities and blatant unfairness arising from the global economy generated a wider audience for left-wing solutions. The debate that erupted in 2016 over Google's tax contribution to the UK government was an emblematic example, one that has echoes across the democratic world.

When the UK's chancellor, George Osborne, hailed a 'brilliant' tax settlement with Google that raised a puny £100 million, he was not being entirely stupid or ideologically reckless. Google generated significant income for the UK in other forms. The company could move its UK operations elsewhere, if it wished. Italy managed to extract a little more from Google and was cited as an example for Osborne to follow. However, the difference between the sums was not very great – not enough to fund public services that were desperately short of cash. What was Osborne to do? Tax the company in a way that provoked it to move elsewhere, and lose all tax revenue and many jobs? There are arguments in favour of such a move, but there are risks, too. These are the dilemmas of the insiders in a global economy. Do they act unilaterally, claiming a moral purpose, only to find that economic growth starts to fall as large global companies look elsewhere?

The Google deal caused such intense outrage because of the profound feeling that had welled up since the crash of 2008, that there was one rule for the hyper-rich and another rule for everyone else. While median incomes had been stagnant, the rewards for the wealthiest continued to soar. The rage this provoked in the democratic world was a key ingredient in the rocket fuel that gave lift-off to Donald Trump on the right, even though he himself was a representative of the moneyed elite. It was why Hillary Clinton found herself having to battle for the Democratic nomination with Bernie Sanders. It was fuelling the rise of populist parties of the left and right across Europe.

Governments are caught in a global economy where one country can undercut another in terms of tax rates in order to attract big businesses. Within minutes of the HSBC bank hinting that it might move its UK operation to the Far East, Osborne started to sound less tough on his future plans for banks. The long-serving Labour chancellor, Gordon Brown, faced the same dilemma: get tough and risk losing business, or offer lower tax rates to attract large corporations. On the whole, Brown opted for the latter.

For the followers of the left outsiders, there were warnings from the recent past. President Mitterrand was elected to France in 1981 on a platform of 'socialism in one country'. Within two years he was implementing a series of U-turns as he discovered that, in an increasingly global and competitive economy, he was powerless to implement his more radical economic policies. To some extent President Hollande has discovered the same. Hollande's election was one of several that exposed the myth – widely and wrongly believed in much of the UK media – that voters automatically turn rightwards after a crash. But his stumbling attempts to implement his policies, including large tax rises for the wealthy, showed how difficult it was to make unilateral economic policies from the left. Soon Hollande was attracting the lowest poll ratings of any recent president.

Like Corbyn, Sanders and others, Tsipras was a beneficiary of the insecurities that arise from a globalized economy, but once in power he quickly also became a victim of its might and rules, which do not recognize a country's boundary or democratic will.

The left-wing outsiders came to prominence and, in some cases, to power raging against an economic order that makes it almost impossible for them to implement some of their policies. Like right-wing outsiders, when they are elected to power they face the thorny dilemmas of the despised insiders.

We have explored why and how the outsiders made their moves, although we are nevertheless surprised each time another figure rises from nowhere. But their appeal is obvious, in an era of change. The mystery is the failure of the mainstream to adapt to change and address the threat of their fragile new opponents. This is the mystery to which we will now turn.

3

CHOOSING TO BE POWERLESS:
THE MAINSTREAM LEFT

When the UK's Labour Party gathered for its annual conference in Brighton in September 2005 it should have been in euphoric mood. Earlier in the year the party had won a third successive general election, a feat without precedent in its history. Instead, the atmosphere was wary and subdued. That was partly because Iraq was getting darker, in the aftermath of the 2003 invasion that the Labour prime minister, Tony Blair, had advocated with tireless passion. Another factor was the intense rivalry between Blair and his chancellor, Gordon Brown, who ached to succeed him as soon as possible.

The third factor was the political direction in which Blair was taking his party. In his speech to the conference Blair hailed globalization, its inevitability and the near-powerlessness of government. He had rarely talked about the role of the state and, when he did so in this speech, he chose to stress the limits of what it could – or should – do in the era of globalization:

> Change is marching on again. Perhaps our children more readily understand this and embrace it than we do. How quickly has the iPod entered the language and the reality of our lives? With what sense of near wonder was the fax machine greeted, just a few years ago, and already overtaken?

> A baby is born. The father takes a photo on his mobile. In seconds relatives around the world can see, and celebrate. A different world to the one we were born into. Faster, more exciting, yet with that come threats, too.
>
> The pace of change can either overwhelm us, or make our lives better and our country stronger. What we can't do is pretend it is not happening.
>
> I hear people say we have to stop and debate globalization. You might as well debate whether autumn should follow summer. They're not debating it in China and India. They are seizing its possibilities, in a way that will transform their lives and ours…
> The character of this changing world is indifferent to tradition. Unforgiving of frailty. No respecter of past reputations. It has no custom and practice.
>
> The temptation is to use government to try to protect ourselves against the onslaught of globalization by shutting it out – to think we protect a workforce by regulation, a company by government subsidy, an industry by tariffs. It doesn't work today.
>
> Because the dam holding back the global economy burst years ago. The competition can't be shut out; it can only be beaten.[1]

Note the personification of 'change' in the opening sentence of this section of his speech. 'Change' was on the march. 'Change' – and not elected politicians – was the agent to make or break voters' lives. Blair was one of the best speech-makers in post-war UK politics. In the case of his post-election conference speech, the elegance of the prose served to highlight his determined passivity as an elected prime minister hailing globalization. Blair could not have been clearer. Change was indifferent to tradition, unforgiving of frailty, and there was little that elected leaders could, or should, do in response.

Outsiders on the right and left were to disagree about this. To those voters worried by the challenge to tradition and who felt suddenly frail, the outsiders offered hope. Blair was one of those on the centre left who had begun his political journey by acting expediently, partly in order to win. He had concluded long ago that for Labour to put the case for more government in most of its policy manifestations was a vote-loser. By 2005 he was a committed believer in the limits of the state. He stated quite explicitly from around this time that the new divide in politics was between 'open versus closed' and not 'left versus right'. On this, he was closer to parts of the mainstream right.

Blair both led and was part of a wider movement on the centre left. In Germany the leader of the Social Democratic Party, Gerhard Schroeder, instigated a series of reforms as chancellor that led to a formal split in his party. In 2003 he launched Agenda 2010, a package that consisted of cuts in welfare spending and a loosening of labour regulations. In several respects he wanted government to do less. Blair and Schroeder were to work closely together, in some ways constructively, as they sought a new definition for the centre left – or what Blair sometimes called 'the radical centre'. Both understood that globalization contained many opportunities and could not be 'stopped' or 'reversed' as if it were a government policy. But they, and others on the centre left, underestimated the degree to which change would leave some voters feeling frail and 'left behind'.

There were many forces beyond the control of elected insiders that rendered them vulnerable and insecure as they sought to govern in the era of globalization. We shall be exploring the unavoidable fragilities in later chapters. As we do so, we shall discover the degree to which the elected insiders, and the experts who advise them, were loathed indiscriminately and unfairly. But in one significant respect, parties on the mainstream left and mainstream right were directly responsible for the rise of the outsiders. They made choices amidst tumultuous change. Partly they chose to be powerless at a point when a significant number of voters were becoming more insecure about work, housing, the quality of public services and their longer-term economic prospects. Individual governments might not be as free as they once were to act unilaterally on behalf of their voters. But they are not as impotent as the insiders chose to be, in the face of global change.

Establishment parties vacated large sections of the political stage and chose to huddle together in a consensus around economic policy-making, the role of government and how best to cope with rapidly changing circumstances. There was no neat symmetry in the move towards a mythical centre. The mainstream left moved towards what they considered to be the vote-winning centre ground, largely defined by the right – only to become trapped as the orthodoxies they embraced became outdated. Significant parts of the electorate had moved on, crying out for help from government. But much of the mainstream failed to notice.

This does not mean there were no differences between a mainstream left government and one led by the mainstream right. In spite of the nervy dance around the 'liberal centre', there remained major contrasts. They were not all the 'bloody same' – a cliché applied dangerously and thoughtlessly across the democratic world. But those differences were sometimes wilfully hidden, because leaders from both sides of the narrowing divide worked on the assumption that being part of a 'centre-ground' consensus would help propel them to government and retain power, once they got there.

For several decades being part of a social and economic liberal consensus seemed to be the safest and most direct route to power. Indeed, from the 1980s until 2008 the consensus seemed to be the *only* available route to electoral success. The emphasis was on smallish government, hailing the gods in the financial sector, and with a focus on how voters should be 'free' to help themselves. Only after the financial crash in 2008 did this consensus – this formal or informal alliance between two parties supposedly at different parts of the spectrum – become a form of incarceration. Even then many of the mainstream leaders failed to realize they were in a trap. They misread the historic significance of the crash and how it was bound to change the dynamics of politics. They saw the nerve-shredding dangers, as banks headed towards bankruptcy and economies sped towards the edge of a cliff. In most cases they did not see that the crash was an epoch-changing event. Indeed, they were surprised and reassured at how quickly all appeared to return to the comforting turbulence of the pre-crash era. As Mervyn King noted prematurely, there did not seem to be an anger that would change politics.

As often happens after a traumatic crisis, the mainstream rulers sought a return to the recent past, when banks flourished and people borrowed recklessly. It was the past they knew, the past of the liberal consensus. Like characters in a 'film noir', they chose to move towards their doom, even though they had already been exposed to the dangers of doing so. The sequence was the same in the UK during the turbulent 1970s. Policies to control prices and wages led to the fall of the prime minister, Ted Heath, in 1974. How did the Labour government act in response? It introduced policies to control wages and prices.

The coming together of the mainstream left and right intensified in the early 1990s, specifically in the United States and the UK, with others following soon afterwards. The ideological consensus was formed for defensive reasons and began with the parties on the left making the first moves. Leading Democrats in the United

States and the Labour Party in the UK had reached the conclusion that they could not win elections by putting overt left-of-centre arguments on the economy. Redistribution and higher public spending through significant tax increases were propositions that lost elections. In fairness to them, they had plenty of evidence to reach that judgement. The Democrats had struggled against President Reagan in the 1980s, with his so-called 'Reaganomics' – light-touch regulatory mechanisms and tax cuts for the wealthy – policies embraced with such noisy, resolute enthusiasm by Margaret Thatcher in the United Kingdom.

Both were electorally invincible. Reagan won two major victories in the United States; Margaret Thatcher won three elections in the UK, including two landslides. In their very different ways, both were teachers, communicators making sense of what they were doing, even when what they were doing made little sense. As if by instinct, untutored by today's ubiquitous spin doctors, both deployed populist anti-government language, which their opponents struggled to challenge. They were setting the people free. They did not want government to take more of the people's hard-earned money than was necessary.

Thatcher explained that her father never spent more than he earned, when he ran his grocer's shop in her home town of Grantham. The government should follow the same path. In reality, Reagan's administrations spent vastly more than they earned, and so did hers, at various phases of her long rule. It did not matter. They had hit upon a language, and enough emblematic policies, to excite sufficient of the electorate to keep them in power. Public services declined, diminishing the quality of life of voters, including affluent ones. The decline had a terrible impact on the economy, with business leaders in both countries pleading for more investment in the creaking infrastructure. But their left-of-centre opponents could not frame vote-winning arguments around a more active state. In the end, they gave up trying.

Bill Clinton was the first to reframe successfully a left-of-centre argument, by endorsing policies that were unthreatening to those middle-class voters who had been brought up on 'Reaganomics' in the 1980s.

Shortly before Clinton's victory, and before the Conservatives' fourth successive win in the UK in April 1992, the former UK chancellor, Nigel Lawson, made an insightful prediction. Speaking in 1991, when the Labour party was well ahead in the polls, Lawson declared that the Conservatives would win the forthcoming election because it was winning the battle of ideas. Lawson added that the party winning the battle of ideas would always be victorious at elections, even if it faced crises en route.

Lawson was right, in relation to the UK. The Conservatives won easily in 1992, albeit under the leadership of the more pragmatic John Major rather than the tonal evangelism of Thatcher. In the US, Bill Clinton was the victor by turning the battle of ideas on its head. He stole from the Republicans the language of economic competence. Above all, he ruthlessly mocked President Bush's pledge at the previous election not to raise taxes. 'Read my lips… no new taxes,' Bush had declared, before he sensibly raised taxes during his subsequent four years in office.[2] Clinton's onslaught was counter-intuitive and successful. Instead of trying to win the battle of ideas by putting a centre-left case for tax and higher spending on its own, he attacked his Republican opponent for raising taxes and, in doing so, raised questions about Bush's integrity, too. This gave Clinton space to be the reassuring candidate – the one who could be trusted, in all senses of the term, to run the economy.

Clinton's campaign was elegantly judged to maximize support. He claimed to be fighting for the 'forgotten middle class'. In his campaign manifesto his pitch was relentlessly focused on a class that happened to comprise most voters, separating off only the very wealthiest:

> For more than a decade our government has been rigged in favour of the rich… While the wealthiest Americans get rich, middle class Americans work harder and earn less while paying higher taxes to a government that fails to produce what we need: good jobs in a growing economy, world class education, affordable health care, safe streets and neighbourhoods…[3]

The juxtaposition worked triumphantly. Clinton spoke for the many and not for the few – as the UK Labour Party was to put it, equally triumphantly, in the 1997 election.

After the Conservatives won the UK election in the spring of 1992, with their fourth successive victory, there was a widespread assumption that Labour would never form a government again. Its leader, Neil Kinnock, had changed his party with heroic determination over nine turbulent years. By 1992 Labour had different positions on Europe, public spending, taxes, nationalization and unilateral nuclear disarmament from those it held when Kinnock became leader in 1983. Kinnock had worked tirelessly on internal reforms and on the way the party was projected to the media. But Labour was still slaughtered, in terms of votes cast, even if the result was much closer in relation to the number of seats each party won.

Understandably and unsurprisingly, two ambitious younger MPs who were prominent in the Labour Party, Tony Blair and Gordon Brown, visited Washington and assiduously followed the Clinton technique. Clinton had won. Labour had lost, again. New Labour was an almost precise lifting of the Clinton strategy. Blair and Brown focused relentlessly, and counter-intuitively, on the 'Tory tax rises', just as Clinton had done in relation to Bush. They stood for the 'many and not the few'.[4] They espoused economic stability and prudence, working with business and the financial sector on ways in which they could move forward together. They pledged to stick to the Conservatives' spending plans for two years and not to change income-tax rates for an entire parliament.

And yet, as is so often the case in politics, as they made their cautious defensive, expedient steps towards what they rightly believed would be fertile electoral terrain, they were also moving in some respects towards their doom. In their determined pragmatism – their search for what Blair regarded as a 'Third Way' – they were responding to the politics of the 1980s and early 1990s, while failing to notice that the demands of political leadership were changing. Their cautious moves led their party to three election victories, but as they looked back, to avoid the vote-losing traps of the past, they failed to see the seismic scale of the new challenges ahead.

Clinton, Blair, Brown and many other European leaders on the centre left sought to work with the booming financial sector, recognizing the revenue-raising capacity of one part of their economies that was expanding reliably. They encouraged this sector to be entrepreneurial and risk-taking and to secure the massive rewards for such seemingly hazardous activities.

In doing so, they were moving inadvertently towards the 2008 financial crash, the tumultuous event that perversely became as great a challenge for the left of centre as it did for the centre right. Many left-of-centre governments were in power when the music stopped. They were in no position to blame light-touch capitalism, when they were the ones who had chosen to step back.

This is explanation, and not condemnation. Without knowing what was to happen next, left-of-centre leaders raised money for public services without making vote-losing tax rises. Here was a way in which the centre left could burnish its credentials by associating itself with the successful money-makers, much admired in the media and beyond. The centre left no longer comprised the money-takers, the mean-spirited politicians who stifled wealth-creating innovation. It was at one with the innovators. It was responding brilliantly to the politics of the 1980s, but was doing so in the 1990s. In its analysis of how to win elections, it was forensically triumphant. In seeking a guide as to how to govern, it was a decade late.

In terms of proposing an ideological explanation for the financial crash, and outlining alternative routes that would lead to a future where such crashes became impossible, the centre left should have been in a powerful position. Instead, in many cases it was as culpable as the centre right. It had chosen to worship at the altar of the bankers, on the assumption that such uncritical homage would reap electoral and economic dividends.

The centre left could not see what was happening in front of its eyes, because it was busy looking back. The consequences of globalization were making new demands. The centre left was scared to seem too interventionist. The people were enjoying easy borrowing; was it going to be the spoilsport? Economies were booming; was it going to regulate in ways that might curtail that boom?

———

In the United States during the 1990s it was President Clinton who lifted the protective barrier that had divided the banks' so-called 'casino banking' divisions from the more pedestrian high-street banking departments. Clinton's move, which came after a fierce lobby from bankers, heralded the birth of so-called 'superbanks'; and those banks flourished in the same way in much of Europe, with no formal division between so-called casino banking and high-street banking.

With a similar flourish, Clinton also signed the Commodities Futures Modernization Act, a move that lightened regulation further in the financial markets – an area that had already enjoyed much freedom under President Reagan. Around the same time, he also beefed up President Carter's much earlier Community Reinvestment Act. This was an Act that forced lenders to take a more sympathetic approach to poor borrowers who were trying to get on the housing ladder.

Like Carter, Clinton acted with noble objectives in mind. There are no elected political villains in this narrative. This is far more complicated and subtly interesting than a story about malevolent or insanely incompetent leaders. It is about left-of-centre leaders trapped by their vote-losing pasts, trying and succeeding in moving on, only to become incarcerated by the ways in which they moved on, failing to recognize that there was new political space that required far more moving on.

Clinton acted in the way he did partly because he wanted the poor to own homes, and few people complained at the time, as loans became available for those without the means to pay them back. Clinton was being defensively expedient, as well as seeking to help the poor for altruistic reasons. He felt he needed to show that a Democrat could work as constructively with the financial sector as any Reaganite Republican. In seeking to reassure voters that he could be trusted with the economy, by working with the biggest agents of free-market capitalism, he paved the way for the likes of Bernie Sanders to make their case two decades later with such passion.

The same nuanced combination of motives trapped the UK Labour government, which had so closely followed Clinton's route towards power. In turn, centre-left parties in the rest of Europe became influenced by New Labour's electoral victories – especially Blair's landslide win in 1997 and his continued popularity in government for the first few years. Instead of noticing how globalization was making new demands on their ideological ingenuity, they all hailed ways of winning that were rooted in the context of the early 1990s.

After Labour had lost the 1992 election, Blair and Brown were among those who attended the post-mortem at the party's governing National Executive Committee. During the funereal meeting, its main polling and focus-group guru, Philip Gould, told them brutally that Labour had lost a fourth election in a row because voters did not trust it to run the economy. He was even more precise. Gould said voters did not trust Labour with their hard-earned money. They did not trust it to spend money wisely, to raise taxes fairly and, while that remained the case, Gould argued, they would never win power. He also added that businesses didn't trust Labour, either, and while it was so mistrusted by the business community it would remain unelectable, because the party needed the endorsement of at least some significant parts of the business community to have credibility in terms of economic policies.

For Labour, the era of mistrust began long ago, and the main mission of Blair and Brown was to become trusted. It was a tragic irony that they left power more mistrusted than any prime ministers who had preceded them. The irony was deeper in that the policies they pursued to restore trust were the very ones that ultimately fuelled irrationally high levels of mistrust.

Gordon Brown was made shadow chancellor in 1992. From the moment he took up this role, partly following Clinton but also his own embryonic ideas, he was determined to go into the next election with an economic policy that could be trusted by the voters. In doing so, he was very clear that Labour could not argue for higher taxes, beyond one or two tax rises that would be guaranteed to be popular – again a technique lifted from Clinton. Taxes on unpopular privatized utilities, for example, were guaranteed vote-winners.

But on the whole Brown knew that he had to work within the framework of the long-running Conservative government in order to give Labour a chance. In the context of the times, he made a perfectly valid judgement. Brown felt that he had to be seen to be close to business leaders, and in particular the hugely respected bankers who were generating such wealth across much of the developed world in the global economy, which was forming fast in front of their half-seeing eyes.

Brown liked to be photographed with bankers. Preparing his every public appearance as if he were planning for war, he would make carefully choreographed public visits when a new bank opened in the City of London. This was New Labour, working with the City of London and not against it. When Brown, as chancellor, sought a protective shield as he skilfully navigated a route towards raising taxes, in order to pay for much-needed improvements to the National Health Service, he asked a banker to chair an independent inquiry as to how taxes should be raised. This was a different age, one in which bankers offered a veneer of respectability when a Labour government was acting daringly. Being associated with bankers was seen as a massive additional boost to these left-of-centre parties. It was not just the centre right that could hold their own with the whizz-kids of the financial sector. The left of centre was a player now.

The coming-together of the Conservative and Labour Parties in the UK, and in other parts of the European Union, and the coming-together of the Democrats and moderate Republicans in the United States gave the chance for left-of-centre parties to create a large tent of support. In the UK, the Thatcher-supporting *Sun* newspaper became a cheerleader for Tony Blair. In the US, Clinton managed to frame arguments with a wider appeal than seemed possible for a Democrat in the previous era, when the Republicans won the presidential elections with relative ease. But the tent was not of a durable, long-lasting quality. Voters entered it with contradictory expectations, and some felt excluded quite quickly.

In the 1990s – the decade of left-wing retreat, during which Margaret Thatcher described Tony Blair as her greatest achievement – there were still significant differences between the two sides. Bill Clinton's policy-making and priorities were distinct from those of his mainstream Republican counterparts. We got a sense of that when George Bush replaced Bill Clinton after his two terms in office. Under Bush, public spending was more constrained, tax cuts were focused on the wealthy, and foreign policy became more recklessly unilateralist. When Clinton came to office he bravely raised taxes, having run a campaign mocking his predecessor for doing the same. He attempted, through his wife, to reform healthcare. In terms of financial regulation, the pressure from Republican leaders in Washington was to move much further to the right, to make regulation a light touch, to the point of a near free-for-all. The right wanted spending cuts, when Clinton targeted spending subtly and yet substantially on poorer parts of the US. Clinton's pitch of economic competence and social justice, a potentially vacuous pairing, seemed to take shape as the economy boomed, the budget was balanced and jobs were created.

In the United Kingdom the Labour government, particularly through the policies of its chancellor, Gordon Brown, was stealthily redistributive and increased public spending by significant amounts. But it did so without framing an argument around what it was doing. Defined by Labour's election slaughters in the 1980s, Blair and Brown never spoke of redistribution in an era of widening inequality, or hailed investment in public services too noisily. They were fearful of falling into old traps around 'tax and spend' and the role of the state. Blair and Brown made more speeches than most prime ministers and chancellors. Only one was about the role of government; the relationship between the state and markets; when markets worked and when they did not. Brown delivered it in the spring of 2003. It was lost in the march towards war in Iraq, and amid a sense that every word he uttered was a bid for the leadership.

The public gap fuelled undeserved disillusionment. One of the defining insights into the rise of the outsiders, and the failure of the mainstream parties, comes from a politician who never witnessed the newcomers' ascent. The UK's former Foreign Secretary, Robin Cook, who died in 2005 was an MP for the Scottish constituency of Livingston, a relatively poor area. Speaking at a fringe meeting of the Labour Party conference in 2001, early in Labour's second term in power, Cook noted that his constituents in Scotland had been beneficiaries of the government's tax credits – credits that boosted the income of the poorest, especially those on low wages in work.

But Cook noted, with prophetic insight, that because the Labour government did not shout loudly about this policy – indeed, did not talk about the policy very much in public at all – his constituents thought their significant increases in income were a mere technical adjustment made by the Inland Revenue. They made no connection at all with the Labour government that had introduced the policy. The arduous work of Brown and many others in establishing tax credits went largely unnoticed, partly because ministers did not want them to be noticed.

The reason why Gordon Brown and Tony Blair did not talk about the tax credits, making the connection between policy formed in London and the beneficiaries, was multi-layered and, again, understandable in the context of the time. Blair was not a great fan of the credits, and chose always to make public arguments that appealed to Middle England and the newspapers it read. In contrast, Brown was passionate about credits. But Brown did not highlight the policy because he felt that Middle England, so crucial in the electoral calculation of New Labour, would disapprove. Middle England voters would be appalled at the idea that their money was being redistributed.

But secretly Brown was redistributing. The fact that large numbers of voters who were the beneficiaries never realized what he was doing explains what happened in Scotland subsequently. One of the most powerful arguments of the Scottish National Party – itself one of the most astonishing examples of outsiders seizing power – was that the parties in Westminster were more or less the same. Labour and the Conservatives both let down Scotland: that was the potent message from the SNP. They were not interested in poorer communities, but were bothered about big business and cosying up to the middle classes of England. In some respects, precisely the opposite was the case.

If anything, Scotland – because of Brown's background as a committed Scot – benefited disproportionately, compared with other parts of the United Kingdom. But no connection was made. Those Scots who voted for the Scottish National Party, and deserted the once-dominant Scottish Labour Party, did so on the false assumption that the Tory and Labour parties in the New Labour era were almost interchangeable. They heard the messages and did not follow the policies. Having decided they were all the bloody same down at Westminster, the course was set. In the referendum on independence in 2014 the more overt left-wing Labour leader, Ed Miliband, was regarded as little different from David Cameron. Miliband's actual views chimed more with the social-democratic pitch of the SNP's leaders. But when he went on a walkabout in Edinburgh, the protesters were out in large numbers, as they would have been for Cameron. At one point Miliband hid in a barber's shop to await calm. His experience was a portent of what was to come. After the referendum, voters in Scotland turned away from the Labour Party in droves towards the SNP, a major factor in Labour losing the 2015 general election.

The muted messages from the New Labour leadership, fearful of alarming its new Middle England voters, formed part of the backdrop to Brexit as well. 'Those politicians at Westminster are all the bloody same... we'll back the outsiders,' was a common refrain. It was a vote against the 'elite' formed of the mainstream left as much as the mainstream right.

While genuine differences between mainstream left and mainstream right were underplayed, the degree of actual convergence mattered, too. There was a coming-together before the crash, one that remained in place afterwards. While many voters despaired at what had happened and were fearful of the consequences, the elected leaders from the centre right and centre left seemed to be making roughly the same point: the bankers were to blame, but the 'people' would have to be punished through unprecedented public-spending cuts.

After the 2008 crash, the framework that had taken shape during the Reagan–Thatcher years – the one that had endured beyond their rule and had sucked in left-of-centre parties as well as right-of-centre ones – was suddenly vulnerable. The crash raised major questions about the relationship between the state and the financial sector in particular, but also about the relationship between the state and individuals.

The crash was required in order to trigger such questions. How can the government regulate more intensively? Should the state own the banks? Before the crash, even raising such questions was politically nightmarish. Governments could have regulated more intensively and they could have intervened to make mortgages less wildly accessible. But it would have taken a brave and prophetic administration to have done so, when the policies of the light regulatory touch were so popular and so apparently benevolent, in their consequences for people being able to buy on credit, including the purchase of houses on relatively low incomes. There was no obvious way in which a government could have become hyperactive with any confidence, without alienating voters. The headlines about a 'nanny state' erupt at the tiniest excuse. Imagine the furore before the crash, if the state had taken away the right of those on low incomes to borrow indiscriminately. What is right and what is politically possible are often unrecognizably different.

The crash changed the dynamics of politics immediately. What was the right thing to do not only became politically possible, but urgently necessary. Yet the centre left was trapped by its immediate past and its failure to form accessible arguments about what needed to be done next. In the days leading up to the collapse of Lehman Brothers, the then Cabinet minister, Ed Miliband, caught the end of a radio interview with two guests pleading for governments to intervene, in order to prevent a financial crash across the globe. He assumed that the interviewees were two left-wingers. To his delighted amazement, one was from Goldman Sachs and the other was from Lehman's, which was heading towards the cliff's edge. Miliband was one of the most left-wing ministers in the Labour government and he had ached to frame arguments about the benevolent potential of an active state. Rightly, he saw the crash as a moment when space was created for left-of-centre arguments to be made. But he misread the mood on another level, underestimating the degree to which left-of-centre governments in power at the time of the crash would be blamed for what happened. Soon Miliband would be a political victim of the crash, and not a beneficiary.

———

There were attempts in many countries, by mainstream left-of-centre parties, to try and suggest that what was happening called into question the orthodoxies that had dominated economic policy-making for so long. But as they themselves had been supportive, or appeared to be supportive, of those orthodoxies, their attempts never had much chance of wider resonance.

The lack of political space to lead a distinct debate about the reasons why the crash happened was matched by what followed. The most common response to the crash was a series of austerity measures, most specifically deep, real-terms cutbacks in public spending. The victims were not those who had caused the crash, but those who were previously in secure jobs, enjoying and benefiting from higher public-spending levels. Once again a semi-consensus formed on the mainstream left and mainstream right around the need for less government, when the crash highlighted the need for more.

Mainstream left-of-centre parties were caught in a different trap post-2008. If they tried to challenge the post-crash consensus that favoured deep spending cuts, they were deemed to be irresponsible and reckless, in proposing spending when borrowing was 'out of control'. But whereas before 2008, and certainly in the early to mid-1990s, the consensus on the so-called centre ground had been a cosy and electorally fruitful terrain, this new consensus around support for spending cuts was as politically dangerous for the mainstream left as challenging it was. The new orthodoxy, known vaguely as 'austerity', appeared to victims of the crash in poorer areas as collusion – almost a conspiracy to continue supporting those who had been responsible for the crash, and punishing those who had not.

Once again there were many nuanced differences between parties in their responses, in terms of the scale of public-spending cuts they proposed and the degree to which they argued that bankers should be penalized and constrained in terms of future policy-making. But the fundamental consensus between mainstream left and right appeared to be still intact. The coming-together provided space for outsiders, both on the left and on the right.

The framing of the pre-crash centre / centre-left ideology – whether it was around the 'Third Way' promoted by Clinton and Blair, or around the view espoused most passionately by Blair while still UK prime minister that there was now no left or right divide – vacated space for those who were, more defiantly, still on the left and right. Until the early 1990s the centre left and centre right engaged in big battles about the role of government: what it could and could not do. Under leaders like Clinton and Blair, that ideological battle became muted or engaged so discreetly that few people noticed. In the empty ideological space, outsiders started to make grandiose claims about what they could do with power.

In abolishing left and right, Blair and those who thought like him failed in the end to strengthen the position of the left-of-centre, but colluded in a weakening of the values that underpin a political party. As Blair found increasing common ground with the Conservatives' new leader, David Cameron, after the 2005 election, he hailed an era of 'political cross-dressing', a metaphor which suggests that, irrespective of party, a leader could – and would – take on the clothes of opponents, and vice versa.

As was often the case with Blair, he extrapolated from his own personal journey a new global phenomenon. By the end of his leadership, Blair was dressing in the clothes more readily worn on the right. So much so that the Conservative peer and *Times* columnist Daniel Finkelstein wrote that one of the many reasons why Tony Blair was popular with Conservatives like himself was because the prime minister was clearly a figure on the centre right.

Blair grasped part of the debate. In the era of globalization, free-trade internationalists like himself, George Osborne, David Cameron and Nick Clegg were on one side. Interventionists and protectionists were on the other. But the simplistic division ignored the new challenge for the mainstream parties. How could they intervene to make globalization work for most voters and retain, or re-create, a country's sense of identity and purpose? The answers to these thorny questions were bound to divide on left and right grounds, even if many of those responding supported open societies and free trade.

When the outsiders claimed that the insiders were all the same, they were talking dangerous nonsense; and yet at times, almost openly, the likes of Blair and Cameron were close to being 'all the same'. When voters hear a leader with that rare privilege of speaking from a pulpit, which can shape the way the country thinks about itself, say that there has in effect been a coming-together of right and left, it is not surprising if they look elsewhere.

Some voters in the UK, as in the US and parts of Europe, suffered falls in their standard of living and unreliable public services, even though they were told (by supposedly different party leaderships) they would have 'choice' in public services and would benefit from economic growth. They now look elsewhere because they have been informed that the two major parties are cross-dressers, are similar, share the same ideas and views. Yet they feel they haven't benefited from the long rule of interchangeable leaders at the top of mainstream left and right parties, with their apparently similar cross-dressing philosophies.

Unsurprisingly in the US, when another Clinton came along to represent the Democrats in the 2016 presidential election, those voters who felt excluded from the consensus that had formed in the early 1990s (of which Hillary's husband, Bill, had been the main architect) also began to look elsewhere. Hillary Clinton was a substantial progressive figure. She would have made significantly different policy decisions from even moderate Republicans. She showed a left-of-centre faith in the state when she tried to introduce reforms to healthcare in Clinton's first administration, and in some of her largely hidden policies that were put forward in the presidential election. She was a passionate progressive in relation to policies associated with social liberalism.

She was also part of the old consensus, the one that started to emerge in the early 1990s. How could she not have been, when her husband was the pivotal instigator? Aspiring leaders never escape from their political upbringing – the era when they became fully formed public figures. Hillary's was formed in the cautious, defensive 1990s when the centre left was conceding ideological ground.

Ironically, the manner in which many commentators from the Democratic wing and the moderate Republican wing – and, indeed, the right Republican wing – coalesced around Hillary highlights the reason why she lost. She had become part of a seemingly apolitical, non-ideological elite, where in the eyes of many, and certainly that part of the electorate who felt excluded and dispossessed, power was almost an end in itself. All of them, in their mutual supportiveness, were in the same political place, or so it seemed, huddled together on terrain that produced the financial crash and the war in Iraq.

The same consensus took shape in the United Kingdom, where quite a few of those who would regard themselves as Labour and followers of Blair welcomed the election of David Cameron, first as prime minister of the coalition, and then with an overall majority in 2015. There are some who worked for Blair in Number Ten who supported Cameron privately in both those elections, and certain columnists in the UK media who switched from Blair to supporting Cameron; they could not cope with either Gordon Brown or his successor in opposition, Ed Miliband, who were seen as dangerously left-wing, being two or three millimetres to the left of the inter-party consensus.

What was missing in that ideological rootlessness – the coming-together of figures from the centre left and centre right in support of free trade, free movement, a free market, a relatively small state, light regulatory governments – was a view about the role of the state, the role of government. In the end this is the fundamental divide between left and right. Both sides have perfectly legitimate arguments, but it's an argument that has been constantly reapplied to changing times, yet was missing in the 1990s and into the twenty-first century.

Hillary Clinton rarely reflected on the role of government. President Obama did, but before he got into power. His book *The Audacity of Hope* was partly an argument about the benevolent impact of government. It was more overtly social democratic than many of the writings of aspiring Democrat candidates who hope to become President of the United States. But once he got close to that position, Obama too adopted a much more cautious framing. Blair and Brown made thousands of speeches, but none on the role of the state, partly because they did not have a clear view, and also out of fear that any talk of 'the state' would seem to Middle England as if they were returning to the dreaded 1970s.

The problem with that caution – apart from the obvious one of leaving space for the outsiders to form their own, very populist approach to the state – is that the omission doesn't leave them with the necessary ammunition to make sense of what's happening, to explain the changing world. If government is viewed as largely technocratic, a Third Way where you navigate between conflicting ideological positions, then what do you do when the order you have embraced appears to collapse, as happened in 2008? What position do you take, in terms of regulating a financial sector that is evidently out of control? Where do you stand when figures who seek a small state, as a matter of ideology, claim to be taking public-spending decisions purely on the basis of a managerial response to the 2008 crash? How do you frame an argument about more spending being necessary, and that government itself can stimulate economies and has a role in delivering public services more effectively?

Leaders on the mainstream left avoid debate about the size and functions of the modern state. As with all defensive evasions, the omission is understandable. To put the case for the state triggers rows about higher taxes, profligate public spending and the stifling of individualism, not least when mediated by a right-wing media. But not to put the case proves to be more dangerous, giving up much of the stage to the outsiders.

These questions are more relevant in a global economy and not less, because the challenge for mainstream leaders is to make sense to many frightened and bewildered voters of globalization's opportunities and dangers. They are ruling in fast-moving times. One of the tasks of a leader is to explain those times. Very few mainstream leaders are great educators. The ability to be a political teacher is not an added luxury, but an essential part of leadership.

The outsiders are better educators. Highly contentiously, sometimes absurdly and often dangerously, they seem to make sense of these sweeping, changing times. The mainstream leaders haven't even tried to do so.

More fundamentally, they have a duty to explain to their electorates how they – as potential or actual leaders – will try to protect them, their voters, from the inevitably destabilizing consequences of a globalized economy; and how they – as individual leaders – will govern in order to make sure everybody gets the chance to fulfil their potential in this unruly new world. That is where the political debate in individual countries should lie. The mainstream left needs to have a sense of where they stand in relation to the state, its size, its responsibilities, its functions, its roles within a global economy, from which there is no turning back. And the mainstream right, too, if it wants a smaller state, needs to explain how that will benefit its electorate: the poor as well as the already wealthy.

But that debate has not just been avoided; there has been an assumption that it should not, and does not, deserve to exist. The divide where insecure, vulnerable mainstream leaders feel safest is one between competence and incompetence. It is one that they are doomed to be trapped by, because at some stage they will appear incompetent or be incompetent, such is the complexity of government. So the wider ideological framing is essential and, ultimately, politically safer. An ideological clarity is in the self-interest of the mainstream, but is almost non-existent.

———

The support for Hillary Clinton among the mainstream centre left and mainstream centre right in the US presidential election was mirrored in the consensus for 'Remain' during the referendum on the European Union in the UK. Here, once again, there appeared to be a coming-together of those who had apparently shared similar views about the economy since the early 1990s.

In Cornwall some Brexit voters were interviewed for a BBC programme during the 2016 referendum. A decorator said the reason he was going to vote 'Out' was that he had heard both George Osborne (then Chancellor of the Exchequer) and Labour equivalents (the former chancellor Alistair Darling, and the former Cabinet minister and special adviser to Gordon Brown, Ed Balls) warn that the benefits of recent years would be lost, if the UK left the European Union. The decorator said, 'We feel we have had no benefits. They must have been speaking to a different audience to us. We can't afford to buy a house here. Our living standards have gone down. A lot of us struggle to find work. The elite supporting Europe have done nothing for us.'[5]

Many of those who voted to leave the European Union may well become victims of the departure, both during the transition towards exiting and in the longer term. But it is understandable, when a group of leading figures from two different parties have come together on many issues, it would seem, in their search for the largely mythical centre ground, that those who feel excluded from that consensus move outside it.

The legitimate wariness of ideological consensus is fuelled by the dangerous, lazy, foolish anti-politics instinct. In the end, it's an instinct that threatens democracy and is not reasonable or based on evidence. But in that coming-together ideologically of the mainstream parties of the left and the right, voters feel with good cause the need for an alternative.

The alternative, from their perspective, takes the form of a cry for the government or other mediating agencies to intervene on their behalf. This is deeply ironic, given that many of the disillusioned are anti-politics and in a way anti-government, which is why the mainstream left became fearful of putting the case for government.

The disillusioned voters tend to respond positively to any campaign that declares government should get off their backs and let them be free. But on a deeper level, their cry is for governments to intervene more. Evidently there is a demand for governments to be more active in order to constrain the free movement of labour. The concern about immigration means so much more than the specifics of immigration, reflecting a deep sense of insecurity as to whether some voters will have a job for very long or whether they will have a job at all; an insecurity about whether they will have provision when they're ill or old; and a need for decent, reliable, affordable public services.

That phrase 'left behind' is a reference to being left behind by government. And in that cry for help the outsiders have found they have all the political space they need. Trump is both a tax-cutting right-winger and a big-government activist. Hillary Clinton had no alternative story to tell in explicit, vivid language, accompanied by accessible, attention-grabbing policies.

Trump was never an outsider. The power conferred on media celebrities, through revered influence, is often greater than the power that despised elected politicians seek to wield. Many elected politicians have no influence or power whatsoever. Still, Clinton was more part of the despised mainstream than Trump, because she was shaped by the era when the consensus formed.

Similarly, in the European Union debate in the UK, there was a group of people who appeared – whether they were Labour or Conservative, or indeed Liberal Democrat – to have ruled the country for decades, all promoting one message on the EU. Meanwhile those who could not be held directly responsible for the failings of the recent decades were on the other side: the apparent outsiders arguing that Britain would be better off 'Out'.

The problem for those who argue that the only relevant ideological debate is 'open or closed' is that their support for openness over the last few decades has inevitably brought about many crises. Although the supporters of the 'open' consensus are sincerely and justifiably terrified by what Trump and the other outsiders represent, they presided over the era of the financial crash, the war in Iraq, the disappearance in many countries of once-vibrant manufacturing industries, to be replaced by far less reliable sources of work and income. The great liberal consensus brought many gains, but also many threats and insecurities and some moments of reckless wild danger. It is not as if they, in their consensual coming-together in favour of 'open', can claim a record of unqualified advancement. After a long period of rule, the chickens come home to roost.

Given that the mainstream insiders are largely in the same space, the critiques of the problems that have arisen in the decades during which the insiders have ruled is left to the outsiders – those who were not part of that governing consensus. The more pertinent debate could, and should, be between the centre left and centre right, but that can only happen when they stop agreeing with each other.

The same problems have arisen for the centre left in Germany, where the Social Democratic Party (SPD) understandably became fascinated by the electoral success of New Labour in the United Kingdom. After New Labour's victory in 1997 the then SPD chancellor, Gerhard Schroeder, launched with Blair, Peter Mandelson and others an attempt at a Third Way governing philosophy. Several commentators on the centre left in Germany argued that the joint 'Third Way' document that followed was much closer to the policies of the Christian Democrats and, to some extent, to the right of them. The SPD have struggled with identity and purpose ever since, and already lacked self-confident direction, which 'The Third Way' document did not address. Even some UK commentators who were supportive of New Labour considered the Anglo-German centre-left initiative to be too right-wing. In the *Financial Times* the political columnist Philip Stephens described the proposals as being far too close to the Thatcherite ideas of the 1980s.

The document published by Blair and Schroeder is of great significance, showing the degree to which the leaders of the centre left had moved towards the right. In the late 1990s they won elections on this basis, but their assumptions and ideas also set the scene for the rise of outsiders. They were too timid, too unquestioning of the status quo, making even those moderate, pragmatic left-of-centre leaders from previous decades, like Harold Wilson and Willy Brandt, seem like wild socialists by comparison. To understand Corbyn, Oskar Lafontaine's move leftwards from the SPD, the continuing political vivacity of the Greens in Germany and, indeed, Austria, this 'Third Way' document is a useful guide.

The document – entitled the 'The Third Way' for the UK and 'Die Neue Mitte' ('The New Centre') for Germany – begins by arguing that in the past, as far as the centre left was concerned:

> The means of achieving social justice became identified with ever higher levels of public spending regardless of what they achieved or the impact of the taxes required to fund it on competitiveness, employment and living standards.

The context in which this was written is revealing, especially in the UK. In 1998, after one year in power, the Labour government was sticking rigidly to the previous Conservative administration's spending plans – ones that were so tight the Conservatives had no intention of adhering to them, if they were re-elected. There was, and always is, the need for relentless scrutiny of the way public money is spent, but services in the UK were in crisis by 1998, partly because of a sustained lack of funding. The opening insight might have had legitimate force if, in the UK, the Labour government had increased public spending on, say, the NHS to German levels. It had not done so. The words are therefore breathtaking in their naïve complacency. Instead of agonizing about how to address much-needed public investment, such concerns were lazily dismissed as the misjudged preoccupation of the centre left.

The same complacency applied in the superficial section on the relationship between the state and markets:

> The belief that the state should address damaging market failures all too often led to a disproportionate expansion of the government's reach and the bureaucracy that went with it. The balance between the individual and the collective was

distorted. Values that are important to citizens, such as personal achievement and success, entrepreneurial spirit, individual responsibility and community spirit, were too often subordinated to universal social safeguards.

No wonder much of the centre left in power was ill-equipped to cope with the financial crash that followed ten years later. In the late 1990s the centre left tended to focus solely, and lazily, on the limits of what the state could do, as if it was still the 1970s, rather than a new era of change that was bound to bring new roles and responsibilities for government. The rest of the document was also written as if to prove that Blair and Schroeder had learned the lessons of the 1970s and 1980s, rather than as a forward-looking document addressing the new demands of globalization:

> The ability of national governments to fine-tune the economy in order to secure growth and jobs has been exaggerated. The importance of individual and business enterprise to the creation of wealth has been undervalued. The weaknesses of markets have been overstated and their strengths underestimated…
>
> Public expenditure as a proportion of national income has more or less reached the limits of acceptability. Constraints on 'tax and spend' force radical modernisation of the public sector and reform of public services to achieve better value for money. The public sector must actually serve the citizen: we do not hesitate to promote the concepts of efficiency, competition and high performance.[6]

As Philip Stephens had noted, Margaret Thatcher would have agreed with every word. Some on the centre left in the 1990s did not seek to win the battle of ideas, but accepted defeat and, in their contrition, hoped to win elections more or less on the same basis as she did. The parties on the centre left that followed this defensive route suffered severe identity crises, and voters became suspicious of their leaderships – leaderships that worked so assiduously hard to win their respect.

Inevitably, neither Blair nor Schroeder followed precisely the ideological path they had unveiled with such confident lack of confidence. In particular, Blair announced suddenly, eighteen months later, that Labour would increase spending on the NHS to the EU average – a huge public-expenditure commitment that would inevitably involve tax rises. But this was how two dominant figures were thinking in 1998, and how they continued to frame public arguments in the years to come.

The same sequence of confused timidity applied more recently in France, where François Hollande led a bewildered administration, apparently ideologically robust when they were elected, exposing in their victory the myth that the left had failed electorally since the financial crash. The left has not failed electorally since the crash, in some of the most economically powerful countries, but Hollande struggled pathetically and moved towards the deceptive safety of a defensive path in the same way that the French prime minister, Lionel Jospin, did before him. Jospin famously said at one point, in a disdainful manner, 'Don't think I am no socialist.' What was he? How did he differ from the centre-right alternatives in France?

——

On the issue of immigration and asylum – those two distinct policy areas that outsiders on the right falsely conflate – the centre-left mainstream has struggled not only to come up with a coherent version of events, but also even to *appear* to have a coherent version of events. The outsiders are utterly incoherent in their approach, but they *appear* to be coherent and speak with conviction. Appearance matters, politics being an art form. The artists give the impression of coherence, even when they have not got a clue what they would do, when faced with the dilemmas of power. Take New Labour's approach to whether the UK should join the euro, in the build-up to the 1997 election. The leadership was as divided and confused by the policy area as the dying John Major government was. But Blair conveyed a sense of clarity and purpose, while mocking the divisions within the Conservative Party. Blair was a political artist – and that is not a derogatory observation. In leadership, artistry is not an optional extra, but is essential. As the outsiders rose, the mainstream lacked artists.

At least, with Blairite defensiveness in the 1990s, there were immense electoral victories for the centre left. The centre left's fearful opportunism in relation to the asylum crisis in particular has left it even less popular. The response to Angela Merkel's generosity, as the Syrian refugees fled the nightmare in their own country, was one of cowardly expediency that led to no electoral benefit.

The response of the then Austrian chancellor, Werner Faymann, was fairly typical. At first Faymann stood shoulder-to-shoulder with the German leader, unwavering in his demand for a 'European solution' to the refugee crisis. This was a good slogan, suggesting that international coordination was the only way forward and that there was a way of resolving the crisis.

Indeed, it was at Faymann's behest that in early September 2015 Merkel agreed to accept the refugees stranded in Budapest's sweltering Keleti railway station and on Hungary's border with Austria. Faymann hailed the gesture, saying that he and Merkel were 'raising borders for humanity' – another good phrase.[7] Faymann was an effective communicator, but then he changed the policy he was communicating about.

In mid-September 2015 Faymann travelled with a delegation to Berlin to consult with Merkel and her top ministers. As the situation worsened during the autumn, and with other European countries refusing to pay more than lip-service to helping out, Faymann was resolute. He said Budapest's rough treatment of the refugees reminded him of the Third Reich. In November 2015, on another visit to see Merkel in Berlin, Faymann warned against a 'competition over who can build the best and highest fences'.[8]

But by then Austria had slowly begun preparations for its own fence, at its main border crossing with Slovenia. Vienna downplayed the move as a 'temporary' measure, designed to better direct the flow of refugees. The real reason for the fence, however, was that the Austrian public was becoming nervous. Between early September and mid-November 2015, some 450,000 refugees arrived in the country. While most of them travelled on to Germany, thousands sought asylum in Austria.

Faymann, who governed in a grand coalition with the centre-right Austrian People's Party, was under pressure to take action. The Freedom Party, a right-wing populist movement, had gone on the attack over Faymann's embrace of Merkel's refugee policy and was climbing in the polls. Before the refugee crisis had fully formed, Faymann's socialists, the People's Party and the Freedom Party were neck-and-neck at about 26 per cent each. By mid-November 2015 the far-right Freedom Party had surged to 32 per cent, nearly 10 percentage points ahead of the socialists.

Efforts to share the refugee burden at the EU level were failing pathetically – a vivid retort to Eurosceptics who believe, wrongly, that the EU tells individual countries what to do. The fractured response to the refugee crisis shows that in some respects the EU is not powerful enough. Though EU members had agreed in September to allocate some 160,000 refugees across the bloc, Eastern European countries and others were refusing to honour the arrangement.

Meanwhile, Faymann was following the political debate in Germany with alarmed dismay. Merkel had been under persistent attack from within her own conservative base. Her approval ratings were plummeting. The Bavarians were demanding that she re-impose border controls and introduce a cap on refugees, but Merkel resisted on both counts.

Despite her assurances, the Austrian coalition began to worry that the German border could close, saddling Austria with all the refugees. While Germany had already introduced some border checks, a stricter regime could threaten Austria's economy. Germany is by far Austria's biggest trading partner, accounting for one-third of its exports.

The turning point came in early December 2015. By then, refugee numbers had dwindled to a couple of thousand per day, from rates of up to 10,000 in October. But instead of taking on all the refugees, as they had in the past, the Germans began turning some back, arguing that the migrants did not intend to apply for asylum in Germany, but in other countries, such as Belgium or the Netherlands.

The Austrian coalition panicked. In March 2016 it announced tough new plans to reject almost all asylum-seekers at its borders. Under the new measures, all asylum claims were to be decided within an hour, at the country's borders. Only migrants who had an immediate relative who had already been granted asylum in Austria would be allowed to enter. Faymann indicated that the country would no longer allow asylum-seekers to cross its territory on their way to Germany. They were closing their borders for the sake of appeasing the electorate. In doing so, the Austrian coalition exposed another myth perpetuated by the outsiders: that the insiders pay little attention to 'the people'. They paid far too much attention. If Germany wanted to accept asylum-seekers, 'they must be picked up from where they are, before they make an illegal journey,' Faymann said, in a betrayal of Merkel, brought about by extreme electoral fragility.[9]

As is often the case when pragmatic mainstream parties concede ground, the betrayal did not make Faymann stronger. He became even more fragile. His hard-line approach boosted neither the coalition's support nor his own standing. Within months he was forced to resign, becoming the first major political victim of Europe's refugee crisis, after accusations from within his own party that he had caved in to right-wing populist demands to build fences on the country's borders.

His standing within his own party had plummeted. At the May Day celebrations in Vienna in 2016 – normally a deeply symbolic day for the party, which has had a strong position in the city since the end of the Second World War – Faymann was booed and jeered, with Social Democratic Party of Austria (SPÖ) supporters holding up placards demanding his resignation. Faymann, who had been in office for nearly eight years, admitted at a press conference in the chancellor's office that he had lost the support of his party and would also be stepping down from his role as head of the SPÖ.

'This country needs a chancellor whose party is totally behind them,' Faymann said. 'The government needs a fresh, forceful beginning. Anyone who doesn't have this support is not up to the job. A lot is at stake. This is about Austria,' he continued, adding that he was 'very grateful to have been allowed to serve this country'.[10]

Faymann's U-turn reflected a much deeper insecurity on the centre left: a sense of rootlessness; the belief, formed with a degree of mountainous electoral evidence, that they had lost the arguments in the 1980s and, to some extent, the 1970s.

In their contrite expediency they had no ammunition to make sense of the changing times. What proved smart in some cases – brilliant strategic pragmatism in the early 1990s up to 2008 – became a calamity for them as they tried to navigate the disruptive consequences of the globalized economy. It left them unable even to find the language to inspire and lead and make sense of things.

Hillary Clinton, in her campaign for the presidency in 2016, talked a lot about her support for diversity and the historic significance of a woman becoming President of the United States. She is a passionate social liberal, who faced a male chauvinist of the extreme variety, and yet in a constraining way social liberalism became the essence of her message. Her campaign theme – 'Stronger Together' – partly suggested a celebration of diversity and tolerance, with a woman seeking to be at the helm. But what did it suggest about jobs and the economy? Such a focus was not, and could not, be enough to make sense of the changing global world.

The same narrow range of ideas applied to the UK's Labour Party after its defeat in the 2015 election – an election that opinion polls had suggested that, one way or another, it would win. When its leading lights came to reflect on the defeat, they had nothing to equip them to make sense of what happened, other than banalities and clichés. Figures capable of thinking deeply and thoughtfully, like David Miliband, the former Foreign Secretary, offered utterly vacuous insights. Miliband declared that his party had, as he put it, 'turned the page backwards' and it was now time to 'turn the page forward' – a meaningless observation, which was not subsequently fleshed out in any depth at all.[11]

Labour's philosopher-king in Parliament, Jon Cruddas, who had been theoretically behind the policy reviews of his party for the previous few years, said in his post-mortem interview, 'it's time for the party to visit some dark places'.[12] What he meant by that metaphor was the need to confront the realities as they were, not as the party might have hoped. But that is a statement of the obvious. It leads nowhere.

The former Labour MP who was, and remains, a historian, Tristram Hunt, wrote in a major article that 'the party is regarded as increasingly irrelevant'.[13] As if any political leader anywhere in the world would argue for irrelevance being its defining creed. In early 2017 Hunt left politics to run London's Victoria and Albert Museum.

None of them had a more detailed, thought-through analysis, based on clear values and policies arising from those values. There is another pattern forming, related to the one that traces the rise of the outsiders. The accompanying pattern shows the failure of social democrats to engage in the deep thinking which can lead to a coherent policy agenda that commands wide appeal. The Labour Party post-2015 was an early indication of the problems that Hillary Clinton came upon, when she was making her pitch in the United States. In what way had she moved on from the early 1990s? In what way was she making sense of the globalized revolution that was transforming the lives of many Americans? In what way did she have solutions that were distinctively social-democratic solutions? Look at what she chose to emphasize during the campaign and you find few answers. That does not mean that she personally might not have had a whole series of detailed policy prescriptions, when in power, but she lacked the language and ideological route-map that could confidently convey them to the wider electorate.

In that space the swagger of Trump's projection, with his indiscriminate use of government when he wanted to make a case for action, his incoherent arguments about lower taxes, at least resonated with an electorate that felt disconnected from the political process, partly because the political process had chosen to disconnect from them.

Reflecting on the early electoral success of the relatively new party on the left in Spain, Podemos, before the rise of Trump or the fall of Hillary Clinton, there was an illuminating exchange between the Spanish party's political secretary, Íñigo Errejón, and the left-wing academic Chantal Mouffe. Their insightful exchanges were extensive enough to form a book.[14] In the depth of their analysis, the strategic focus with a clear view about the need for an electoral strategy, there is a seriousness of intent that has echoes in a very different context with the sort of intensely smart, strategic conversations that those mainstream centre-left figures from the early 1990s had with each other.

Blair and Clinton, Blair and Brown in the UK – all of them were trying to find a way back for the centre left after a decade at least of terrible electoral setbacks and apparent ideological defeat. They addressed, with energy-draining focus, the failings of their parties in the recent past, without noticing that the recent past had been overtaken. The discussion between the Podemos duo was different, reflecting on the potential of the left-wing outsiders to take power in one form or another, but they were doing so with an emphasis on how that might happen. This was not a conversation in the abstract. The exchanges were rooted in what was electorally possible, as well as the ideas on which the left-wing outsiders could make their moves. In reflecting on the space that was available, Mouffe made this observation:

> Believing that your vote will make a real difference, this is fundamental. This is interesting because the current post-political model of consensus at the centre removes from politics one of its key elements, its partisan nature. As we have seen, in order to belong to an 'us' there needs to be a 'them.' And what 'them' means in the field of democratic politics is an adversary. I think that in many countries one of the reasons that fewer and fewer people are interested in politics and there are increasing levels of abstention is that the difference between centre-right and centre-left is so minuscule that people feel that there is nothing at stake. Let me remind you of a staggering electoral episode. In the very first round of the 2002 French Presidential elections Jean-Marie Le Pen eliminated the Socialist candidate Lionel Jospin. I used to joke with my students that the difference between Jospin and Chirac was the same as that between Coca-Cola and the campaign against Pepsi. Jospin, who is of course a very decent person, had the very bad idea of proclaiming during the campaign against Chirac, 'I am not a Socialist.' Thereafter most of my friends told me that they wouldn't be voting for him in the first round but only in the second round. People didn't get mobilised for Jospin because there was no passion involved, and it was Le Pen that got through to the second round, leaving the Socialists out in the cold.

This is far too sweeping a summary in many respects. There are, and were, large differences between those standing on the mainstream left and those on the mainstream right. The election of one or the other would trigger significant policy differences. However, she is right to make the observation that the perception of the consensus is strong and, ultimately, dangerous. Parts of the electorate see those who rule, or seek to rule, in Paris or Madrid or London or Washington as the same. And the outsiders – whether they are the

Scottish Nationalists or Podemos in Spain – will make that point repeatedly. Although a lazy or wilfully self-interested distortion, this would not resonate unless they had some ammunition to make it do so. The coming-together with part of the right's agenda that was so fruitful for many on the centre left in the 1990s had become a hugely complex problem for it.

The political secretary of Podemos, Errejón, responded by saying:

> This is because nothing of any substance was in dispute. The most important decisions are taken by unelected powers in a remote sphere that is far removed from any potential control by citizens. Meanwhile political representatives come to resemble each other more and more, and their constituents less and less. In the absence of any contestation over ideas and projects, democracy languishes and resignation spreads, and disaffection also breeds as the crisis of representation deepens and institutions are increasingly under the sway of powerful minorities.

This is both an observation and, of course, a political message. It was in some respects the message that Alex Salmond and Nicola Sturgeon from the SNP used so powerfully in their rise to dominance in the politics of Scotland, where in effect during the first Scottish referendum on independence they argued, 'Look at London and Westminster, at Cameron, the [then] prime minister, at Miliband, the [then] leader of the Labour Party – they're all the same, they've all colluded, they've all signed up to a programme of austerity in response to the financial crash, which was brought about by a set of policies and assumptions that both the major parties had been wholly supportive of.' That perception of power concentrated in a few hands with a shared set of assumptions that continue, irrespective of what happens in elections, is part of what fuels the anger and disillusionment with the mainstream parties. Evidently those mainstream parties have not done enough to challenge that sense of disillusionment and anger.

Mouffe noted: 'That is precisely what is needed in politics: something substantial has to be at stake, with citizens having a choice between clearly different projects.'

It could be argued that in the United States they couldn't have had a clearer choice. There were so many vivid differences between Trump – a figure who had never held public office, who had treated women with contempt – and Hillary Clinton – a public servant, feminist and someone who had held high office. Yet because she was seen as being part of that early 1990s consensus and hadn't broken away from it, the choice, bizarrely in such a wacky election, became a relatively narrow one. Perhaps if Bernie Sanders had been the Democrats' candidate, the choice would have been more vivid, clear and tangible to those who felt disillusioned. But we will never know what would have happened if Sanders had stood. All we do know is that the choice was not one that propelled Clinton to office.

Continuing their dialogue, the political secretary of Podemos went on to say:

> In my opinion, with this post-political narrowing of democracy the majority of decisions and the most crucial ones are being taken in places that are out of reach of popular sovereignty. And what is then left for popular sovereignty is merely to choose between variations on the same consensus, not to decide between alternatives. They cannot make a real difference to the lives of citizens. And it is certainly unlikely to galvanise any kind of passion. It is unsurprising in these circumstances that people abandon politics to the experts or leave it at the mercy of intricate machineries.[15]

In some respects this is a false analysis, because what has happened is that people – far from abandoning politics to the experts – are quite openly rejecting the views of experts. Or perhaps, because politics appears to be in the hands of experts who got some policies badly wrong, there is now a revolt against those with specialist knowledge. This is the point when political debate becomes impossible. An expert can assert something, only to be told that we have had enough of experts. There is no answer to that. The collapse of democracy follows.

In the 1990s the mainstream left managed to elect formidable political leaders, silver-tongued communicators with a forensic sense of strategic objectives. But they were not visionaries. They could brilliantly analyse the recent past and adapt their parties accordingly, but they could not see very far ahead. When they could – and the likes of Bill Clinton and Tony Blair had a deep sense of the global revolution that was erupting around them – they lacked the ideological depth to adapt. They governed in complex times, when few were inclined to recognize complexity. But they also made choices. In doing so, they gave space to outsiders on both the left and the right.

4

CHOOSING TO BE POWERLESS: THE MAINSTREAM RIGHT

The stakes were high for President Obama as he delivered his State of the Union Address in January 2011. The next presidential election would be held the following year, and much of the euphoria that had greeted Obama's first victory had evaporated. Intense disillusionment – the unavoidable sequel to euphoria – was starting to take hold. The disappointment arose partly because Obama faced right-wing Republicans in Washington who believed, with ferocious ideological verve, in the virtues of a smaller state. Out of conviction rather than a desire to humiliate an opponent, they sought from the beginning to narrow Obama's space to make economic policy. In response to the republicans' onslaught, Obama cautiously put the case for government as a benevolent force in his speech to mark the start of 2011. He did not do so with the unqualified confidence of President Trump, the right-wing outsider who loathes government and politics, yet pledges to spend and govern on an epic scale. Obama navigated a Third Way, first by showing the benefits of capital spending:

> We will put more Americans to work repairing crumbling roads and bridges. We will make sure this is fully paid for, attract

private investment, and pick projects based on what's best for the economy, not politicians.

Within 25 years, our goal is to give 80 percent of Americans access to high-speed rail, which could allow you to go places in half the time it takes to travel by car. For some trips, it will be faster than flying. As we speak, routes in California and the Midwest are already underway.

Within the next five years, we will make it possible for business to deploy the next generation of high-speed wireless coverage to 98 percent of all Americans. This isn't just about a faster internet and fewer dropped calls. It's about connecting every part of America to the digital age. It's about a rural community in Iowa or Alabama where farmers and small business owners will be able to sell their products all over the world. It's about a firefighter who can download the design of a burning building onto a handheld device; a student who can take classes with a digital textbook; or a patient who can have face-to-face video chats with her doctor.

Obama was smart enough to frame an argument about spending as being part of the anti-politics fashion. Cleverly he stressed that he was doing what was best for the economy, and not for politicians. Then he went on to make clear that his ambitions for infrastructure would be accompanied by a freeze on current spending:

All these investments – in innovation, education, and infrastructure – will make America a better place to do business and create jobs. But to help our companies compete, we also have to knock down barriers that stand in the way of their success…

I am proposing that starting this year, we freeze annual domestic spending for the next five years. This would reduce the deficit by more than $400 billion over the next decade, and will bring discretionary spending to the lowest share of our economy since Dwight Eisenhower was president.

This freeze will require painful cuts. Already, we have frozen the salaries of hardworking federal employees for the next two years. I've proposed cuts to things I care deeply about, like community action programs. The Secretary of Defence has also agreed to cut tens of billions of dollars in spending that he and his generals believe our military can do without.

I recognize that some in this Chamber have already proposed deeper cuts, and I'm willing to eliminate whatever we can honestly afford to do without. But let's make sure that we're not doing it on the backs of our most vulnerable citizens. And let's make sure what we're cutting is really excess weight. Cutting the deficit by gutting our investments in innovation and education is like lightening an overloaded airplane by removing its engine. It may feel like you're flying high at first, but it won't take long before you'll feel the impact.[1]

The simile at the end of this austere section was as smart as the declaration that he was not planning investments in order to benefit politicians. The image of removing the engine of an overloaded plane is a vivid and accessible way of highlighting the dangers of seeking a balanced budget too speedily. Obama was a rare example of a leader on the left of centre who could make complex arguments more vividly accessible.

The argument made no headway with leading Republicans in Washington. As usual, Obama was in a battle over his budget plans. The then chairman of the House Budget Committee, Paul Ryan, had been chosen to give the official Republican response to the President's nuanced address in January 2011. Ryan was utterly dismissive: 'We hold to a couple of simple convictions,' he said. 'Endless borrowing is not a strategy; spending cuts have to come first.'

To Ryan, Obama's words were anathema. In a conversation three days later with James Pethokoukis, a conservative blogger for the American Enterprise Institute, he had harsh criticisms for the president. 'His comments seem to derive from a naïve vision,' Ryan said, based on 'an idea that the nucleus of society and the economy is government, not the people'. Obama's 'big-government spending programmes fail to restore jobs and growth,' he went on, and amount to 'a statist attack on free communities'.[2]

Ryan did not explain which mediating agencies he assumed would empower 'the people' – the missing link of small-state right-wingers across the Western world, as David Cameron discovered when he struggled to implement his 'big society' after becoming UK prime minister in 2005. Instead Ryan pursued his ideological course on the assumption that he was speaking for 'the people', even though Obama had won one presidential election by a wide margin and was to be elected for a second term.

The following year, as Obama and Congress fought to near-deadlock again over economic policy, Ryan published *The Path to Prosperity*, his budget proposals for the coming year. With the enthusiastic support of senior Republicans, he proposed $5 trillion of spending cuts, opposed some of Obama's proposed tax rises, and proposed to bring the deficit to below 3 per cent of GDP by 2015, an objective that would involve real-terms cuts on an unprecedented scale for several years. At the same time he was dismissive of what he portrayed as Obama's profligacy. Once again the deadly dance was played out, the tentative centre-left president against small-government Republicans.

Ryan and senior Republicans in Washington were part of a wider pattern on the mainstream right. In the UK, David Cameron and George Osborne pledged to wipe out the deficit in a single parliament after they were elected in 2010, and again in 2015 when they had a tiny majority. In France, President Sarkozy implemented real-terms spending cuts in some public services after the financial crash of 2008, so much so that some of his opponents sought to blame him for the inadequacies of the police and intelligence services, as France suffered a series of terrorist attacks long after he left power in 2015 and 2016. It was 'Sarkozy's cuts', they argued, that explained why police and the intelligence services struggled to cope.

Parts of the mainstream left chose to be powerless as an act of defensive expediency. They did not believe they could win elections by putting the case for government. Parts of the mainstream right took the same passive route, on the basis of assertive ideological self-confidence. Most markedly, the Republican leadership in Washington in the pre-Trump era worked on the assumption that not only should they seek smaller government as a matter of conviction, but that their principled leadership was a route to enduring popularity. They thought they had hit upon the dream ticket, matching conviction with electoral success. Voters were anti-big-government. They were choosing not to spend and intervene. They were choosing to be powerless. Bingo!

Parts of the mainstream right well beyond the US had come to believe passionately in their own populist accessible language about small government 'setting the people free' – that deceptively reassuring and superficially uplifting slogan. It had some cause for this view. When voters were asked in opinion polls and focus groups whether they wanted to make decisions for themselves, and for the state to get out of their lives, most responded positively. Similarly, when asked whether they believed that governments spent too much and wasted their hard-earned money, they enthusiastically concurred.

However, such emotive, distorting questions, with their inevitable answers, do not even hint at the full repertoire of voters' complex desires, needs and hopes. When deep public-spending cuts are implemented, the state becomes more detached from the voters it is meant to serve. As a result, some voters feel 'left behind'. In a reverse sequence to the populist support for small government, they demand that the government acts to protect them. If the government cannot do so, or chooses not to do so, they turn to the likes of Donald Trump, the right-wing statist who pledges that he – through his own actions as a personification of the state – will transform their lives. It is not only poorer voters who feel let down by small government, by the mainstream right choosing to be powerless. Business leaders demand greater investment in infrastructure and some hope for an active industrial strategy, with governments intervening on their behalf. The relatively well-off in apparently thriving metropolitan areas worry about schools, housing and health provision. Vast swathes of the electorate start to feel detached when the state fails to deliver. The populists on the right make the connections between voter and state, or at least do so in their language and the pledges they make.

Trump is in a very different place from much of the Republican Party as represented in Washington. Under his presidency, Paul Ryan is the House Speaker, the Republicans' highest-ranking official. If Obama had come up with some of Trump's spending plans, Ryan would have worked sleeplessly to block them. In his obsessive focus on the need for cuts, Ryan is the type of Republican who has done much to reduce the capacity of the federal government, and indeed the governability of America.

The long years of penny-pinching and paralysing gridlock in Washington have created the impression that government is nearly impotent in relation to domestic policy, provoking that great sense of frustration and abandonment that made Trump's candidacy so potent. Voters were not grateful for the persistent opposition of leading Republicans to public spending. Instead, they turned to a public spender in the form of Trump. For his own part, Trump is almost legendarily bored by budgets and policy detail. This is part of his appeal. Republican stringency has not been electorally potent. Tax cuts for the wealthy, and reduced spending on public services, have inevitably hit the Republican base as much as any other section of the electorate. The consequences of those cuts – the smaller state, the degree to which Obama's plans were undermined or blocked – contribute to an anti-politics rage, even if the anti-state Republicans act out of a belief that politicians should leave it to the people to make their own way.

It is the conviction that government cannot do very much and, when it tries, it is only inefficient that Trump and his supporters challenged, albeit inadvertently. President Reagan's small-state conservatism was kept in check partly by his own pragmatic instincts and by the expedient requirements of Washington politics in the 1980s. In the years that preceded Trump, the opposite applied. The ideological demands of the Republican right made it much harder for an expedient president to rule cautiously. Obama's presidency coincided with a period when ideas arising from the Tea Party shaped the thinking at the top of the Republican Party in Washington, and hardened traditional conservative instincts into an unyielding, dogmatic approach to the pivotal issues of government spending and taxation.

Trump recognized, again perhaps instinctively rather than as a thought-through governing philosophy, that what voters dislike is not the principle of active government – indeed, they have been crying out in some ways for *more* active government – but its failure time and again to deliver what they seek.

Even the last Republican president before Trump, George W. Bush, seems nuanced and sophisticated in his attitude towards the state compared with Ryan and other senior Republicans from the Obama era. Bush was a figure of the right and was well to the right of his father, the Republican president who had ruled before him. But, as governor of Texas and then as president, Bush at least tried to harness state power to improve schooling for poorer children. It was only when the ardent small-state conservatism of the Tea Party began to consume the Republicans during the Obama years that even such moderate activism, as practised by Bush, became anathema to much of the party.

As the Tea Party began to make waves, at least internally within the Republican Party, the prominent conservative commentator William Kristol argued in 2008, when Obama first became President of the United States, that conservatives, as he put it: 'Should think twice before charging into battle against Obama under the banner of small government conservatism'.[3]

Astutely he recognized that, though the ideology sounded attractive in theory, Republican presidents, one after another, had discovered it wasn't a successful formula for governing. Kristol pointed out again in 2008 that 'five Republicans have won the Presidency since 1932. Eisenhower, Nixon, Reagan and the two Bushes. Only Reagan was even close to being a small government conservative.' And of course Reagan wasn't very close at all, in practice. He cut few spending programmes and let the deficit soar. Reagan's relaxed approach to the deficit gave Clinton the space to argue that he would seek a balanced budget and therefore portray himself as the figure of economic competence against the Republican record of the Reagan era.

Fleetingly, after Reagan left office, the potentially potent phrase 'big-government conservatism' originated as a description that wasn't a term of abuse. It was used along with 'progressive conservatism', a phrase that became very popular in parts of the UK later, and 'opportunity conservatism'. This was the model that, to a limited extent, George W. Bush sought to follow, or wanted to, when he first took office. Bush deployed the term 'compassionate conservatism' as he sought victory in his first presidential election. But during the Bush presidency and with the rise of Obama, the small-state ideology took hold in the Republican Party.

In his own eccentric way, Trump's views mark a significant leap from that ideological attachment towards the small state. Only in his case the government is wherever his mood takes him. He shows no interest in agencies of delivery other than himself. Indeed he shows no interest in the mechanics of delivering in any form. There was no detail as he promised to make the US great again. Instead, he hailed the individual might of the presidency – or his presidency – accompanied by a substantial increase in public spending, especially capital spending.

The same space that Trump occupied – terrain vacated timidly by the mainstream left in the United States, and with ideological fervour by the Republican mainstream in Washington – was to some extent leapt upon in the United Kingdom by UKIP. The qualification is important. Like most right-wing outsiders, UKIP have leapt all over the place. Their claim to espouse active government was fleeting and opportunistic. UKIP's leadership began to promise, at least implicitly, a form of big-government conservatism as it put the case for the UK to leave the EU. In effect, its message in many different policy areas was: 'Look at what a British government could do, if freed from the shackles of the European Union.' Even those Conservative Cabinet ministers who joined the Brexit campaign and were theoretically advocates of a small-state liberal conservatism began to face the logic of their other arguments and put the case for bigger government.

Nigel Farage and the two most prominent Cabinet ministers campaigning for 'Out', Michael Gove and Boris Johnson, argued that the state must intervene to curtail the free movement of labour. That was their most overt campaign for government intervention. Forget about their support for the purity and efficacy of markets. Forget about their wariness of government as a highly active regulator of markets. They wanted the state to decide how the labour market should work.

In one TV appearance Gove, not known previously for his enthusiasm for state intervention in industry, argued that the government would be freer to save the threatened Tata steelworks from closure, if outside the EU. With the passion of a Tony Benn-like figure, he argued that EU laws made it more complicated for the UK government to intervene, but outside the EU the government would be free to save an industry threatened with closure as a result of cheap imports from China. He sounded like a politician from the 1970s, a decade that Gove and many others had almost defined themselves against. But they had become big-government interveners as a consequence of their support for Brexit and the need to argue that a government independent of its obligations within Europe would have new powers with benevolent consequences. Suddenly they became big-government conservatives, leaving behind their Thatcherite soulmates at the top of the Conservative Party, or having to do so in order to make sense of their support for Brexit.

As part of its statist weaponry, the 'Out' campaign claimed mendaciously that the NHS would have an additional £350 million to spend a week, once free from EU budgetary demands. The leading campaigners, who had not been known as ardent supporters for higher spending on the NHS, knew that many voters who were inclined to support 'Out' wanted to hear how a UK government would protect them, after a long period in which they had felt left behind – that revealing phrase which begs another pivotal question: Left behind by whom, and from what? In one form or another, the answer to both those questions was that it was the state and its mediating agencies that had left them stranded. Like Trump, the leading Brexiteers – in targeting those who felt disillusioned and left behind – became right-wing statists.

Under the leadership of David Cameron from 2005, the Conservatives 'modernized' in a very limited way. Cameron and his close ally, George Osborne, who became Chancellor of the Exchequer, regarded modernization largely in terms of the need for the party to become more socially liberal. They met this objective in many significant ways, but it was the wrong objective, a narrow response to a much wider challenge, one that required much deeper thinking about the party's attitude towards the state and the purpose of government. Like leading Republicans in Washington, they chose not to make more significant ideological moves in relation to the state.

The Conservative Party would have seemed preposterously outdated if it had not become more socially liberal in its attitudes towards women, gays and ethnic minorities, not just in theory, but in selecting more women candidates, younger representatives and MPs from ethnic minorities. Cameron and Osborne were successful in making their party more representative of the UK as a whole and more socially tolerant. A Conservative Party conference in 2014 or 2015 was recognizably different from one in the early 1990s, when those attending were fairly old, mainly men, and white. There were many younger party members, ethnic minorities and women at party conferences, and to some extent that was also true of the Conservative parliamentary party by the time Cameron resigned as leader and prime minister in the summer of 2016.

But Cameron and Osborne remained determinedly Thatcherite in their view of the state, almost as hard-line as the Washington Republicans. They were sometimes subtler than the Republicans in their capacity to surprise. In 2015 Osborne announced with a flourish the introduction of a national Living Wage, a proposal that the Labour Party did not fully espouse, out of fear of appearing too left-wing. Osborne also became belatedly a cheerleader for some major spending projects, such as the introduction of high-speed rail to the UK's outdated transport system. But such ambitious acts could not, and did not, obscure the relentless message: the deficit must be wiped out speedily, even if such drastic action were to take the engine out of the plane, to deploy Obama's simile. Osborne was constantly trapped by his ambition to cut the size of the state, and by his hope to be a reforming chancellor on the centre ground. His proposal to launch a Living Wage was also accompanied by such severe cuts in welfare spending that they were defeated in Parliament, with many Conservative MPs regarding them as too brutal. They also remained Eurosceptic enough not to challenge their party on Europe until it was far too late. And yet it was the Conservative Party's militant, obsessive Euroscepticism that had brought down a succession of party leaders. These self-proclaimed modernizers did not want to address that issue.

As such, they were far more timid internal reformers than Neil Kinnock, the Labour leader in the 1980s who dared to challenge his party on all the thorny issues of that era, from ending support for unilateral nuclear disarmament to scrapping Labour's opposition to the UK's membership of the EU.

It was the failure of Cameron and Osborne to discover a new approach to public spending and tax, the size and role of the state that undermined their modernization project most of all. Up until 2001 public services in the UK had become desperately under-resourced, following decades of inadequate investment, for a variety of reasons. There had been much lower spending levels than the average in the European Union, and services were poor. In the 1970s the Labour government had been forced to impose cuts by the International Monetary Fund, as it lapsed from one crisis to another. In the 1980s and 1990s the Conservative governments chose not to increase investment in public services at the rate of most equivalent countries in Europe. The Labour government elected in 1997 pledged to stick to tight Tory spending plans for its first two years, and only started to make significant improvements towards the end of its first term and then during the second.

But Cameron and Osborne sought no new view on the state, when they took over their party. Instead they did something different. They tried to give the impression that they had a new approach, while retaining the old one. Cameron cleverly adapted Margaret Thatcher's famous statement that there was 'no such thing as society'. In his opening speech as leader in December 2010, Cameron argued there was such a thing as society, but it was not the same as the state. This was precisely the same argument as Margaret Thatcher's, while appearing to challenge it. Thatcher had pointed to other mediating agencies, such as charities, to deliver public services. Cameron made exactly the same point while pledging to cut government spending on charities, an early contradiction that highlighted the shallowness of his leadership.

The key event for Cameron and Osborne, as it has been for so many of the political figures trying to come to terms with the global economy and newly daunting challenges, was the financial crash of 2008. Before that, they had affected support for the spending levels of the Labour government, which – contrary to mythology – were not reckless and excessive. Cameron and Osborne had pledged to run a budget whereby they would use 'the proceeds of growth' for both spending increases and tax cuts. This was a vague formula that gave them plenty of space to do what they wanted, but even with all its flexibility, it was a formula that did not last beyond the financial crash of 2008.

Cameron had briefed journalists, during his leadership contest in 2005, that he would stick to Labour's spending plans and that nothing would persuade him to change his mind. He noted that his recent predecessors had made similar early claims and then reneged on them very quickly. In his first party conference speech as Conservative leader in 1997, William Hague repeatedly declared that it was time for his party to 'move on' from the recent past. Three years later Hague announced an unfunded Tax Guarantee, implied big spending cuts and prepared to fight an election in which he would insist it was time to 'save the pound'. He was slaughtered in 2001. When he replaced Iain Duncan Smith in 2003, Michael Howard delivered a victory speech insisting that the party had to change, but soon he was advocating the familiar mix of tax and spending cuts. Cameron insisted he would not do that. He would be stronger. But in 2008 he changed tack, as his predecessors had done, and returned to his party's comfort zone.

Cameron and Osborne used the financial crash to reframe Conservative Party policy-making, moving from acceptance of Labour's spending levels to proposing immediate real-term spending cuts in some areas. They leapt to the right of Thatcherism. There were no real-term spending cuts in the 1980s under

Margaret Thatcher, even though she was an advocate of smaller government.

The duo claimed they made their moves because they had to – that the deficit that arose following the financial crash gave them no choice. They deployed a technocratic argument that disguised a degree of ideological conviction about the virtues of a smaller state. It was a perfectly legitimate position for figures on the right to take, but what blurred the argument was their claim to be something else: figures on the centre ground, progressives in British politics. They never made the case overtly for the virtues of a smaller state as an ideological objective, but evidently they were making choices. Other leaders responded very differently to the financial crash and argued for a fiscal stimulus. Indeed, support for a substantial fiscal stimulus was initially the response of most mainstream leaders. Cameron and Osborne were virtually the only leaders of a mainstream party arguing for spending cuts in response to the crisis. They claimed to be modernizers. If the vague, overused term means anything, it must be about moving a party on from its recent past. Cameron and Osborne did not move their party on enough. They represent one last attempt to revive Thatcherism or, as one of their senior allies put it at the time, in private conversations with journalists, 'We are reheating Thatcherism.'

In doing so, they gave space to outsiders on the right to claim a passion for active government. It was Farage who articulated his contrived passion to save the NHS in its present form. Given that the mainstream left in the UK felt compelled to follow Cameron and Osborne and put a similar case for some spending cuts, they also gave a boost to left outsiders, too. Ed Miliband, the Labour leader after 2010, and Ed Balls, ultimately its shadow chancellor, had worked as Treasury advisers for many years during the Labour government. In some respects this was a political disadvantage for them, because they were associated with the economic crash that had happened under the Labour government's watch. But they also had the depth of knowledge, economic expertise and ideological conviction to recognize that there was a Keynesian solution to the crisis. A fiscal stimulus was introduced in 2008 and Balls was arguing, after Labour left office in 2010, that a further very large stimulus was required.

But the paralysing focus groups told them they were seen as being reckless with the voters' money. George Osborne, in forming some clever soundbites about not giving the keys back to those who had crashed the car – vivid phrases that were economically absurd – trapped the mainstream Labour leadership into coming close to supporting the Cameron–Osborne spending proposals. Osborne was an educator politician, seeking to explain what he was up to. Miliband and Balls found no equivalent language. They did not follow Osborne precisely. Indeed, Osborne followed them, cutting more modestly than he implied in his absurd promises to wipe out the deficit speedily. But voters who were not following every twist and turn closely would have formed an impression of a very similar approach between the two sides. Indeed, that was the partial aim of the ambiguous Labour leadership: to give the impression of 'financial responsibility' by being seen as tough on public spending. They wanted to get that impression out there because they did not think they could win an argument about the economic benefits of a more balanced approach. As it turned out, Osborne was also sending out confused signals, talking tough but repeatedly failing to meet his targets to wipe out the deficit by a wide margin.

———

But words matter. The publicly declared positions form a narrative. Those who found space to the left and right of the 'austerity consensus' were UKIP and, ultimately, the Labour leader who was elected after that party's general-election defeat in 2015: Jeremy Corbyn. Here the parallels with the United States, and to some extent other parts of Europe, are precise. The UKIP leadership followed arguments very similar to those of Donald Trump. They were nationalist, at times they were protectionist while proclaiming support for free trade, and yet they promised higher levels of capital spending, pledging also to protect the welfare budget for the indigenous population and to spend more on the National Health Service, although a few years earlier they had advocated privatizing parts of it.

The far right in Europe contorted in a similar fashion, noting the space left to them by the mainstream right. Shamelessly performing political U-turns, it became an advocate for high spending on health, welfare and capital.

The election of Trump, and Brexit, highlighted the degree to which the small-state approach of Cameron and Osborne in the UK, or of senior Republicans in Washington, had become outdated, both as an electoral strategy and as an economic policy.

Trump recognized the space to put an argument about the state, as did Sanders from the left. The victims of the 2008 crash were not the bankers who had caused it, but voters dependent on relatively high levels of government spending. The outsiders framed arguments that were partly potent because of their accessible language. 'I stand for the people left behind,' said Trump many times during the campaign.

Once he was elected, Trump's economic advisers also exposed the weakness of the fashionable consensus around the so-called 'austerity' packages that followed the 2008 crash. The weekend after his victory the *Financial Times* published an article by one of Trump's economic advisory council members, Anthony Scaramucci, suggesting that Trump would finance his new spending plans – and they were massively ambitious – with 'historically cheap debt and private–public partnerships'. He insisted that, in doing so, Trump would reduce the deficit by stimulating economic growth. He was proposing a familiar Keynesian argument that some of the mainstream left across Europe, and indeed in parts of the United States, had ached to make, but apart from Sanders, and subsequently the likes of Corbyn, Syriza in Greece and Podemos in Spain, had failed to do so.

Scaramucci went on to argue that 'Economies around the world are fighting deflation largely because of a post-crisis movement towards fiscal austerity. We can close the wealth gap in America by replacing emergency level interest rates with fiscal stimulus.'[4]

This was immediately recognized as being a tectonic shift, and it took an outsider on the right to make it, or one of his economic advisers who understood economic policy. And the case could only be made with credibility partly through the heady confidence brought about by victory, and partly because the space was there for the case to be made.

By the summer of 2016, those in power since 1997 in the UK were suddenly out of government, just as brutally rejected as Hillary Clinton would be in the US. Blair, Cameron, Osborne, Clegg and their senior advisers had similar views on the role and size of the state, public-service reform and the European Union. Cameron was the self-proclaimed heir to Blair. But the determined opponents of the 2008 fiscal stimulus, Cameron and Osborne, were gone now: Cameron left politics and Osborne was on the backbenches. In the Labour Party the followers of Tony Blair's politics were unsure what to say or do. Some of them left Parliament, in a very different response to Labour's dissenting MPs in the 1980s, when some formed the SDP or stayed in their party, ready for the long haul. Nick Clegg, former leader of the Liberal Democrats, was also a mere backbencher, putting the case for Europe as articulately as ever, but one of the tiny Liberal Democrat parliamentary party. The once-mighty Liberals were politically homeless. Blair, Osborne, Clegg and Peter Mandelson sometimes reflected that they had more in common with each other than with some in their own parties. Blair came closest to reflecting this publicly, in the context of their shared opposition to Brexit. Writing in *The New European* in October 2016, Blair issued a rallying call: 'Build the centre in all political parties. Organize and persuade. This is a world which changes fast.'[5] In an interview for the BBC to coincide with the article, Blair argued that centrists in different parties who shared similar ideas were suddenly powerless and without a clear common agenda, beyond their alarm about the implications of Brexit.[6]

Cameron's successor, Theresa May, is closer in some respects to being a genuinely modernizing prime minister, finally moving her party on from Thatcherism. She is the first Conservative leader for many decades to put the case for the state. In her first party conference she declared that it was time to put the case for the good that the government can do – a sentence that would not have been uttered by her more libertarian predecessors. She is closer to the politics of Macmillan and Heath, one-nation Tories. Her challenge is to make the sentiments apply in policy terms, amidst the turmoil of globalization and Brexit.

There are many other reasons why mainstream parties became so vulnerable so quickly, with the rise of the outsiders. They faced complex and nightmarish dilemmas, in an era when few voters were willing to recognize complexity and context. But the nervy, cautious expediency of parts of the left, and in some cases the ideological submission on the left, was a matter of choice. Arguments could have been made, and language deployed, for more daring interventionist policies to attract a wider appeal. On the whole, leaders on the mainstream left across the democratic world chose not to make them. On the mainstream right they could have recognized that modernization – that fashionable political term – should take the form of new views about the state, rather than continuing with an ideological attachment to small government and spending cuts, on the assumption that such an approach would always be popular and economically successful.

Leaders always struggle to adapt in changing times. They are brought up on a set of assumptions and rarely change them, even when external circumstances are unrecognizably different. Towards the end of his life the former UK Labour prime minister, Jim Callaghan, who ruled at the conclusion of the unruly 1970s, noted that successive governments made the same mistakes during that turbulent decade. 'We were brought up in the 1930s and our overwhelming priority was to prevent the unemployment of the decade, the poverty and wasted lives, ever returning. We looked back to our pasts for guidance and did not see what was happening in front of our eyes.'[7]

What was happening was that well-intentioned corporatism, as advanced by Edward Heath, Harold Wilson and Callaghan himself, was not working. The UK was struggling to compete with the rest of its competitors both inside and outside the EU. Trade unions were refusing to respond to enforced pay policies. Yet each government imposed a pay policy and sought to intervene to save failing industries, rather than accept the high unemployment that had scarred the 1930s. During the 1979 election Callaghan detected a 'sea change', in which deeper forces made his defeat inevitable. The currents were deep, and Margaret Thatcher had new ideas on how to swim with them. There was a similar sea change after the 2008 crash and the wider tidal waves arising from globalization, but leaders turned to the immediate past for guidance – the world they knew – just as UK leaders had done in the 1970s.

For the rest of this book we will reflect on the mountainous challenges that politicians face, not least those in mainstream parties. We need to understand the dilemmas more clearly, as democracy becomes more fragile. But the mainstream leaders, and aspiring leaders, partly chose to leave space on the political stage at a moment when the world was clearly changing and the challenges were unrecognizably different from those of two or three decades earlier. They stuck to a similar approach, a similar assumption that elections were won on the centre ground, without recognizing that the centre ground from two decades ago had ceased to exist in the way it did then. They chose to be powerless. That is where they are culpable, in the rise of the outsiders.

5

THE POWERLESSNESS OF POWER

In April 2009 the world's most powerful leaders were heading for London to attend the latest G20 gathering. The Group of 20 is the international forum that brings together the world's leading and emerging industrial economies. It builds on the meetings of the Group of Eight (G8), originally established as the G7 in 1976, but renamed after the admission of Russia in 1998 – an international forum for the eight major industrial economies. It comprises: Canada, France, Germany, Italy, Japan, Russia, the United Kingdom and the United States, although in 2014 Russian membership was suspended following the country's annexation of Crimea. The G8 seeks cooperation on economic issues that are facing the major industrial economies, while the G20 reflects the wider interests of both developed and emerging economies. Both convey a sense of muscular power.

The security arrangements alone suggest awesome might. Scotland Yard described its G20 policing plan for the conference in April 2009 as one of the largest and most complicated public-order operations it had ever devised. Around 84,000 police hours had been allocated to the entirety of 'Operation Glencoe', the title for the G20 security strategy. All police leave was cancelled in London for the duration.

Outside the M25 motorway, officers from Bedfordshire, Essex and Sussex had roles in securing the arrival and transfer of delegations to their embassies and hotels. Inside the capital, police coordinated the movement of these entourages and created a security-friendly, sterile environment at the ExCeL centre, the base in East London for the talks.

The G20 marked Obama's first visit to London as president. In his honeymoon phase, Obama had the charisma of a film star and the weighty authority of a newly elected president. The UK's prime minister, Gordon Brown, was hosting the event, having worked sleeplessly in the preceding months seeking agreement for a major stimulus package in the aftermath of the financial crash of 2008. The Chancellor of Germany, Angela Merkel, the President of France, Nicolas Sarkozy, the Prime Minister of Italy, Silvio Berlusconi, and the Prime Minister of Australia, Kevin Rudd, were among the world leaders in attendance.

At the end of the summit, Gordon Brown unveiled a $1.1 trillion (£747 billion) rescue fund for the global economy. At a press conference with Obama, he declared: 'This is the day the world came together to fight back against the global recession, not with words but with a plan for global recovery and reform.'[1]

The event appeared to symbolize authoritative machismo of an almost cinematic quality. Leaders flying in from across the world; security so tight that every available police officer was on duty; the celebrity chef Jamie Oliver cooking dinner for the leaders, on the eve of the summit; protesters cordoned off at a safe distance; leaders giving press conferences, one after another; trillions of dollars being spent – this was a gathering of the mighty.

Or so it might have seemed. On one level, it was. Here were leaders of government seeking to find a way through the nightmare of the financial crash. Only they had the power to navigate such a route. Yet the external glitter, the lofty theatrical entrances and exits, and even the fiscal stimulus proclaimed at the end of the G20 were deceptive.

Already Obama's hands were being tied. Republicans in Washington wanted a much speedier reduction of the US deficit. From the beginning of his reign they were seeking deep cuts, rather than a spending stimulus. Along with Brown, Obama might have wanted an internationally coordinated fiscal stimulus on a large scale. But his opponents in Washington were ready to strike. Some had no intention of giving him a honeymoon, in terms of his economic plans. Away from the glitz of a Jamie Oliver dinner in London and meetings with doting leaders from around the world, Obama was soon to enter a form of legislative hell in the US.

The host of the summit was the UK's prime minister, Gordon Brown. He had higher hopes for the final package, but could not persuade the likes of Sarkozy and Merkel to sign up to a more expansive stimulus. The French and German leaders were much keener on new forms of financial regulation than they were on spending or borrowing more money. The summit of the mighty was not unified, and therefore could not be as effective as Brown had envisaged. Brown was already in a weak position domestically, with senior figures in his government plotting against him.

Being a human being, he had also hoped the summit would strengthen his position as prime minister. It made no difference. Those who saw Brown privately in the immediate aftermath noted melancholy rather than exuberance in the moody leader. Brown recognized that UK voters could not relate to the still-significant advances made at the summit. They were worried about their own jobs and the cost of living. He sensed, with justification, that the voters he ached to impress regarded the summit as an irrelevance. Some blamed him for their own insecurities, and continued to do so. Within weeks of the summit Brown's press secretary and close ally, Damian McBride, was forced to resign, after being involved in passing on salacious, unproven gossip about senior Tories to an embryonic polemical website. Brown was personally devastated to have lost McBride and was badly damaged by the association. As headlines raged about McBride and Brown's brutal approach to politics, the seemingly all-powerful summit was a distant memory in the UK. By the end of the same year and the beginning of the next, Brown faced another attempted internal coup. In 2010 he lost the general election and never returned to power.

The Australian prime minister, Kevin Rudd, who attended the G20 summit in London and was supportive of Brown and Obama's proposals, was ejected from power the same year. He was the victim of a successful internal coup and was replaced by Julia Gillard. She did not last very long, either.

The Italian prime minister, Silvio Berlusconi, attended the summit at a time when his hold on power was already precarious. He was by then the subject of several police investigations. Within a few months of the summit, in October 2009, Italy's highest court ruled that he could not be immune from prosecution because he was prime minister. Berlusconi was now in even deeper trouble than usual.

Sarkozy ruled uneasily in France for a few more years after the summit, until he was defeated in 2012, the first president for thirty years to last just one term. In such turbulent times his successor, President Hollande, also survived only a single term. Merkel lasted much longer, but soon after the summit she tottered as she faced an impossibly demanding set of challenges, from the crisis in the eurozone, to the refugee emergency and the threat posed by international terrorism.

The elected leaders of the G20 summit were fragile and insecure. They might have been debating how to spend trillions, and had been cordoned off with the tightest security operation in the Western world. But the choreography of this G20 summit, and all such gatherings, was an illusion.

———

Most leaders of elected governments are nowhere near as powerful as they appear to be. Quite a lot of them struggle to stay in power for very long or to maintain a level of popularity that enables them to follow their convictions as far as they wish. Instead, they are forced to twist and turn pathetically. Democratic rule was never easy. Ruling has become even harder as globalization takes hold.

The gap between the way elected insiders are perceived and the reality of their neurotic, tentative hold on power is darkly comic. Tony Blair's former press secretary, Alastair Campbell, noted that when he attended the G20 summits of international leaders, the media portrayed them as grand gatherings of the intimidatingly powerful. Here were leaders with a swaggering muscularity, deciding what to do next with their global might. Campbell observed at first hand that such gatherings were very different from that perception: a weekend away for anxious leaders worried about forthcoming elections, the state of the economy in their countries and in the wider world, security issues, the media. The 'insiders' had good cause for their neuroses. However strong some of them might appear to be, they governed most of the time in a weak political context.

Few of them dared to explain the reasons for their fragility – a trap that made them even more vulnerable. Most felt obliged to appear mighty and omnipotent, to feed the impression of strength. They could not admit to vulnerability, fearing that such an admission would be taken as a sign of hopeless weakness or would become part of a self-fulfilling prophecy, in which public exploration of the constraints upon them would sap their authority and make them even more powerless. They were trapped. If they sought to explain their vulnerabilities, they would become even more vulnerable. Instead, the elected leaders gave interviews in which they insisted on how well they were doing, and how optimistic they were that their policies were transforming people's lives for the better. In doing so, they seemed detached from the hard realities or, even worse, indifferent to them.

There was a classic example of the dilemma in the UK at the end of the summer of 2008, as the global economy moved towards its apocalyptic crisis. The then newish prime minister, Gordon Brown, was already under immense political pressure and wanted to hit the ground running after the summer holidays, a rare moment in the year to make a fresh start. He had given upbeat briefings on the state of the UK economy to British journalists accompanying him on a visit to the Olympics in China. He ached for some sense of optimism, after a turbulent few months.

Unknown to him, his chancellor, Alistair Darling, had given an interview to *The Guardian* in which he warned that the global economic conditions were the worst for sixty years. He was being open, and in some ways was stating the obvious. But when they were published, his words became self-fulfilling. The pound fell like a stone on the Monday afterwards. Brown's plans to sound upbeat – a message that can also fuel a degree of fleeting economic buoyancy – were scrapped as he instructed Darling to mount a defensive retreat.

Who was right? Darling was speaking some truths aloud. But Brown was not being loftily detached, in not wanting his chancellor to be so candid; he was so neurotically in touch that he knew his personal ratings had slumped and that he was threatened by plans for an internal coup. He needed momentum. Pointing out the dark gloom ahead was not his idea of momentum, although, in an ironic twist, the subsequent crash did give him a new sense of purpose. He became a political beneficiary of the worst crisis in sixty years.

The gulf between actual and perceived power is a gift for the outsiders. From the outside, they can make soaring claims. Instead of challenging their mendacious pledges, the frustrated, angry voters hail their visions. It is the expedient long-haul of the insiders that voters choose to view with disdain. As the outsiders become more boastful about what they can achieve, the insiders feel obliged to make bigger claims, too. That is another part of the trap into which they have no choice but to fall. After the battle of words, or during it, the insiders are judged on the basis of implementation. At which point their claims fall apart. Implementation of policy never goes to plan, especially at times of sweeping change over which they have limited control. There is Obama, battling pathetically with Congress to pass a budget over which he has already compromised a thousand times. Or there is Cameron, forced to hold a referendum he does not want to hold. Take a look at Merkel, twisting and turning over asylum-seekers and Greece's tenuous membership of the eurozone. These are the familiar images from democratic politics. They are the twists and turns required to stay afloat. But most voters do not follow the reasons for these twists and turns. Some prefer to view with disdain the pathetic wobbling of those they elected. And over in a politically safe corner is Trump, promising single-handedly to make America great again. Then in Germany, France and Holland there are the right-wing populists with their unyielding resolution to make their countries great again, too.

In response to the unavoidable chaos of policy implementation, some voters view the apparent strength of the leaders of elected governments and detect, wrongly, an insulated arrogance as the mighty insiders fail to deliver. Voters become more disdainful.

Arrogance is rarely a problem for leaders. Quite often they are nowhere near arrogant enough. The trappings of power can go to the head of some leaders, but even they suffer insecurities. They do not want to lose the trappings of power. Even when opinion polls suggest the insiders are doing well, they wonder how much longer they will remain at the top. The apparently lofty insiders face the verdict of opinion polls, focus groups, elections between the general elections, internal party strife, parliamentary obstacles and impossible tensions within their own governments. At the click of a finger, global investors can move huge sums of money from one part of the world to another, while the elected insiders have to scramble over another thousand hurdles before a policy is implemented – if it ever is implemented.

The causes of these impotent, nerve-shredding insecurities take many forms. One of the most fundamental arises from the theoretically noble democratic constraints that are imposed on the powerful. With a dangerous irony, these democratic constraints threaten to undermine democracy. They render leaders impotent when they need to be powerful. They demand of leaders expedient compromise, when some voters are ready to be disillusioned in a nanosecond, regarding a messy, incremental approach as an act of betrayal.

While the outsiders proclaim with a charismatic swagger, the insiders navigate around mountainous obstacles that sometimes block their way or force them to veer off from their intended direction. They age visibly as they make their stressed-out moves, while feeling compelled to make clear to voters that they are strong and bold. Like the outsiders, they insist they are leading voters to the Promised Land, even though voters note that they are meandering awkwardly. In an age of mistrust, some voters conclude that the meandering contortions are deliberate and wilful, not an unavoidable necessity.

In parts of Europe, constitutions were framed after the Second World War in ways that deliberately made governing the equivalent of an obstacle course. Electoral systems were established that made coalition almost inevitable. The noble aim was to prevent the rise of extremism or allowing extremists to dominate a single government. The objective was not only noble, but the only one available after what had happened before, when a different breed of outsiders took hold. Nonetheless, the consequences are not wholly benevolent in the era of globalization. Coalitions are formed from different parties, quite often one from the mainstream right and the other from the mainstream left. Leaders of the parties that form such coalitions have no choice but to compromise, to the point where the distinct purpose of their own parties is unclear and they appear to be without principle. In eras of greater trust, parties are hailed for seeking to work together. Coalitions often enjoy a honeymoon period, on that basis. But in the era of extreme mistrust, coalitions fuel the voters' disdain.

Forbes magazine named the German chancellor, Angela Merkel, as the most powerful woman in the world, as she started out on her third term at the end of 2013. In some respects she was.

Germany was the dominant power in the European Union, and Merkel was at the helm as the supposedly powerful leader of her country, the long-serving leader who, virtually single-handedly, can make the EU work as a political and economic force. But she faced forbidding constraints on her actual power, beyond the draining dynamics of coalition.

She was a vivid example of a strong leader in a weak context. Always note the background against which a ruler seeks to govern, before assessing the scale of their power. From the fragile euro to the refugee crisis, and on to the threat posed by terrorism, the EU was tottering. As Merkel sought solutions, she was viewed with a growing wariness and disdain by parts of the German electorate. Far from being powerful enough to say what she believed or to follow her convictions, she needed to keep her grand coalition together – one that included social democrats to the left of her. Meanwhile, a party well to the right of her, a conveniently long way from the dilemmas of national power, started to make waves on the back of the Syrian refugee crisis.

In seeking resolution through tortuous negotiation and compromise, she alienated voters who wanted straightforward solutions and strong leadership. Some voters moved to the extremes, partly as a consequence. The hesitant compromises were the inevitable dynamics of democratic politics. But a growing section of voters across the democratic world did not see the contortions in such a light, struggling leaders seeking resolution through politics rather than through force. They saw only the weakness of the individual, or individuals, at the top.

Merkel was not alone in her relative powerlessness. She was surrounded by the powerless in power. In Austria the country's two main parties – the Social Democratic Party and the centre-right

Austrian People's Party – which together made up the governing coalition, were humiliated in the 2016 presidential election. Disillusioned voters selected candidates from the far-right Freedom Party (FPÖ) and the Green Party to contest the election, both parties uncontaminated by power. The main parties of the coalition were unrepresented in the presidential election. In supporting two outsiders, the voters were rebelling against another grand coalition, another government tottering grandly.

In contrast, the outsiders in Austria retained their ideological purity. The parties from the centre left and centre right became impure as they governed erratically, changing their positions on the refugee crisis and coming to terms with the aftermath of the financial crisis. This was not a time for grandeur in the grand coalition.

Alliances between the main centre-right and centre-left parties in Europe were labelled 'grand' because they used to command mighty majorities: around 80 per cent of the electorate. The adjective was absurdly misplaced. In most countries, the majorities of grand coalitions were dwindling or disappearing. In Germany by the end of 2016 polls suggested that Merkel's governing coalition of Christian Democrats and Social Democrats commanded jointly around 50.5 per cent of support – a tiny majority of the electorate. Their association was harming each of them, and yet they were doomed to remain associated as they moved towards the next national election.

The two parties were trapped together partly because alternative partnerships were more nightmarish. Critics of grand coalitions in Germany and elsewhere predicted that both the bigger parties would suffer. Every time Germany's two main parties have formed a grand coalition, they have inadvertently strengthened the extremes. The grand coalition from 1966 to 1969 boosted the National

Democratic Party of Germany (NPD), an ultra-right party. It also generated enough discontent to give rise to an extreme leftist movement, out of which the Baader-Meinhof terrorist network emerged. Similarly the 2005–9 grand coalition led to a surge in support for the Left Party and the Greens. The main beneficiary of the latest grand coalition that took office in 2013 was the AfD, the right-wing anti-immigration party.

Doomed to repeat this pattern, Germany ended up with a grand coalition in 2013 partly because the two main parties reject possible deals with extremist groups. Their reasons for doing so are reasonable and, in theory, self-interested. Why give rivals to the right and left the credibility of power? But in the pursuit of reason and self-interest, the mainstream parties were the victims in the midst of heightened irrationality. The grand coalition was the only arithmetically feasible constellation able to command a majority. The extremists were free to make waves outside the constraints of power. The SPD rejects a coalition with the Left Party at national level. The CDU rules out governing with the AfD. That leaves the four centrist parties – the two coalition partners, plus the smaller Greens and the liberal Free Democratic Party – as the available partners for government. In such circumstances, and in spite of its many fragilities, the AfD had the space to become a significant and influential opposition party.

Of the two coalition parties in Germany, the SPD's decline on the centre left is most marked. By the end of 2016 polls suggested that support for the country's oldest party had slumped to less than 20 per cent, compared to 40.9 per cent in the 1998 elections. Entering a grand coalition as junior partner allowed the SPD to punch above its weight. Joining Merkel's government seemed the pragmatic thing to do. The party paid a heavy price.

THE RISE OF THE OUTSIDERS
THE RISE OF THE OUTSIDERS

The Christian Democrats are probably doomed to govern for some time to come. They will continue to face the dilemmas of power, at a point where the complexities are great and the appetite of voters for understanding the challenges is tiny. An extension in power for the Christian Democrats might prove to pave the AfD's path to national government some time in the future. Merkel has no choice but to be the assiduous deal-maker, while the far right has the luxury of outlining shallow but intoxicating visions.

———

Across much of the European Union countries are governed by increasingly fragile coalitions. As support for bigger parties falls and newer parties compete for voters, election results are bound to be less decisive. Formed in a spirit of resolute hope, the governments of varying parties struggle to maintain their early optimism, each party infecting the other by association and the humiliating agonies of near-impotent power.

The Greek coalition, the one that was swept aside by Syriza in January 2015, came to power a few years earlier promising economic stability, as a direct result of opposing mainstream parties working together in government. During his heady honeymoon, the centre-right Greek prime minister, Antonis Samaras, declared that the government's goal was 'to get the country out of the crisis and to have the sacrifices people have made pay off. This is a government of responsibility, a government that is here to make big changes.'[2]

Initially, voters were relieved. Here were parties working together for the good of the country. The junior partners included the socialists, Pasok, a party that had governed with seeming authority on its own, winning a historic landslide in 1981. But the coalition struggled to achieve economic stability. Instead, it was compelled to impose sweeping spending cuts, without voters feeling much – or any – gain from the pain. A prime minister who promised much found he could do little.

Within a few years Pasok became even more involved in a coalition that had laid off 15,000 public employees, among them high-school teachers, school guards and municipal policemen, and also passed a bill instituting the Single Property Tax and the auction of houses. When Greek voters turned left, they looked beyond a mainstream party diminished by shared power.

Other coalitions in the EU are formed with similar optimism, only to become unpopular in the face of sweeping external forces. All of them have been shaped unavoidably by the need for constant compromise, hopes being raised in the early phase of inter-party cooperation and then hopes dashed, when tough policies are implemented.

Even the UK elected its first coalition since the Second World War in 2010, following the long-drawn-out disillusionment of voters after the early, dangerous, Obama-like euphoria that greeted the election of New Labour in 1997. The ingredients were the same as they were in the rest of Europe: the rise of smaller parties, the decline in support for the two bigger parties and sweeping economic change.

The dynamics were the same, too. The coalition virtually destroyed the smaller partner, the Liberal Democrats, at the subsequent general election in 2015 – the fate of smaller parties in coalitions. The party was nearly wiped out for appearing to betray all it had claimed to stand for, in the previous election in 2010. Its leader, Nick Clegg, resigned the day after the slaughter in the 2015 election. For five years he had been deputy prime minister. Suddenly he was a former leader and one of just eight MPs representing his near-moribund party in the House of Commons. A year later, in 2016, Clegg published an illuminating book in which he put the case for pluralist politics, while noting that the smaller parties in coalitions across Europe are nearly always punished in subsequent elections.[3]

He could have pointed out that the bigger parties were made more vulnerable, too, including his Conservative partners in the UK. The Conservative prime minister in the coalition, David Cameron, may have won an unexpected tiny majority in the UK's 2015 election, but he never accomplished his declared aim of reforming his party in any significant way. He was a curiously ghostly leader, and part of the reason for that ghostliness was that his energy was sapped keeping the coalition together – two parties locked in an awkward dance. A young and inexperienced prime minister, Cameron kept them on the dance floor for five years, becoming an adroit manager rather than a commanding leader. After losing the referendum on Brexit in 2016 he left politics altogether. The ghostly leader became invisible.

His fate partly reflected his unformed political personality. Like Blair, Cameron became a party leader and prime minister at far too young an age, and without the experience of fighting internal battles, as Blair had done between 1983 and 1994, when he grew politically. But the context played its part, too, in Cameron's shapeless leadership: managing a coalition in an era when the two bigger parties were in decline, and when neither had much hope of winning alone with a big majority. His successor, Theresa May, acquired an early reputation for being close to omnipotent, but that was because her main political opponents were in disarray. With a tiny overall majority and Brexit to navigate, May had very limited room on the political stage.

The expediencies and apparent weaknesses of leadership in coalition politics make the outsiders seem more worthy and principled than they are. But their principled convictions are an illusion. If outsiders join a coalition, they have no choice but to become pragmatic and appear weak. But most of them are on the outside, appearing to be strong. For the elected insiders, the struggles with purity of conviction are constant. Cameron's tiny space on the political stage was emblematic. Farage could say what he liked about Europe, and did so, most days of the year. Cameron was in a coalition with the pro-EU Liberal Democrats, while leading a party with lots of MPs who agreed with Farage. Cameron might have had Old Etonian self-confidence, but that was not enough to free him from the incarcerations of power.

The traps became more dangerous following the financial crash in 2008. Mainstream parties on the left became part of coalitions that were imposing spending cuts. Mainstream parties on the right had to accommodate the supposedly opposing views of their partners on the left. From a voter's point of view, what were the differences between them?

There are inevitably many significant differences, or else the politicians in question would not have chosen to join one party over another. This should be a statement of the obvious. But the differences are much harder to discern when parties rule together, or try to do so. Into the space where battles between the mainstream right and left might once have been fought come the outsiders, with their self-confident ideological distinctiveness.

The financial crisis in 2008 heightened disillusionment with mainstream politics, making it harder for one party to win election victories outright. The unavoidable need for parties to work together heightened the disillusionment further. Here was the circuitous trap formed by circumstance, and not by the misjudged choices of mainstream leaders. In government, policies were implemented that were in marked contrast to what party leaders had pledged, prior to an election that brought about the need for a coalition government. The gap was inevitable, given that party leaders in the government had to come up with agreed positions. Party leaders are not all the bloody same. But in coalition they have to unite around the same policy.

It was in the hope of ruling with fewer impossible obstacles that the Italian prime minister, Matteo Renzi, made his fatal moves at the end of 2016, the worst possible year to seek approval for fewer constraints on government. Here was another vividly emblematic sequence. In effect, Renzi proposed to abolish the powerful Senate in the Italian parliament and to give the party that won the most votes in elections for the Chamber of Deputies a great many additional seats, allowing the formation of a stronger government. Given that Italian governments do not last very long, making long-term policy-planning almost impossible, the proposals had some logic to them. But Renzi was also wildly optimistic to assume they would be given the go-ahead in a referendum. Reason plays little part in referendum campaigns. Referendums become unavoidably stormy political battles, rather than seminars on the rights and wrongs of a particular proposition. Votes are cast for a thousand different reasons, often unrelated to the question being posed on the ballot paper. In this case, Renzi was proposing the worst of all questions in the anti-politics era: Will you give me, an elected insider, more power? At least that was how the question was bound to be perceived, and how it *was* perceived.

Renzi lost the referendum by a humiliating twenty-point margin at the end of 2016. His defeat made Cameron's loss of the Brexit referendum by four points seem like a victory. Prime ministers hold referendums because they are weak. The outcomes of these referendums make them weaker still.

At the time of writing, sixty-five governments have ruled Italy since the end of the Second World War. Three prime ministers have been at the helm since Silvio Berlusconi's government in 2011: Mario Monti (he served seventeen months), Enrico Letta (ten months) and Renzi (thirty-three months). All were put into office through presidential crisis-management or by political intrigue, not by voters.

Renzi sold his reforms in the name of strong government. In theory, voters – not least voters in Italy – yearn for strong government rather than constant change. But at the same time the anti-politics mood is so intense that they do not want strong government as yearned for by orthodox politicians. Renzi was a moderate left-of-centre figure and not a megalomaniac. But he was recognizably part of the mainstream, an elected insider. As such, he handed a gift to the Five Star Movement, the anti-politics party that is neither right nor left, with a comedian as its standard-bearer. Five Star can be allowed to be strong as it is not recognizably political; it is anti-politics. But if its leaders become elected rulers on the national stage, it will not be allowed to be strong for very long. Voters will turn against Five Star, too.

David Cameron's decision to offer a referendum on whether the UK should leave the EU was a consequence of several neurotic-inducing constraints on his apparently laid-back and self-assured leadership. All of them highlight how difficult leadership has become, not just for him, but for any leader of an elected government. Cameron's party had become nearly impossible to lead, over the issue of Europe. In the early phase of his leadership Cameron suggested that his party should stop 'banging on' about Europe – hardly an act of assertive reform. He did not dare to resolve policy differences over the UK's membership of the EU, but urged instead near-silence on the issue, a darkly misplaced aspiration. In the build-up to the 2015 election Cameron feared, with good cause, that voters and more of his MPs would defect to UKIP. Two MPs had already done so.

Defections are traumatic for leaders and their parties, and are nearly always a sign of decay. Opinion polls are increasingly unreliable. Defections are a more accurate guide as to a party's fate. In the 1970s and 1980s in the UK there were defections away from the Labour Party, as it was slaughtered in general elections. From the mid-1990s there were defections to the Labour Party, as it marched towards a landslide win. The switching of sides points to a broader direction of travel, which is why Cameron and Osborne ached for defections to their party early in their leadership. They never persuaded a single MP to switch sides, but lost two of theirs to UKIP.

As well as having to manage his own party, Cameron, like all prime ministers, faced the challenge of elections between general elections. Such elections can have almost as much impact on elected leaders as a general election itself. In the 2008 elections to the European Parliament, UKIP secured more votes than any party: a seismic event that can be seen retrospectively as a sign that the UK would vote to leave the EU, when given the chance. Cameron did not read the vote in quite that way. Instead it confirmed his view that he had been right to offer a referendum on the EU, to keep his party intact and to attract back voters heading for UKIP. He assumed he could win the referendum, and that the offer of one would be a vote-winner while calming his party down. He was half-right. The offer calmed his party down a little, but he lost the referendum. He was dealing with forces beyond his control. In trying to deal with them, he lost control altogether. He became powerless.

Mid-term elections of any sort tend to be authority-sapping for elected leaders. Merkel's CDU party suffered severe setbacks in regional elections, triggering doubts about whether she would, or should, survive much longer. She continued to do so, but with less authority, forced to twist and turn even more than usual in an attempt to appease her right flank, as well as the so-called centre ground.

At least Merkel had the fortune, or misfortune, to remain in power. In Australia recent prime ministers would ache for such longevity. Australia was recently served by five prime ministers in five years, a symptom and cause of instability in a tough political culture, where leaders were obliged to seem stronger than they were. All the ingredients appeared to be in place for an elected prime minister to rule mightily in Australia: twenty-three million people, a continent all to itself, with abundant natural resources, a constitutional monarchy, robust rule of law. Instead, Australia became the land of the bloodless coup. Malcolm Turnbull, a suave self-made millionaire, former lawyer and tech entrepreneur, replaced the deeply divisive Tony Abbott, who had defeated Labour's Kevin Rudd at the 2013 general election. Rudd himself went to that election just after he removed Julia Gillard in a ruthless internal coup, having had time to plot his revenge on Gillard, who had replaced him in similarly brutal fashion in 2010. Each of the five prime ministers arrived with proclamations of sweeping ambition. The more precarious they became, the more assertive they felt the need to be. By the end of their brief periods at the top of Australian politics, their overwhelming objective was to hang on.

Ready to be disillusioned, voters noted the contrast between declared ambition and near-impotence. Some voters started to look elsewhere, impatient of hearing nuanced explanations about the inevitable fragility of leaders in democracies. Even Turnbull – the fifth prime minister in the fast-moving sequence, who had the swagger of a leader on a mission – survived only on the basis of deals done with other unreliable parties to hold the coalition together. Like other leaders, he was not as strong as he seemed.

Elected prime ministers and presidents are doomed to be vulnerable most of the time, even if in Australia the level of fragility was unusually acute. Such instability can be caused by a thousand factors, ranging from ambitious rivals to sheer incompetence. Whatever the cause, instability at the top gives space to outsiders to seem strong. Pauline Hanson, the leader of the right-wing One Nation party in Australia, has been on a political path that is as whacky as that travelled by UKIP leaders in the UK. She was expelled from One Nation in 2002; a court found her guilty of electoral fraud in 2003, a verdict that was subsequently overturned; she finally re-joined One Nation in 2013, becoming its leader again the following year. In the 2016 federal election she was elected to the Senate, where she had a platform along with three other representatives from her party, to espouse her populist views with an unqualified confidence that contrasts with the enforced twists and turns of insecure prime ministers, who are often fighting for their political lives.

In September 2016 Hanson generated headlines across the world by warning that Australia was in danger of being swamped by Muslims, and told those who were unwilling to give the nation their undivided loyalty to 'go back where you came from'. Twenty years after saying that Australia was at risk of being overrun by Asians, Hanson used her first speech to parliament since being re-elected in July 2016 to declare: 'I'm back.'

In her opening speech she said that while Australia had embraced migrants from all over the world, many of whom had integrated into society, Islam had had an impact on Australia like no other religion. 'Islam cannot have a significant presence in Australia if we are to live in an open, secular and cohesive society,' said Mrs Hanson, who famously ditched her fish-and-chip shop to represent Queensland, ahead of her first foray into national parliament:

> If you are not prepared to become Australian and give this country your undivided loyalty, obey our laws, respect our culture and way of life then I suggest you go back where you came from... If it would be any help I would take you to the airport and wave you goodbye with sincere best wishes.[4]

Hanson showed a Trump-like capacity for mischievous provocation, which was attention-grabbing in its accessibility. Safely out of power, she can stir the pot without having to contemplate the practical consequences. She seems strong because she expresses views strongly. The contrast between the weakness of fragile prime ministers and the apparent strength of outsiders is as dangerous as the one between elite elected insiders and noble outsiders who are safely distant from the dilemmas of power.

The outsiders are liberated from the constraints of government. They can say what they like, when they like. They offer an alternative to the hard grind of democratic scrutiny, or appear to do so. Although they are weak, they fight elections unconstrained. They have space because the anti-politics mood becomes an anti-democratic refusal to accept that elected leaders cannot wave wands or prevail through will and charisma alone. In the UK, Nick Clegg used to spend hour-long interviews and phone-ins trying to explain that he was the leader of the much smaller party in the coalition, and therefore could not implement all that was in his party's manifesto. He might as well have been speaking Latin. It is easier, and in some ways more fun, for voters to express cathartic anger than seek to understand. Clegg made big misjudgements, but he secured no understanding for his overall position of a leader trapped in a coalition with a bigger, ideologically right-wing party. He was trapped not by his choices, but by the voters who had made, by some margin, the Conservatives the largest party in the Commons after the 2010 election. The voters blamed Clegg, although they had made the choice.

Elected leaders give space to the outsiders partly because they are doomed to do so. While they oscillate indecisively, with transparent agony and vulnerability at a time of threatening change, the outsiders leap unconstrained onto the stage. As the outsiders leap, democracy is under threat, not because they are formidably strong, but because their impact on some voters makes it so much harder for elected insiders to explain the checks and balances that render them powerless.

———

The gap between perceived might and actual power is arguably at its widest in the US. Every four years a victorious president is hailed as the most powerful leader on earth, possessing almost a spiritual force, and yet he spends huge swathes of subsequent presidential time struggling to get measures passed through a determinedly assertive Congress. One of the ironies about perceptions of Hillary Clinton as the ultimate lofty insider is that she knew better than most the limits of elected power. Her husband, in his first term as president, asked her to pioneer reforms in healthcare. She got nowhere with them.

Partly she herself was responsible for the paralysis, in becoming trapped by unfocused detail. But the opposition to the principle of reform was always going to be too great. Obama's biggest achievement was passing reforms to healthcare, but it took a titanic effort, and compromises that threatened to render the changes next to useless. As it turned out, the reforms were more substantial than Obama's right-wing opponents had hoped, and some still have their eye on dismantling the Affordable Care Act that was passed in 2010. Trump has his eye on it, too.

Republicans, with their newly discovered ideological zeal, never let go, even once the law had passed. 'Why is there still such a fuss? Well, part of the problem is the fact that a Democratic president named Barack Obama passed the law,' Obama himself declared, during various speeches towards the end of his second term, conveying a frustration at odds with the perceptions of a US president being the most powerful leader in the world.

'Now that I'm leaving office, maybe Republicans can stop with the 60-something repeal votes they've taken and stop pretending that they have a serious alternative and stop pretending that all the terrible things they said would have actually happened when they have not, and just work with the next president to smooth out the kinks,' he told one rally in Miami. That was before he knew who the next president was going to be.[5]

Here was Obama still having to plead, after the law had been passed, following agonizing, sleepless acts of compromise:

> The law has ended the insurance industry's most pernicious practices, fostered improvements in the way doctors and hospitals deliver care and brought the number of Americans without coverage to a historic low. Some state markets appear to be working just fine, and at least a few insurers are making money.

181

The law's achievements don't make the problems any less real. But they do put those problems into perspective – and suggest that fixing them is worthwhile.[6]

The battles over Obamacare and other items of presidential legislation were straightforward, compared with Obama's attempts to pass budgets with relatively modest levels of spending. Obama was facing the small-state Republicans, the ones who believed their ideological purity was electorally popular, until their spending cuts had a direct impact on voters' lives, paving the way for Trump to pledge spending at levels that Obama would never have dared. The supposedly mighty president headed powerlessly towards the 'fiscal cliff' on several occasions.

The concept of a 'fiscal cliff' is itself a vivid illustration of the stifling limits on presidential power. In the battle between president and Congress at the end of 2012, the term referred specifically to more than $500 billion in tax increases and across-the-board spending cuts that would have been triggered in the following year alone, unless Obama and the Republicans had reached an alternative agreement. Ben Bernanke, the chairman of the Federal Reserve, who was not known for catchy phrases, had coined the metaphor 'fiscal cliff' the previous winter to warn of the dangerous, yet avoidable drop-off ahead in the nation's fiscal path, if president and Congress failed to do a deal. The phrase stuck, as agreement on budgets proved nearly impossible in most years of the Obama presidency.

Since Reagan's administration in the 1980s presidents and Congresses had occasionally agreed a self-imposed future crisis, to force themselves to agree on unpopular tax and spending actions – a reckless form of discipline. For a president who could at least see the case for government spending, it was a double bind. Trigger swingeing cuts, by a failure to reach agreement, or do a deal with the Republicans that would include large reductions in government spending. There was little scope for significant increases in public spending, even though Obama argued throughout his presidency that the economy as a whole could benefit from investment in capital and some public services, particularly health and education.

'There's a stalemate, let's not kid ourselves,' noted the Republican Speaker of the House of Representatives, John Boehner, during one set of nerve-shredding negotiations in the autumn of 2012, a few months before the then chair of the House Budget Committee, Paul Ryan, published his alternative proposals, which included deep spending cuts and a speedy elimination of the deficit.[7] During that particular stalemate Obama spoke euphemistically of 'prolonged negotiations'. These were not talks between relatively like-minded figures, such as those that take place between Cabinet ministers from the same party in other countries, or between different parties in a coalition with a broadly agreed course. These were attempts to get agreement between two different political species: a moderate Democrat administration slightly to the left of centre, and ideological Republicans that made Reagan's small-state conservatism seem like a vision of reckless socialism. Obama had to act as if he were still fighting an election campaign, when seeking to avoid the fiscal cliff's edge. Appealing to voters during a visit to Pennsylvania in the autumn of 2012, he declared, 'It's not acceptable to me and I don't think it's acceptable to you for just a handful of Republicans in Congress to hold middle class tax cuts hostage simply because they don't want tax rates on upper income folks to go up.'[8] As if fighting an election, he claimed to speak for the many and not the few. But he was not fighting an election. The mighty president was seeking to get legislative approval for his modest budget plans.

The battle went on as the cliff's edge was approaching, at the end of 2012. 'The proposal that was presented to Republicans yesterday has the strong support of the majority of American people,' declared a deputy White House press secretary. 'So all we're waiting on right now is House Republicans to acknowledge one very simple thing, which is that tax rates on the wealthy must go up to get this deal done.'[9] A senior House Republican spoke of the 'sad lack of respect with which the president treats the Congress', as if respect must manifest itself with pathetic presidential submission.

There is a very big difference between healthy scrutiny and paralysis. The US constitution too easily makes paralysis prevail over checks, counterbalances and robust forms of accountability. To some of his early ardent fans, Obama has been a disappointment. That is partly because he was doomed to disappoint. He had no political space in which to meet some of the early expectations.

Obama was elected in 2008 on the back of the empowering slogan 'Yes, we can', words that imply a triumph of the collective will. Very quickly he discovered that 'No, he could not'. Even his relatively modest measures aimed at stimulating the US economy after the 2008 crash moved him towards the fiscal cliff. A few years later Obama, speaking at a Democratic Congressional Campaign Committee in 2014, argued that the Republicans had been recklessly obstructive since even before he took office:

> Their willingness to say no to everything – the fact that since 2007, they have filibustered about 500 pieces of legislation that would help the middle class just gives you a sense of how opposed they are to any progress – has actually led to an increase in cynicism and discouragement among the people who were counting on us to fight for them.[10]

But who can blame the Republicans? They are leaders of strong conviction, with the power at least to block a president who does not share their vision of a small state. Why not exert such power? They are not the problem. Their power to do so is the problem. When president and Congress are broadly of a similar mindset, the constitutional rules work well. The president is still held to account. Compromise is often required. Scrutiny is impressively forensic and intensive. But when there is an unbridgeable clash of views, governing becomes almost impossible. A president is bound to disappoint those who voted for him. Other agents in the US economy – parts of the private sector, financial markets – will exert more power than a president struggling to overcome impossible obstacles.

In an interview with *Vanity Fair* towards the end of 2016 Obama was candid about the constraints of power:

> With that power, however, also comes a whole host of institutional constraints. There are things I cannot say. There are things that… that I cannot say, not out of any political concerns, but out of prudential concerns of the office. There are institutional obligations I have to carry out that are important for a president of the United States to carry out, but may not always align with what I think would move the ball down the field on the issues that I care most deeply about.[11]

Like several of Obama's farewell interviews, this one with the historian Doris Kearns Goodwin was gloriously reflective. In a competitive field, this quote was the most revealing. Here was supposedly the most powerful leader in the world admitting that his sense of office sometimes prevented him from moving the 'ball down the field' in the areas that he cared about most deeply. After eight years Obama was reflecting on the powerlessness of power.

He had lost his principled beliefs amidst the glamour of office. The office constrained him. He could not be himself.

On a much smaller part of the political stage, the then leader of the UK Labour Party, Neil Kinnock, was asked the following question in a BBC interview in 1988: 'As leader of the Labour Party you are reviewing the party's commitment to unilateral nuclear disarmament, but what is your personal position?' Kinnock had been a passionate supporter of unilateralism, but without hesitation he replied, 'Being leader of the Labour party and having personal views is a contradiction in terms.'[12] He was no longer allowed to have personal views. He had become a leader and was powerless to be himself any longer.

Now that Trump is in the White House, Democrats and quite a lot of Republicans view with relief the constitutional constraints in Washington – the democratic safeguards and separation of power delicately put in place with such admirable commitment to pluralist democratic politics by political artists in the late eighteenth century. Under Obama, they might have been obstacles to progress. Now they are perceived with less frustration as noble barriers that might block the instincts of the outsider in the White House. But it was the constraints that partly gave space to Trump in the first place.

Obama did not meet the hope that he generated, because he could not do so. He won two elections by a wide margin, in terms of the popular vote and in states secured in the electoral college. After which there were too many hurdles in his path, fuelling the instinct for disillusionment. As he has acknowledged, Obama might have played Washington more skilfully, working Congress with the tireless guile of Lyndon B. Johnson. But, as Obama has also insisted, he gave his all, as did his senior advisers, working through endless nights to get some of his policies through all the hoops. There was a clash of ideologies that neither guile nor charm could smooth over. The constitution had created a clash between two immovable objects. In relation to the economy, together they moved towards the cliff's edge, their energy sapped as they sought some form of unsatisfactory resolution. In contrast, the non-elected outsider – Trump the candidate – could promise to build a wall or impose a tariff or build roads, and there were no obstacles to block the words. The words were unimpeded. While Obama seemed weak at times, Trump appeared to be a mighty alternative. Partly it was the US constitution that made Obama weak.

There are other impossible constraints on elected governments. One recent UK Chancellor of the Exchequer noted privately that what happened in China, in terms of economic growth, would have more impact on the UK economy than his next budget or the one after that. Yet such budgets seem of overwhelming importance, as if the economy of the country in which it is delivered will be shaped by the words of a single individual from a single government. The chancellor must make boastful claims about the performance of the economy, to reassure markets and lift the morale of his party and of potential supporters in the electorate. There is always an election or a referendum around the corner. When the boasts seem at odds with voters' lives, they fume about the politician's mendacity or detachment from reality. The politician is *so* in touch with reality that he has no choice but to make exaggerated claims, in the hope that they become self-fulfilling.

For those countries in the eurozone, there are even more constraints than there are over those that are not members. The individual governments have no control over interest rates. The European Central Bank has as much power over economic policy as some elected governments. In the UK, after the 2016 Brexit referendum, the non-elected Governor of the Bank of England, Mark Carney, had more power and influence in the immediate aftermath than any elected Cabinet minister.

In Italy, Matteo Renzi's lost referendum was indirectly about the woeful performance of the Italian economy as a member of the eurozone. The referendum was in itself a constraint on power, the biggest of the lot. It brought about the resignation of Renzi. Cameron held three referendums while he was UK prime minister, not because he was a convert to direct democracy, but because of deeper fragilities. He held one in order to keep his party together (the referendum that he lost on the EU); another in an attempt to keep the United Kingdom together (the one he won, but sort of lost, in Scotland, in that the SNP thrives in its aftermath); and one more to keep the coalition together (the referendum on electoral reform that Cameron won and Clegg lost). None of Cameron's referendums resolved the issues they were held to address. Each had the opposite impact, fuelling divisions over the question that was put to voters.

More referendums are likely, in the era of mistrust. Leaders do not feel confident to make major decisions. Arguably, they are not trusted to do so. In the era of mistrust, elected leaders are acutely conscious of how they are perceived. The mistrust leads to another form of paralysis: a fear of acting boldly. Leaders yearn to be popular and understandably worry about their levels of unpopularity. As they act hesitantly or with a nervy evasiveness, the mistrust rises further. They are the powerful without power, in an era when the lives of voters are changing fast. Voters ache for mediating agencies to protect and guide them, and yet they do not trust the most accountable mediating agency – the elected insiders. Voters can remove a government and often do. They can insult politicians and often do. The elected politicians must make decisions with no easy answers in the context of globalization, knowing that they are not trusted to make a decision on matters big or small. As a result, they offer wary voters the chance to 'take back control'. Voters seem to like the idea. Who would not do so, when asked whether or not they would like to take back control of their life? To pose the opposite highlights the potency of the offer: would you like to *lose* control of your life? But the offer is much more ambiguous than it sounds.

6

———

TAKING BACK CONTROL

The phrase 'taking back control' became ubiquitous in the era of the outsider. Like the phrase 'those who have been left behind', repetition obscured its meaning. Seizing back control of what, and by whom? These are pivotal questions relating to where power lies and who exerts that power – questions that lie at the heart of the outsiders' ascendancy and the crisis in mainstream parties. Donald Trump persistently asserted throughout his campaign that it was necessary for America to take back control. One of the leading strategists for the 'Out' campaign in the Brexit referendum, Dominic Cummings astutely recognized that this single phrase was a vote-winner. Who does not want to be more in control? Early in 2017 Cummings wrote a vivacious and historically rich account of how 'Out' had won the referendum during the previous summer.[1] He did not argue that 'deep forces were in play' and that the result could easily have gone the other way. But he did note the power of the slogan and the way it connected so conveniently to many themes, from immigration to top executives' spiralling pay, with no agency seemingly able, or willing, to exert control. But each time that assertion was used with a swagger that suggested precision, no one specified very clearly what they meant by 'control' – not even Cummings, who wrote more precisely than most.

The same words were used also on the left in parts of Europe, as well as by Trump and the Brexiteers. In Greece, as he was seeking to pass a budget in the Greek parliament – a programme that contained a series of expedient compromises forced on him by the demands of power – Tspiras declared, 'We are doing this so we can take back control.'

This was also one of the big themes in the early days of Podemos in Spain. As it began to make waves, Podemos' central message was a call for democratic and parliamentary control of several bodies, including the European Central Bank.

All the vivid phrases that punctuated the rise of the outsiders had the same meaning, and lack of meaning. When outsiders noted that voters who were 'left behind' wanted some form of representation, and when those seeking to be their representatives insisted it was time for them to take back control, they opened up a series of policy questions that had been left unanswered since the 1970s. What role should, or could, governments play in intervening in the global market? How could individual governments protect those who could no longer rely on traditional forms of employment? Should governments intervene to protect some traditional industries that were run efficiently but were threatened by cheap imports? In other words, how could governments help voters feel that they did have some sense of control over what happened to them and ensure that not too many of them were detached and 'left behind'.

The backdrop that generated the cries for help was the revolution in working patterns and communications. Communities bound by work that was fast disappearing became fractured. Unsurprisingly, there were political consequences. Any change, deep or shallow, impacts quickly on those supposedly cocooned in affluent capitals, even if they have not noticed the tumultuous waves. In the United

States' presidential election, Trump beat Clinton amongst white voters without a college education by 39 percentage points – a margin larger than Ronald Reagan's against Walter Mondale, when Reagan won his 1984 landslide to give him his second term.

Trump not only beat Clinton by nearly fifty points among blue-collar white men, but by almost thirty points among non-college-educated white women. The areas where he particularly flourished were in the so-called Rust Belt of the United States: Wisconsin, Pennsylvania and Michigan. Polls suggested that one of the regular swing states seemed more febrile than usual during the election. One commentator observed that there were 41,767 reasons for the unpredictability of the state – and that was the number of lay-offs reported, due to the large number of plant closings since the beginning of 2015. Trump appeared to have an answer to such closures, in the form of protectionism. He would seize control of the global market by imposing tariffs on cheap imports, thereby protecting US producers. He did not explain how he would deal with the higher prices that would arise and the demand for wage increases to meet the increased cost of living, the sequence arising from trade wars. But he did have an answer to those worried about work in the swing states. He would intervene to protect their jobs. Backed by small-state, free-market Tea Party types, Trump was the interventionist. He did not have answers in relation to the consequences of protectionism. Outsiders were not very interested in consequences.

The challenge for the elected insiders was multi-layered. It was not only cheap imports from economic superpowers like China that threatened old work patterns. The technological revolution was also transforming the way jobs were defined. Uber would not have happened without an app that capitalized on new forms of technology from the mobile phone to satellites, which bring together driver and customer. The orthodox taxi driver felt threatened by the competition. Both would be undermined, if driverless cars are given the go-ahead. While we wait to be driven by machines, accountants are being replaced by virtual accountants. Paid journalists compete with unpaid bloggers. No one gets paid for tweeting. Emails replace the delivered letter. Local branches of banks are closing, as online banking takes over from contact with paid staff. In towns and cities, coffee shops are full of people with their laptops seeking new ways of working and earning. Not so long ago the coffee-drinkers would have been in staff jobs, secure enough to obtain a mortgage and to plan ahead. Now they improvise. They are the lucky ones. In many areas there are no thriving coffee shops, and no demand for those innovative enough to make inroads with their laptops. The old jobs have gone and there is nothing very much in their place – an emptiness that feeds on itself. If people are not earning very much, they do not have much spare money to spend. Local shops and restaurants close. That means more local people without work, and less demand for labour in any form.

The increasingly fractured work patterns in the United States have been repeated across the European Union. In Spain, youth unemployment peaked at more than 50 per cent. In Greece, unemployment was the highest in the European Union and rose at some low points to more than 30 per cent of the adult population.

In much of the democratic world there has been an accelerating increase in service-sector employment, both in low-skilled customer-service work and in high-skilled knowledge occupations, and a corresponding drop in manufacturing employment. This has contributed to a polarization of the workforce in many countries, with more high-skilled and low-skilled jobs, but fewer requiring mid-level skills. At the same time, young people are finding it increasingly hard to get a foothold in the labour market, and the proportion of the workforce employed on full-time permanent contracts has shrunk.

Labour markets have been fundamentally transformed as digital technology has destroyed a wide range of routine jobs, while creating new employment opportunities for highly skilled workers. Major technological revolutions have always been associated with some places moving ahead while others are left behind – that phrase 'left behind' recurring once again in the context of whole regions.

Over past decades, metropolitan regions such as Berlin, London and Stockholm have surged ahead in Europe by transforming the technologies of the digital revolution into new industries and jobs. At the same time, some former manufacturing cities, once the prospering places of the industrial age, have struggled to reinvent themselves, as a wide range of routine work has become automated, a pattern that will intensify. Urban areas, with their dense economic activity, are becoming hubs of development because they connect the entrepreneurs, innovators and investors who are required to create jobs in the twenty-first century.

Against the backdrop of increased communication and transportation, the continued importance of physical proximity offered in these cities may have seemed oddly unnecessary. However, although mobile devices, social networks and high-speed wireless broadband have made communication over vast distances possible at nearly no cost at all, face-to-face interactions are still the key engine-driver of innovation and growth.

The digital revolution gave birth to a wide range of new jobs for app developers, software designers and search-engine optimizers. Places that managed to create these kinds of jobs grew faster as a result. New high-tech industries, however, have tended to be highly concentrated. Across the industrialized world, metropolitan regions that were successful in transforming new technologies into new jobs have been pulling way ahead, while other areas have seen jobs disappear, leading to regional decline. Indeed, some observers of the UK Brexit campaign argued that the way of explaining the UK now is not in terms of class divisions, but in terms of regional divisions and tensions.

After the election of Trump and post-Brexit in the UK, there was a justifiable interest in the book *Hillbilly Elegy*. The author, J. D. Vance, wrote evocatively of growing up in a poor Rust Belt town, and highlighted the struggles of the white working class, the disappearing jobs, the lost sense of identity and community. Partly the book highlights the trauma of aspiration: escaping poverty in Kentucky's Appalachian region, but struggling to adapt in Ohio. The themes extend well beyond the US. The former UK chancellor, George Osborne, cited the book as a must-read, as he sought to make sense of the Brexit result. As the US anticipated the possibility of a Trump victory, US columnists were citing *Hillbilly Elegy* as a biblical text, the book that made sense of lost securities and identity amongst the white working class.[2] As Obama put it, at his final press conference as president in January 2017, when asked why he felt voters had backed his successor: 'They feel forgotten and looked down on… you don't want to have an America in which a very small sliver of people are doing really well and the rest are fighting for scraps.'[3]

Obama cites a wider inequality as an explanation for Trump. Agonized liberals study *Hillbilly Elegy*. And in the UK books on UKIP are read for insights into the appeal of a party where its senior members have punch-ups and its leaders do not last very long, except for one who continues to bounce back, having announced his resignation. The readers are right to investigate, but they are in danger of overlooking an important twist. The focus on the white poor in the US and parts of Europe risks obscuring a wider point. Quite a lot of affluent city-dwellers felt left behind too – those supposedly flourishing in the new global and communications revolution. The pressures on them were similar in some respects to those struggling with change in poorer areas. They were dependent on unreliable public-transport systems. They worried that their children, now in their twenties and thirties, could not afford to buy or rent adequate accommodation, even if they were well paid. Income levels are less relevant than property ownership, in some cities. In the globalized economy Russian oligarchs could buy houses as an investment that inflated the entire housing market, and then not live in them. No one, or no institution, appeared able to regulate or control such wild market distortion, or was inclined to do so.

Early in 2016 a senior figure at a think tank reflected with me on his typical day, living and working in London. He did so as part of a wider discussion on how, even in booming London, little worked as it should. Although he was on a decent salary, he and his family could afford only a small house in Hackney, once a relatively poor area but, following gentrification, now an area where homes sold for millions. His mortgage swallowed up much of his income. Each morning he took his young child to a crèche. The crèche was local-authority controlled and had originally been opened so that poorer parents could go to work. But the council was making big cuts in its budget and therefore had to charge high fees for the childcare. Although the crèche had been built for poorer families, many could not afford the charges and it had become a middle-class crèche. He then took a train to work. The trains were unreliable and expensive. When they failed to arrive, he was not sure who to complain to and whether the complaint would have any impact. Was it the train company, Network Rail, the government or the regulator that could act on his behalf – or none of them? No institution was accountable. He started to look for schools, post-crèche. There had been much talk from Blair and Cameron of 'choice' for parents. There was no choice. Most schools suffered from teacher shortages. One school had acquired a good reputation that fed on itself, attracting the most motivated parents. Its open days were the equivalent of attending a rock concert, and for most parents there was no chance of their child getting in. His job was not a secure one; he was on a contract that was dependent on funding from generous donors from the public and private sectors. The donors were less generous, with all the economic uncertainties. Those feeling left behind, unsure how to hold providers to account, included some in the booming cities. Over a cup of tea, those left behind in the US Rust Belt states and in parts of England where voters felt 'left behind' and ignored would have discovered common ground.

In these supposedly flourishing modern cities, voters also struggled to secure a doctor's appointment. They also found that it was difficult to get reliable, secure work, even if their income was much higher compared with those in the left-behind regions. The urban insecurities were one reason why quite a lot of the big cities moved to the left. London became a reliably Labour city when Labour's support was falling fast elsewhere. New York elected a left-wing mayor. Struggling with the costs of childcare, poorly regulated and overpriced transport, insecure work and soaring accommodation costs, the voters cried out for a body to take control.

The Twitter-feed of commuters in London and the South-East was a cry for help that was almost as intense as it was from those who chanted Trump's name at his presidential rallies. Desperate travellers made cathartic tweets to the companies supposedly responsible for providing trains. 'Where are the trains this morning? I am late for work for the fifth day in a row'; 'What has happened to this service? Who is in charge?' These were impotent tweets of despair. No one was in control – not the commuter dependent on reliable trains, when they were wildly unreliable; not the government that privatized the railways; and not the train companies, which tended to blame the company responsible for maintaining the tracks. Who was in charge? Here was another power-related enquiry that explained the disconnection between the insiders and the voters. The question was a unifying one, as potent in cities as the Rust Belt as in poorer parts of Europe.

The unifying disconnection raises another question: If even those who are benefiting from the new globalized economy feel powerless, why is it that the mainstream parties struggle so hard to make sense of these changing, fractured work patterns, and to put together a programme of policies and ideas that address the fears of not only those in the left-behind regions but also those in the flourishing cities? If they were able to do so, there is a coalition of support available to them that would win any general election in the Western world.

The changes are starkly obvious. The insiders must have been living on another planet, if they were not aware of them. But on the whole they chose to emphasize the potential benefits and underplay the negative consequences. Even the arduously cautious struggled at times not to be insensitive. Hillary Clinton famously said at one point in the presidential campaign, in praising the future for alternative forms of energy and developing an argument around greenery and climate change, 'We're going to put a lot of coal companies and coal miners out of business.'[4] She was making a point that would appeal to environmentalists and was speaking the truth, in that it was unlikely that in fifty years' time the United States would be using much, or any, power from coal. Nonetheless, her publicly declared insight reflected a failure to recognize the sensitivities of those who were still dependent on the old jobs. Given that every public word she uttered was considered in advance for its vote-losing potential, the utterance shows that she underestimated the insecurities arising from such changing patterns. To take her example, while climate change brings responsibilities and opportunities, it also becomes a threat to some traditional jobs. In those traditional jobs were many former long-time voters for the Democratic Party.

Even the silver-tongued insiders struggled with the downsides of globalization. Obama, with his power of oratory and language – a figure who, in his writing before he became president, was comfortable with making left-of-centre arguments about the benevolent potential of the state – did not always rise to the challenge of being optimistic and yet alert to the downsides. In praising the expansive developments of Silicon Valley, he was almost dismissive of those working-class voters who were anxious about globalization, declaring on one occasion: 'We're part of an interconnected global economy now and there's no going back from that.'[5]

He was obviously correct, but where were the qualifying sentences that would reassure those being forced from old jobs that they would be able to work again? Obama was equally dismissive of the arguments of Bernie Sanders, which resonated briefly but powerfully in the campaign for the nomination to become the Democrats' presidential candidate. Obama described Sanders as 'A talented but ageing politician who simply refused to accept the new democratic map.'[6]

'The new democratic map' was framed by President Clinton in the late 1980s and early 1990s. Clinton had sought to come to terms with the consequences of globalization by partly accepting them. In another of his farewell interviews, with his friend and former senior adviser David Axelrod, Obama was more reflective both about Sanders and about the politics of globalization. He described Sanders as a centrist, compared with the position of some of his right-wing Republican opponents. Obama also suggested that he would spend some of his post-presidential freedom seeking to find out why it was that some voters did not make the connection between significant policies that he had instigated and the impact on their lives. He had highlighted another factor in the rise of the outsiders and the decline of the mainstream: the breakdown in the connections between the elected representatives, their policies and the governed.[7]

———

Obama is not alone in seeking to make connections and to discover when the link between the state and some voters has been severed. The UK's current Conservative prime minister is more wary of globalization than Blair was when he made his conference speech in 2005 – the address in which he argued that for a government to intervene would be as fruitless as seeking to prevent summer moving on to autumn. Theresa May's address to the financial elite in Davos in January 2017 suggested that she is to the left of Blair in her argument. She is the break with the past, the Tory modernizer, addressing – in words at least – the fragilities brought about by globalization.

The qualification about words, rather than actions, is important. It was Blair who intervened in the labour market by introducing a minimum wage. Blair was the prime minister who transformed some lives by investing in the NHS. From opposition, May opposed both measures. But the framing of an argument from the prime ministerial altar does shape political debate and policy-making. She frames the argument as a believer in government:

> Talk of greater globalization can make people fearful. For many, it means their jobs being outsourced and wages undercut. It means having to sit back as they watch their communities change around them.
>
> And in their minds, it means watching as those who prosper seem to play by a different set of rules, while for many life remains a struggle as they get by, but don't necessarily get on.
>
> And these tensions and differences are increasingly exposed and exploited through the expansion of new technologies and the growth of social media.
>
> But if we are to make the case for free markets, free trade and globalization, as we must, those of us who believe in them must face up to and respond to the concerns people have.
>
> And we must work together to shape new policies and approaches that demonstrate their capacity to deliver for all of the people in our respective countries.
>
> I believe this challenge demands a new approach from government. And it requires a new approach from business too.
>
> For government, it means not just stepping back and – as the prevailing orthodoxy in many countries has argued for so many years – not just getting out of the way. Not just leaving businesses to get on with the job and assuming that problems will just fix themselves.
>
> It means stepping up to a new, active role that backs businesses and ensures more people in all corners of the country share in the benefits of its success.
>
> And for business, it means doing even more to spread those benefits to more people. It means playing by the same rules as

everyone else when it comes to tax and behaviour, because in the UK trust in business runs at just 35 per cent among those in the lowest income brackets. And it means putting aside short-term considerations and investing in people and communities for the long-term.[8]

May was modest compared with Trump's statist ambitions, but both were part of a new era: a response to the liberals' complacency in the face of globalization. In arguing for protectionism, Trump asserted that decades of free-trade policies were responsible for the collapse of the American manufacturing industry. He was feeding on the growing perception among many Americans that globalization had brought more pain than gain, while mainstream leaders were highlighting the degree to which gains had been made.

Opinion polls in some marginal states suggested that poorer voters resented the outsourcing of jobs to cheaper markets as much as they felt threatened by immigration. Against that backdrop, Trump's stance on trade became the clearest of his economic policies, albeit without specifics on how it was going to work, in terms of imposing tariffs. But here was an individual who was going to change and intervene in the chaotic work patterns that were erupting around parts of the United States, or at least that was the impression he partially generated.

Trump was dismissive during the campaign of the North American Free Trade Agreement, the agreement that lowers trade barriers between the US, Canada and Mexico. The deal was negotiated by George Bush and was enacted in the 1990s by Bill Clinton – the coming-together of mainstream Republicanism and the New Democrats as personified by Clinton. Trump was even more dismissive of the Trans-Pacific Partnership between twelve countries around the Pacific Rim, excluding China – although he was dismissive of arrangements with China, too – and of the agreement being negotiated between the US and the European Union. Trump also made clear his anger with China, arguing that since China had joined the World Trade Organization, Americans had witnessed the closure of more than 50,000 factories and the loss of tens of millions of jobs. Trump dumped the TPP in one of his first moves as president.

Such was the bizarre nature of the contest between Trump and Clinton that he was rarely challenged on specifics. Now that he is in the White House, Trump has unilateral powers to withdraw the US from the North American Free Trade Agreement, the World Trade Organization and the embryonic Trans-Pacific Partnership. But it is far from clear whether he can secure what he has vaguely called 'great deals' to replace those arrangements. Nor has he explained that if tariffs are imposed on goods coming into the United States, then the same will apply to those going out, making it more difficult for some in the US to export, and leading in all cases to significant price rises in goods. There is always a downside to the swagger of the outsider, but only when the policies are tested by power.

In the 2016 presidential election Hillary Clinton was in some respects as interventionist as her opponent in her policy proposals, although they attracted little attention. Clinton had worked through plans to seize back control from the unfettered markets. But she did not have the language, passion or enough weighty emblematic policies to reassure the victims of globalization.

Some of the detail was at least as radical as Trump's. Clinton planned a major national infrastructure plan, which would have allocated $27.5 billion annually to improve roads, bridges, public transport and the rest. This is a proportionately bigger sum than the timid mainstream parties dared to propose in the UK election in

2015. She planned an expanded childcare plan, an early-education plan that would have invested $27.5 million a year for states to make pre-school available to all four-year-olds. And she proposed to spend $16.6 million a year to identify and treat children with disabilities, by expanding an existing set of institutions. She had an energy plan that would pay $9 million annually to repair oil pipelines, reduce carbon emissions and fund health and retirement for coal-workers. She was interested in strengthening, rather than abolishing, Obama's Affordable Care Act. And she had various plans for long-term growth as well. Some of her tax proposals, although very cautious in true Democrat style, were also not without significance, in their capacity to raise a fair amount of additional revenue.

But the sums were relatively small, and few voters noticed, or chose to notice, because the focus of the presidential contest was on the allegations around Trump and those surfacing about Clinton's emails. There was virtually no debate towards the end of the campaign on economic policy, the differences between the two candidates and some of Clinton's more radical proposals.

Arguably her proposals were not radical enough, but the idea that she represented solely some defence of an inadequate status quo is simply not the case. The same applies, in varying degrees, to programmes put forward by mainstream parties on the left and right in elections in recent years. But they struggled with an ambiguity over how to present them. Were they being technocratic and managerial, big-tent politicians with little or no ideological edge? Were they motivated, like the outsider, by conviction and deeply held values? Clinton began by being cautiously managerial and then sought to be less technocratic, in response to Sanders. In the UK's 2015 election the Labour leader, Ed Miliband, could never fully decide whether to be the radical left outsider or the reassuring centrist. The German and Austrian social democrats have suffered from the same dilemma. In most cases they seek to resolve it by being both, projecting contradictory and unconvincing public personalities. In contrast, the outsiders say what they think.

There was another reason why mainstream parties failed to come up with more radical propositions to challenge the consequences of the globalized economy. The options were all problematic, complex and difficult.

Mainstream leaders had to explain how the money they pledged to invest in capital spending, or alternative forms of employment for insecure workers, would be raised. The key issue in any general election is how the government plans to tax and spend. The pressure is always to propose tax cuts rather than increases in public spending. People might yearn for specific increases in public spending, but in a general election they tend to be against public-spending increases and in favour of the immediate hit of tax cuts. Tax cuts can be announced and materialize in the next month's pay packets. Public spending rises can take years before they lead to tangible improvements in voters' lives.

How does a mainstream government protect workers in one industry, when consumers benefit from cheaper imports? What happens if banks or large global companies threaten to move elsewhere, if a government imposes taxes or a regulatory framework that they regard as punitive? What is the solution to genuine worries about the free movement of labour, when countries' economies and public services are dependent on immigrants? How can a government pledge a commitment to full employment when technology wipes out jobs? How to address widening inequality in a global economy without undermining economies?

Immigration was the policy area that united the populist phrases about 'take back control' and being 'left behind' – the anguished questions posed by globalization – into a deceptive whole. There was little control over the free movement of people in Europe. Immigrants from other countries could arrive, seemingly without any form of regulation. Meanwhile jobs that were once secure could be swept away and replaced, either by no job at all or by a fractured jobs market where insecure vacancies might arise fleetingly, only to be taken away again. The lack of housing in some areas was another factor. So was the creaky health provision in countries with elderly populations where demand was – to use that phrase again – out of control, compared with the capacity of governments, or indeed the private sector, to provide what was required.

At each point of actual or potential connection with the state a vulnerable patient, a young person looking for a job or somewhere to live, or an older person used to having reliable work with the prospect of that work forming a lifetime's career wondered what was happening and where control lay, in a world which, to them, seemed to have moved quite quickly out of control.

When Theresa May outlined why the UK was leaving the EU she suggested, as part of a pivotal speech on Brexit in early 2017, that British voters were more bothered about holding their government to account. As she put it, 'The public expect to be able to hold their governments to account very directly, and as a result supranational institutions as strong as those created by the European Union sit very uneasily in relation to our political history and way of life.'[9] May was the latest Conservative to become close to the views of the late Tony Benn, the left-winger who put accountability at the heart of his political ideas. Who was accountable to whom? Benn applied this to put the case against the European Union. But the question applied more widely in the era of the liberal consensus, when the role of the state was underexplored. Who or what was accountable, when voters could not find adequate affordable accommodation, or waited a month to see a local doctor, or struggled to work when trains were cancelled? By pledging to act on several fronts and to intervene in labour markets, the outsiders were implicitly offering to be held directly to account.

In the real world, immigration might not be a factor (or not a significant one) in explaining poor public services, housing and insecure jobs. Indeed, health provision could not be expanded in more affluent countries without immigrants. Housing is in short supply partly because not enough homes are being built in countries where the demand is high. Doctors are hard to get to see because there are not enough of them. Much of the anger about immigration is about the failure of governments to deliver adequate public services, or perhaps the refusal of voters to pay the levels of tax required for high-quality provision.

But 'immigration' is an easy target – an all-encompassing policy that brings to life arguments about 'control', when working patterns are changing in front of our eyes. It is changes to working patterns that generate intense insecurity. Immigration is not a cause, and is more often a symptom of the demand for workers in economies that boom, as work patterns change. But for mainstream leaders to disentangle the distinctive themes proved to be too tough a task. They became caught up in the emotive mix.

There is another fundamental reason why mainstream leaders have struggled to come up with long-term policies to protect those who feel the need to take back control. Voters do not trust politicians. In an era when difficult long-term decisions must be made – not least in terms of public spending, whether it is capital spending or current expenditure – politicians are not trusted to take them. Mainstream politicians aching for respectability, seeking that mythical centre ground that creates more problems for them than solutions, are more mistrusted than at any time since the end of the Second World War. And it is in this era of mistrust that they need to be bold and more open-minded and responsive to change. While that mistrust continues, they will find it extremely difficult to be able to respond.

Once again we return to the issue of 'trust', the theme that paralyses mainstream leaders. In their paralysis, the mistrust deepens. Trust, and the lack of it, is part of the reason why mainstream leaders have failed to rise to the demands of sweeping change. That is clear. What is less clear is *why* leaders and politicians are viewed with levels of mistrust that make them even more powerless.

7

TRUST

Increasingly 'trust' is the prism through which politics is viewed. We look through that prism and decide, or assume, that the politicians we see are not worthy of trust. Voters trust celebrities, artists, rock stars, footballers and other non-elected public figures, in some cases to the point of deification. They speak in admiring terms of a footballer earning £250,000 a week. They fume about MPs earning £70,000 a year. Elected leaders are tormented by questions about trust and integrity.

At least they tend to be, after their early honeymoon period, when levels of 'trust' can be dangerously high, making the chances of disillusionment even greater, as leaders struggle to deliver promises made in election campaigns and to please voters, who are quick to blame them and to assume they are being ignored by those they elected.

There are some exceptions. In 2016 *The Economist* magazine reflected that a distinctive culture in Italy had enabled Silvio Berlusconi to thrive as prime minister:

> At the height of Silvio Berlusconi's power, as the billionaire-politician brushed scandals and lawsuits aside with the ease of a crocodile gliding through duckweed, a professor at an Italian university described... how the terms *furbo* and *fesso* helped explain the then-prime minister's survival. In those bits of Italian

society from which Mr Berlusconi drew his strongest support, it is a high compliment to be deemed a *furbo,* or a sly, worldly wise-guy. The *furbo* knows how to jump queues, dodge taxes and play systems of nepotism and patronage like a Stradivarius. In contrast the *fesso* is the chump who waits his turn and fails to grasp how badly the system is rigged, or how much of his taxes will be stolen. The *fesso* might cheer a new clean-air law in his city, naively taking an announcement by the elites at face value. The *furbo* wonders who in the environment department may have a brother-in-law with a fat contract to supply chimney scrubbers. Mr Berlusconi's fans saw him as the *furbo* to end all *furbi.* He showed that he heard them, offering them crude appeals to wise-guy cynicism, as when he asserted that any Italians who backed his centre-left opponents were not just mistaken, but were *coglioni* or, to translate loosely, 'dickheads', who would be voting 'against their own interests'.[1]

Berlusconi might have defied the trend in a freakish way, retaining or increasing support as criminal investigations over his conduct piled up, but Italian politics has been shaped and reshaped by a wider mistrust of party politics. In some recent elections more than one hundred parties or movements fielded candidates. Berlusconi's own career reflected the loose party ties. His party was first called Forza Italia and later became People of Liberty (PDL) when it merged with the National Alliance (AN). It was founded largely on the same rhetoric as so many other parties in Italy: aloof from the corrupt political landscape, in this case in the form of a fresh face from the business world. Berlusconi soon seemed very different. With numerous scandals attached to his name, he struggled to win support by offering himself as a 'clean' candidate. That made room for a new proliferation of parties on the right, which included Civic Choice of Mario Monti, a new Christian Democrat party, and others.

The rise of the Five Star movement in Italy is based partly on a rejection of all orthodox political parties and their methods of doing politics. Some voters in Italy do not trust any orthodox politicians and their parties any more. They trust those who were outside politics and who claim to be a movement rather than a party.

In the era of mistrust, some voters choose to trust the outsiders, both in Italy and across much of the Western world. Grateful voters assume that at last they have leaders who speak for them, and therefore they cast aside the prism of trust. They cannot trust all that Trump has said and done, because he already reneges on some campaign pledges. Far from locking up Hillary Clinton, he invited her to his inauguration dinner and praised her in his speech to the diners. His presidency suffered the early resignation of his National Security Adviser in February 2017, after leaks suggested that he tried to cover up talks with Russia and misled the vice-president, Mike Pence. More trivially, Trump has exaggerated the scale of his victory in the presidential election and the size of the crowds who attended his inauguration ceremony in Washington. If more mainstream leaders had behaved in a similar fashion, they would be in deep trouble – not just in the media, but amongst the voters who had placed their faith in them. Instead, when Trump held a rally for supporters in Florida in February 2017 he was hailed as a hero: the president as the performer of a one-man show. At one point Trump brought a member of the audience onto the stage. The fan declared, with the celebrity president next to him: 'Mr President – we the people, our movement is the reason why our president of the United States is standing here in front of us today. When President Trump during the election promised all these things that he was gonna do for us, I knew he was gonna do this for us.'

The crowd chanted in response, 'USA, USA...' Their patriotic ecstasy is a reminder that in politics 'trust' is deeply subjective. They had chosen to trust their hero and, in the early days of the presidency, they were not going to let the evidence get in the way. Similarly, mistrust forms and intensifies – sometimes without evidence – if voters decide they have been let down. Trusting a leader who is evidently untrustworthy is fairly dangerous. Choosing to mistrust elected leaders, mistaking the complexities of engaging in democratic politics for mendacity and criminality, is even more so.

For understandable reasons, parties within a coalition can contaminate each other. But democratic politics can now contaminate individuals who become politicians, whether they are in a coalition, outside one, or just getting on with their ill-defined jobs. No doubt there are many reasons why people become politicians, including vanity and the thrill of political theatre. But few do so to behave criminally or to act mendaciously for the hell of it. Why would they want to do so? There are easier ways to get rich or famous.

The explanation is partly about us (not the elected politicians), and the way we choose to view politics. We make choices, too. Look at the reactions to mainstream political leaders when, for whatever reason, they leave politics. Almost immediately they are viewed differently.

When Hillary Clinton made her speech in the aftermath of defeat in the presidential election in November 2016, commentators praised her without their usual forbidding qualifications. One wrote revealingly that Clinton 'was never able to show she was something more than the hyper-prepared, super-smart best student in the class. And then she managed to show more of herself in her concession speech, the latest example of politicians doing their best when they've lost something they wanted so badly.'[2]

In fact, her concession speech was exactly the same, in tone and substance, as the main campaign speeches Hillary Clinton had been making for the preceding two years. The difference was not in Clinton herself, but in the way listeners and viewers chose to perceive her. When she was seeking to be president she was polluted by politics and mistrust, viewed as a striving, ambitious, cold and calculating woman. In some quarters she was regarded also as a corrupt, secretive, criminal candidate. But when she had lost and was no longer stifled by politics, she was perceived as a human being. On Twitter, as she made her concession speech, commentators and voters from around the world were proclaiming, 'If only Hillary Clinton had spoken like this during the campaign, she might have won.'

She *had* spoken like this during the campaign. But in the aftermath of her defeat she was seen as a different person, a public figure with authenticity, wit and grace. She was viewed in such a light because she was stepping outside the political arena.

In the UK there are similar examples, as vivid as, and in some cases wilder than, those in the United States. In a competitive field the most bizarre was the experience of the former Labour politician Ed Balls, who had been a senior adviser in the Treasury to the long-serving chancellor, Gordon Brown, and went on to become a Cabinet minister. As a politician, he was so unpopular that he lost his seat in the 2015 general election, even though he was one of the more prominent national political figures. He had been shadow chancellor in the Labour shadow Cabinet for much of the 2010–15 parliament. As a politician, Balls was viewed – wrongly – as a political thug. When his name was mentioned, voters responded to this caricature: 'Oh, Balls, he's a bully', 'Oh, Balls, he beats up other politicians.' He could never escape that caricature while he remained in politics, which meant that, like Hillary Clinton, when he spoke on his brief with great expertise, voters either did not listen or chose not to believe him. He was mired in the era of mistrust.

In reality, Balls was an economist who became a politician, a rare and much-needed combination. He had a hinterland, a zest for life and he was loyal to those he respected, even when that loyalty did not help his own career, and often hindered it. None of this was seen while Balls was in politics, although he tried hard towards the end of his political career to make voters and the media recognize a different side to him.

Yet when Balls decided to become a contestant on the hugely popular BBC TV series *Strictly Come Dancing*, he was a near-instant much-loved celebrity. Some, including the former Labour leader Ed Miliband, who had no time for Balls, described him as a 'national treasure'. Balls – overweight and not a natural dancer – competed with natural dancers and the country started to love him. People who had turned against him as a politician were phoning up the BBC to declare their vote in favour of him, in order to keep him in the dancing competition – a vote that meant he remained in the series until the final rounds. After he was voted out of the contest, he was hugely in demand: presenting awards to film stars, taking part as a star guest on TV programmes. As a politician, some voters turned off when he spoke. After his TV appearances as a dancer, they paid to see him live, when the *Strictly* competitors toured the major stadiums. Balls was the big draw at the O2 Arena.

After Balls had lost his seat in the 2015 election, some voters came up to him and declared they were pleased he had been defeated. Being a human being, Balls suffered following that brutal rejection. But when he became a hit on the dance floor, he was greeted like a rock star when he appeared in public places. There was talk of him returning to politics and becoming the next leader of his party.

This is a dangerously perverse sequence. Voters could agree or disagree with Balls, as a politician (or indeed with Hillary Clinton), but he was impressively involved in some of the epic decisions of recent decades. He was a central figure in the UK government's ultimate decision not to join the single currency – the euro – one of the historic decisions made by a British government in recent decades.

In his twenties Balls was chiefly responsible for putting together a left-of-centre economic framework similar to that of the Democrats in the United States, who were working closely with Larry Summers, as an economist and academic. Both he and Summers are too easily blamed for the financial crash. In the UK the framework, partly defined by Balls, gave the Labour government the space to increase public spending after its election in 1997. Normally a Labour government had no such space, moving from crisis to crisis until it loses the next election. Again, voters can agree or disagree with what Balls did or failed to do, but this was epic policy-making that affected the lives of every single voter in the United Kingdom.

Balls was also involved in the careful planning that led to a unique tax rise in order to pay for increases in spending in the National Health Service, announced by the then chancellor, Gordon Brown, during his budget in 2002. The funding led to improvements in healthcare. The additional cash may have led to terrible inefficiencies as well. But unquestionably lives were enhanced by the sweaty, nerve-racking, energy-sapping manoeuvres en route to that announcement. Balls was at the heart of the strategy behind the scenes, where he was a dominant figure in the UK Treasury. During that period he was viewed with either indifference or loathing. When he went onto the dance floor, he was adored.

Politics contaminates. Once liberated from politics, although these public figures are then unable to implement their noble hopes and visions, politicians can become adored.

The same sequence applied to the former Conservative leader William Hague, another illuminating example from the UK. When Hague was leader of the Conservative Party between 1997 and 2001, he was viewed with disdain bordering on contempt. Newspapers – some of which now support the Conservative Party – portrayed him brutally on their front pages as a dead parrot, an image from the famous John Cleese sketch about a dead parrot in *Monty Python's Flying Circus*. When Hague made speeches or gave interviews they attracted very little attention. As far as there was media coverage, it was derisory. Hague was slaughtered in the 2001 election and resigned as leader of his party.

Almost immediately he became hugely popular. People who would have turned away from his speeches as a party leader now queued up to pay huge sums of money to hear him as an after-dinner speaker. Hague was hired for many thousands of pounds to tell a few jokes. He told good jokes for nothing when he was party leader.

Hague also took lessons to become a pianist, and people wanted to hear him play the piano – a pursuit that humanized Ed Balls too, but only after he left politics. Hague began to chair celebrity quizzes, including the famous BBC news quiz, *Have I Got News for You*. At one point in the years that followed his terrible humiliation at the ballot box, Hague took part in a phone-in on the BBC during which one caller phoned in to say, 'You would make a brilliant leader of the Conservative Party.' To which Hague replied, after a polite pause, 'I have already been a leader of the Conservative Party and I don't think it went very well.' He became a former leader tipped to be a future leader, and it was only during the period after he had been a leader that he became popular, no longer infected by politics at the top.

When the mainstream leaders reach a peak in France, they are often viewed with similar derision. President Hollande attracted such low personal ratings in the opinion polls that he chose not to contest a second election – a humiliating calculation. This was largely a reflection on his mediocre and weak leadership, but he had entered the dangerous arena and become loathed more quickly than he deserved to be. Once French presidents leave politics, they get streets named after them. In the fray, they are not trusted.

The default position of intense mistrust is revealed in another dark context. After the terrorist attacks in Paris in the autumn of 2015, Hollande had no choice but to become an apolitical leader. The presidential response to such a tragedy does not demand political acts from the left or right. In the immediate aftermath of tragedy, a president cannot trigger a great political row. There is inevitably a unifying focus. Soon there might be debates about security and competence, and all the other contentious issues that accompany the threat from international terrorism, but at first there is an apolitical unity. In that context – a non-political one – Hollande's popularity briefly rose. The popularity was measured in terms of trust, as it always is in the anti-politics era. Trust in Hollande rose from 15 per cent before the attacks to 35 per cent the following month, in December 2015. It was a short-lived bounce, after which his ratings fell to freakishly low percentages again.

Voters no longer trusted him once he emerged from the setting of a national tragedy. Hollande was fleetingly seen as a leader who could be trusted, not because he himself had changed, but because voters had chosen to see him in a different light.

In Germany, Angela Merkel too is judged in terms of trust, but in a way that shows the evasive ambiguity of the word 'trust'. Merkel's enduring appeal is based on a claim to trustworthiness in its simplest form. In effect, her message to the German electorate has at times been summarized in two words: 'Trust me'. By this, she means that she can be relied upon to rule competently.

A leader who proposes such a relationship risks a negative response when they are seen to be incompetent. When she says, 'Trust me', what she means is, 'I will deliver what I say, I am a reliable leader.' Probably what she does not mean is: 'I will not be corrupt or a liar.' On the whole, voters work on the assumption that Merkel is not corrupt and mendacious, and therefore she does not need to make that point. In other countries, leaders often fight a battle over trust, when they are seen as corrupt, liars and war criminals. This is especially the case in the UK.

But even in Merkel's case, the issue of trust has stretched to what one German newspaper described as 'breaking point'. Inevitably this followed her compassionate, and economically astute, refugee policy. Merkel herself acknowledged her changed relationship with parts of the electorate and spoke in terms of 'trust' when she lost a key regional vote, in her home region of Mecklenburg-Vorpommern. Voters in her region abandoned the established parties, including the Christian Democrats, and moved towards the German anti-immigration right-wing alternative, just as Austrian voters had done in the 2016 presidential contest. Merkel responded, again using the term 'trust': 'We must all think hard about how we can win back trust again. And of course, in the first place that means me. I am the party chairman, I am the chancellor.'[3]

She did not talk about winning back 'respect' or 'support'. Like all democratically elected insiders, she was looking at how to regain trust. In early 2015, before her refugee policy, Merkel had a popularity rating of 75 per cent. That was down to 44 per cent, her lowest rating in five years, in the summer and autumn of 2016. She framed her response through the nightmarishly distorting prism of modern politics: the prism of trust.

Perhaps she meant that she would need to prove her competence again. Like other highly emotive terms, such as 'asylum', 'immigration' and 'taking back control', such phrases have an evasive ambiguity and tend to be conflated. But 'trust' at its most fundamental – and 'mistrust', in its more common application when applied to modern democratic politics – must also have a connection with 'integrity'. If voters are to trust leaders, they must feel there is a fundamental integrity; and if they mistrust them, they must regard them in some way as mendacious, or worse. This is obviously very dangerous, not just for Merkel, but for the future of democracy.

The focus on 'trust' is unique to politics, although it extends to other public institutions. A newly appointed chief executive, or an aspiring one, does not make a pitch in terms of 'trust'; he or she speaks of ambition and innovation. A head teacher does not begin his or her reign at a school by insisting they are worthy of trust. A newspaper editor does not proclaim that he or she can be trusted with the overwhelming pitch. But in politics it has become necessary to do so.

———

There has always been a degree of disdain for elected politicians. There is nothing new in voters viewing warily those they have chosen as their rulers. The wariness is reflected in satire, going back centuries, and in protests that reflect a resolute anger over a particular policy or issue. The distancing between electorate and leader is reflected in the almost inevitable disillusionment after a government's early honeymoon euphoria is replaced by terrible ratings in the opinion polls. The whole idea of a 'swingometer' – whereby there is an almost inevitable swing from governing party to the main opposition party, as disillusionment sets in – is further evidence that rulers are doomed to be unloved. The sequence from honeymoon to disillusionment has been common in democratic politics for as long as democracy has existed, in some form or another.

But more recently an intolerant intensity has accompanied the familiar disillusionment – a loathing of politics and politicians that is dangerous and undermines democratic politics.

In the UK a series of recent prime ministers arrived in office determined, above all, to prove their integrity, but left with questions about trust overwhelming all others. Securing trust was almost their main political mission. In their bid to be trusted, the mistrust deepened.

John Major, the Conservative prime minister who succeeded Margaret Thatcher in 1990, made great play of his ordinariness – his upbringing in a working-class part of south London. Much of it was authentic. Major went into politics with a fascination for what could be achieved by power, and a degree of ideological conviction as a relatively moderate Tory. He did not have the qualities to be a titanic leader, but he was not a crook. Yet his government was overwhelmed by allegations of 'sleaze'. Opinion polls suggested that 'sleaze' came close to topping the list of voters' concerns about Major's government. Some of his ministers and MPs were culpable in various ways; and one, Jonathan Aitken, served a prison sentence. But perceptions of 'sleaze' under Major went beyond a series of freakish and unrelated cases.

The term served to condemn virtually the entire government. When, as a minister, William Waldegrave tried to explain why ministers might not be able to tell the truth in relation to, say, the strength or weakness of the currency, he was widely condemned as a liar, advocating mendacity as a matter of policy. In fact he was speaking the truth in explaining how a chancellor might fear devaluation privately but, if he were to express his worry in public, would make devaluation more likely. In his vivid memoir, published in 2015, Waldegrave spoke of how tormented he felt as the media, ranging from the *Financial Times* to the *Evening Standard*, wilfully misreported his words.[4]

Amidst new levels of hysteria, John Major launched, in his desperation, a poorly thought-through 'Back to Basics' crusade. He was referring to domestic policies and was not intending it to be an attack on the so-called 'permissive society', but subsequently any Tory MP having an affair (or thought to be having an affair) was accused of immoral hypocrisy. Major never meant his silly slogan to be applied in this way, but that was what happened, after an inept briefing from one of his staff. MPs who were not conventionally married were now in trouble and 'sleazy' in their hypocrisy.

The British media sensed weakness and tormented Major, as one allegation after another surfaced about various ministers and Conservative MPs. None were directly aimed at Major or were about him, but in the end he was the victim, as his then opponent, Tony Blair, suggested that he led a government 'mired in sleaze' – an allegation that Blair was later to regret making, as he too became overwhelmed by allegations relating to 'trust'.

Blair was so determined to prove his own and his government's integrity that he said early on in his premiership that he and his ministers had to show they were 'whiter than white'. Preposterously, he declared that even perceptions of impurity were unacceptable – a sign of how irrational 'mistrust' had become. That was another comment he was to regret, because no minister can control perception. A minister can be pure, but perceived as impure. Obviously it would be unfair under those circumstances to sack that minister or for him or her to resign on those grounds. Indeed, Blair himself was soon perceived as impure. If he had acted on his pledge, his resignation would have had to come within months. There were allegations that he changed policy to help a Labour donor, Bernie Ecclestone, in the autumn of 1997. Blair denied them, but the perception of wrongdoing was in place.

Blair was investigated by the police towards the end of his leadership in a way that shone much light on the distorting impact of mistrust. The cause of the Scotland Yard investigation comprised questions raised by an SNP MP over whether Blair had acted illegally, in honouring some of the political donors to the Labour Party. Many other leaders had honoured donors in a similar way, but Blair, post-Iraq, seemed easy prey, and a wholly inexcusable police operation was mounted on flimsy evidence and a vacuous legal basis. Blair was interviewed by the police and several of his close allies were arrested, sometimes early in the morning, although none were charged. The investigation collapsed when the Crown Prosecution Service ruled that the evidence accumulated by the police was not worth taking as far as a trial.

The very attempt to do so was part of a culture that assumed criminality too readily in relation to public figures. The reporting of that particular investigation was depressingly predictable. BBC outlets in particular ran reports citing 'police sources', quoting them piously as if they were beyond reproach. The 'sources' complained on one occasion about how Number Ten was obstructing their noble investigation. The accusation triggered a long report on *Newsnight* about how Blair and others were 'spinning' the investigation, choosing to be questioned by police when other big news stories were in play, even though the report had been prompted by police sources 'spinning' nonsense to the BBC. The dynamic was a symptom of the anti-politics era and contributed to it. The brave police officers were portrayed as taking on the mighty elite. In reality, the investigation was closer to a police fantasy. The officers who embarked on the investigation were probably not overtly 'anti-Labour' or 'anti-Blair'. They were part of the anti-politics culture, too, enjoying the heroism granted to those who take on the elected insiders.

Arguably the leap towards mountainous disdain began with the impeachment of President Clinton, a similar story to the pathetic police investigation of Blair, but on a much more epic scale. This was overtly political, whereas no Conservative was directly involved in the attempt to investigate Blair; indeed, many Conservatives spoke out against the senior officer who was playing the star role.

In contrast, it was almost as if some Republicans in Washington could not accept Clinton's election. Here was a Democrat imposter disturbing the natural order in which Republicans won presidential elections. They had been brought up politically on a series of Republican victories, and instead of seeking to oppose Clinton purely in terms of policy – although of course they did that as well and prevented Clinton from implementing many of his proposals – they took to other devices to undermine a Democratic outcome.

The impeachment of Clinton in 1998–9 remains one of the most extraordinary events in the United States' history. Kenneth Starr, the independent counsel, but a Republican supporter – strongly encouraged by the support of other senior Republicans in Washington – pursued Clinton obsessively. Starr began by investigating one alleged scandal, the so-called 'Whitewater Affair', concerning real-estate investments. Although that was investigated assiduously and continued to haunt Hillary Clinton in her 2016 campaign, there was nothing Starr could find to bring down either of them. Instead of giving up, he pursued Bill Clinton over his affair with Monica Lewinsky, during which he contrived a set of circumstances whereby Clinton was impeached.

Many years later Starr expressed a degree of regret about what had happened and described Clinton as the most gifted politician of the baby-boomer generation: 'Clinton's genuine empathy for human beings is absolutely clear. It's powerful, it's palpable, and the people of Arkansas really understood that about him. That he genuinely cared. The "I feel your pain" is absolutely genuine.'[5]

There is an illuminating book on the whole affair, called *The Death of American Virtue: Clinton vs. Starr*, by a law professor, Ken Gormley. It is a long book and details insightfully what happened. Although Gormley does not in some respects condemn Starr, he concludes that this was the beginning of the sharp division between Republicans and Democrats. The division was formed over the issue of trust and integrity – the killer of democratic politics.

Bill Clinton's experience came to haunt and torment the separate candidacy of Hillary Clinton in 2016 in ways that were bizarre. She did not have an affair with Monica Lewinsky, and she was not impeached. She was not found guilty during the 'Whitewater' investigation. Yet in the televised presidential debates, when Trump wanted to deflect attention from his own infidelities (or allegations of infidelities) and self-described 'locker-room banter' about women, he would demand of Hillary: 'What about Bill Clinton and his treatment of women?' It was as if she had become bound up with the same degree of culpability as Trump and, arguably, Bill Clinton himself.

In terms of her policy proposals, Hillary was not heard in the campaign, partly because she had to spend a lot of her time deflecting imprecise allegations of corruption. There was no evidence of corruption in her use of private emails – the latest saga to convey sinister, behind-the-scenes Clinton scheming. Her use of private emails was almost certainly a consequence of all the earlier allegations. There became a paranoid secrecy in the Clinton court, partly because they had cause to become secretive; they themselves did not know whom they could trust, and so they became more controlling, less open and that in itself fuelled suspicion. It is the impossible catch-22 in the era of mistrust.

———

Another epic event that quickly became an issue about 'trust', rather than about a leader's judgement or policies, was the war in Iraq. The war was a calamity. What happened raised many major questions, and the political leaders had much to answer for. Yet very quickly the multi-layered causes were reduced to issues and questions about whether Bush and Blair lied in order to take their countries to war.

In the UK the media became obsessed with the idea that the so-called New Labour government focused almost exclusively on 'spin' – presentation in the media – rather than on actual policy development. While New Labour's nervy leaders were far too preoccupied about how they were faring in the media, some of them were also absorbed in policy-making. But that policy-making, and even the internal differences over policy, was underplayed in the UK media. We ended up in a surreal position, before the war in

Iraq, when quite a lot of the focus was on the way the government presented a policy rather than on the policy itself. By implication the media, including the BBC, was suggesting that voters should not trust the government because it was spinning mendaciously.

The focus was dangerously disproportionate. Every prime minister employs press officers to present the government in the best possible light. If advisers working for a prime minister sought to present him or her in the worst possible light, they would be acting oddly.

Blair's press secretary, Alastair Campbell, in particular became an obsession with the media. Even though it is true Campbell sought to present Blair positively, so did the first Labour press secretary to understand the modern media, Joe Haines, who worked for Harold Wilson in the 1970s. By the time Blair came to power, the BBC employed far more managers, producers and reporters at its Westminster base in Millbank than Blair employed spin doctors. But BBC editors, unable to join in with newspapers cheering or jeering partisan policy areas, could obsess about spin and trust without seeming biased. They leaned neither to the left nor to the right in targeting issues of trust and spin. As a result, long before the war in Iraq, the BBC obsession meant that virtually any ministerial announcement was reported partly on the basis of how it was presented. The substance of the policy was underplayed.

The question of whether Blair lied to justify war in Iraq, with the help of Campbell, was therefore one that was guaranteed to make tumultuous waves. On 29 May 2003 a BBC reporter, Andrew Gilligan, generated headlines with a series of reports that began with two so-called 'two-way' interviews on the BBC's *Today* radio programme with the presenter John Humphrys. It was not just the two-way interviews that caused the storm. The BBC headlines throughout the day implied that senior intelligence officials were disowning the government's dossier on the alleged weapons of mass destruction [WMD] that Blair had published in advance of the war in Iraq. Such was the controversy that *The Mail on Sunday*, brilliantly quick at adding petrol to the flames, commissioned Gilligan to write an article in which he wrote that Alastair Campbell was to blame for 'sexing up' the intelligence.

The entire sequence has become part of a highly charged mythology, to the point where any attempt at a brief look at the evidence is almost pointless. It has done more to undermine trust in the 'elected insiders' in the UK than any other factor. Yet while Blair has many questions to answer about his judgement, depth and genuine political courage in relation to the war, his integrity became the only issue. Blair was rarely questioned about whether he understood the tensions in Iraq and the wider region, in advance of the war or after it. He showed little sign of doing so. Instead he was constantly asked whether he was a liar – the default question for parts of the UK media when elected politicians are in trouble.

It is necessary to examine what happened when Gilligan detonated his explosive grenade, because the saga shows how mistrust can be fuelled in British politics – and politics across the democratic world – with deadly imprecision.

Here is a transcript of part of Gilligan's two-way interview at 7.30 that morning, a highly listened-to slot on the BBC throughout the UK. It was his second 'two-way' in the programme. What comes across most strikingly is not sensational revelation, but a lack of clarity between presenter and reporter as to precisely what the revelatory story is all about:

JOHN HUMPHRYS: Our defence correspondent Andrew Gilligan has found evidence that the government's dossier on Iraq that was produced last September was cobbled together at the last minute with some unconfirmed material that had not been approved by the security services. Now, you told us about this earlier on the programme, Andy, and we've had a statement from Ten Downing Street that says it's not true. 'Not one word of the dossier was not entirely the work of the intelligence agencies,' says Number Ten. Sorry to submit you to this sort of English, but there we are. I think we know what they mean. Are you suggesting – let's be very clear about this – that it was not the work of the intelligence agencies?

ANDREW GILLIGAN: The information which I'm told was dubious did come from the information agencies, but they were unhappy about it because they didn't think it should have been in there. They thought it was not corroborated sufficiently and they actually thought it was wrong. They thought the informant concerned had got it wrong. They thought he had misunderstood what was happening. Let's go through this. This is the dossier that was published in September last year. Probably the most substantial statement of the UK government's case against Iraq. You'll remember that the Commons was recalled to debate it. Tony Blair made the opening speech. It's not the same as the famous 'dodgy dossier', the one that was copied off the internet. That came later. It was quite a serious document that dominated the news agenda that day. And you open up the dossier and the first thing you see is a preface by Tony Blair that includes the following words – 'Saddam's military plan allows for some WMDs to be ready within 45 minutes of an order to deploy them.'

Now, that claim has come back to haunt Mr Blair because, if the weapons had been that readily to hand, they probably would have been found by now. But you know, it could have been an honest mistake. But what I have been told is that the government knew that claim was questionable even before the war, even before they wrote it in their dossier.

I've spoken to a British official who was involved in the preparation of the dossier and he told me that in the week before it was published, the draft dossier produced by the intelligence services added little to what was already publicly known. He said: 'It was transformed in the week before it was published to make it sexier. The classic example was the claim that weapons of mass destruction were ready for use within 45 minutes. That information was not in the original draft. It was included in the dossier against our wishes, because it wasn't reliable. Most of the things in the dossier were double-sourced, but that was single sourced, and we believe that the source was wrong.'

Now this official told me the dossier was transformed at the behest of Downing Street, and he added: 'Most people in intelligence were unhappy with the dossier because it didn't reflect the considered view they were putting forward.'

Now I want to stress that this official, and others I've spoken to, do still believe Iraq did have some sort of weapons of mass destruction programmes.

'I believe it is about 30 per cent likely there was a chemical weapons programme in the six months before the war, and considerably more likely there was a biological weapons programme. We think Blix [Hans Blix, head of the UN Monitoring, Verification and Inspection Commission] downplayed a couple of potentially interesting pieces of evidence. But the weapons programmes were quite small. Sanctions did limit the programme.'

The official also added quite an interesting note about the result, since the war, of the capture of some of the Iraqi WMD scientists. 'We don't have a great deal more information yet than we had before. We have not got a great deal out of the detainees yet.'

Now the 45-minute issue is not just a detail. It did go to the heart of the government's case that Saddam was an imminent threat, and it was repeated a further three times in the body of the dossier. And I understand that the parliamentary intelligence and security committee is going to conduct an inquiry into the claims made by the British government about Iraq and it is obviously exactly this kind of issue that will be at the heart of their investigation.[6]

This exchange is worth dissecting carefully as it shows how mistrust in leaders is fuelled by journalistic muddle. Let us begin with John Humphrys' confused opening question. Humphrys suggests that the dossier was 'cobbled together' at the last minute. Was all of it cobbled together? How does he know? It was compiled speedily, but with a lot of senior figures working on it carefully. The stakes were high. It was not put together casually, as Humphrys implied.

Then he asks Gilligan: 'Are you suggesting that it was not the work of the intelligence agencies?' What does he mean by 'it'? The entire dossier? One single piece of cited intelligence?

The question is woolly and makes no sense. The Joint Intelligence Committee signed off the dossier, therefore it was evidently the work of the intelligence agencies at the most senior level. No one had ever claimed that it had been the work of every employee of the vaguely defined 'intelligence agencies'.

Gilligan does not answer Humphrys' vague question. It is left to hang in the air, conveying a sense of scandal without specifying quite what the scandal is. Instead Gilligan focuses solely on the claim that Saddam possessed WMD that could be ready to strike within forty-five minutes. Gilligan's reply that the intelligence agencies were unhappy with the information is nowhere near as explosive as Humphrys' opening question implied. Intelligence can be wrong. Not surprisingly, 'intelligence agencies' were worried that this particular assertion was unreliable and did not want it in the dossier. Gilligan adds that 'what I have been told is that the government knew that claim was questionable' before it was included.

Given that all intelligence is 'questionable', this is not revelatory. We knew at the time that Blair was choosing to believe the intelligence, when he did not have to do so. His opponents were arguing in public that they believed the intelligence was 'questionable'. Robin Cook was one of those making such a case to Blair in private, and then subsequently in public after he resigned. Blair never claimed as scientific fact that the intelligence was 100 per cent correct. He was in no position to do so. He said he believed that Saddam had WMD, and here was the intelligence to back up his view. Blair was wholly wrong, but he was advancing a case, not claiming scientific proof that he was correct.

The next part of the BBC exchange is, retrospectively, sensational for the opposite reason than is normally claimed. Gilligan's source backs the dossier in all other respects except the forty-five minute claim. So the big story is that a British official was relaxed about most of the dossier, because the intelligence was double-sourced. This is the only reference to a source – a British official 'who was involved in the preparation for the dossier'. But those who had been directly involved in the preparation had signed it off. Again there is vagueness. How involved was the source?

Then it all gets even more confused, when Gilligan asserts sweepingly that the still vaguely defined 'agencies' were unhappy with the whole dossier, even though they believed that Saddam did possess some WMD.

So 'most people in intelligence' were unhappy. That is a lot of people, but Gilligan had earlier referred to just one source. And yet the source – 'this official' – did believe Iraq had WMD. Gilligan then returns to the specific concerns about the forty-five minute claim and suggests that this gets to 'the heart of the matter'. Does it? In his desperation over his dependence on intelligence, Blair used every scrap he could find to make his case that Saddam posed a threat. In his foreword to the dossier he highlighted this particular threat. It was up to us how much weight we gave it. The context could not have been clearer at the time. This was Blair's case for war against Iraq. But in the months leading up to the war there was little focus on the forty-five minute claim. It was never at the 'heart of the matter'.

For such a highly charged issue, this was a slapdash 'two-way', and the one quoted here was less contentious and confused than the earlier interview that had opened the programme. Was Gilligan, or perhaps Humphrys, suggesting that the dossier had nothing to do with the 'intelligence agencies'? Was Gilligan focusing solely on the claim about WMD that could be used within forty-five minutes? Was he reflecting the view of a single source? How involved was that source?

Later that day Robin Cook, who resigned from the Cabinet because of his opposition to the war, told friends that he despaired of the Gilligan report. Cook knew the pivotal question was why Blair had become so pathetically over-reliant on intelligence that was known to be unreliable. Suddenly the BBC had made the leap to making claims that the dossier was a work of fiction, sexed up in Number Ten against the wishes of the 'intelligence agencies'. Cook could see a red herring diverting attention from the real saga.

The diversion was so immense that, more than a decade later, it shaped the way Blair was perceived by the media and by many voters. He became the prime minister (and then former prime minister) who had lied his way towards a calamitous war.

All hell broke loose after Gilligan's broadcasts. Blair was on a visit to Iraq when the imprecise allegations were made. He and Alastair Campbell were both bewildered. Had Sir John Scarlett, chair of the Joint Intelligence Committee (JIC), briefed Gilligan, in an act of strange betrayal? What precisely were they being accused of? Then, the following Sunday, Gilligan hyped up his allegations in *The Mail on Sunday*. The first two columns of the first page of the article carried a photograph of Alastair Campbell, with a smaller photograph of Gilligan below and these words in the headline: 'I asked my intelligence source why Blair misled us all over Saddam's WMD. His response? One word... CAMPBELL.'[7]

Here was a senior BBC correspondent asserting, as an assumed truth, that 'Blair misled us all over Saddam's WMD' and offering an explanation from his 'source' – Campbell. Again there was confusion in the article. Because the seniority of the source is unclear, no one could make a fair judgement. But the BBC had lent its weight – the weight of supposed impartiality – in deciding that Blair had 'misled us all' in making the case for war: a sensational allegation.

But the assumption that Blair lied in advance takes some explaining. Did Blair say to his closest fellow crusaders that he would lie about WMD, even though the lie would be exposed when the weapons were not found?

Of course he did not. The sequence was more complex. Blair was desperate to put, and win, a case. He deployed the evidence to win it. He was not conducting a BBC seminar on whether or not to invade Iraq. He needed the backing of voters, the media and most of his party in order to stand timidly shoulder-to-shoulder with President Bush. He could not lead in a different way.

So, like a lawyer in a tight corner, Blair put his case on the basis that the intelligence suggested that Saddam possessed WMD. As he was engaged in an act of persuasion, he did not spend time pointing to the many qualifications in the intelligence. He could not afford to put the case for the opponents of war; the opponents were doing that already. Contrary to the Gilligan reports, he placed such disproportionate focus on the intelligence, with the cooperation of senior intelligence officials on the JIC. There are many important questions that arise. Why did Sir John Scarlett cooperate so willingly? Why was the intelligence so wrong?

These questions were not asked. Instead, a row erupted between Number Ten and the BBC over whether Blair lied in order to justify war.

The Conservative Party did not benefit from the growing perception that Blair lied to justify war. It was in no fit state to be a beneficiary at the time. Instead the seeds were being sown for the rise of outsiders – the nationalists in Scotland and UKIP. And the disillusionment with the once-deified Blair, the prime minister who had pledged to restore trust in politics, fed a wider disdain. Prime ministers ceased to be believed. A few years later, in the Brexit referendum, David Cameron made many warnings about the dangers of leaving the EU. More voters preferred to trust Nigel Farage. If trust becomes a defining issue, then elected prime ministers are doomed to be viewed as untrustworthy at some point in their tenures. The space opens up for outsiders.

Inevitably the Bush administration too got trapped in questions around trust and Iraq, and the missing weapons of mass destruction. And yet the reasons why Bush and Blair came to focus on WMD were far more complex than just a lie to persuade voters to back the war. Although, certainly in Blair's case, he was obsessed with persuading enough MPs on his own side, and voters, to support him, the democracy-poisoning issue of trust is too simple to explain it.

There is no question that, after 11 September 2001 and the terrorist attacks in the United States, Bush and his administration began to focus almost immediately, and without reason, on Saddam and removing him. There was talk, almost within days, from some of Bush's senior figures in that divided, incoherent administration saying that Iraq must come next, even though they had not at that point dealt with Afghanistan – and of course never did fully do so. Without the intervention of Blair, they would probably at some point have acted unilaterally, or with others, and invaded Iraq without consulting the United Nations.

Blair was, in many ways, an insecure prime minister who felt that, as a Labour leader, he had to be in alliance with the United States when military conflicts arose. He had no great specialist knowledge of the Middle East, but he had a deep awareness of why Labour lost elections in the 1980s. One of them was the sense that Labour could not be trusted on matters of defence and the alliance with the United States. The other guiding philosophy Blair had was a shallow one: the Third Way, navigating between left and right and between different problems, to come up with a solution that as many voters as possible would regard as acceptable. In this case, Blair decided that he had to support the United States, but also that he wanted to carry as many people with him as possible, not least in his own party. The way to navigate this particular Third Way was to persuade the United Nations to back a possible war in Iraq. The only way Blair could do that, and persuade Bush to back him, was to focus on Saddam's apparent non-compliance of various UN resolutions in relation to his weapons of mass destruction. The focus on WMD became inevitable when Bush agreed to Blair's proposition that he set out on a UN route to deal with Saddam.

Whether or not there were WMD, and whether or not Bush and Blair were convinced there were WMD, is largely irrelevant. There was evidence from the intelligence that there were WMD, and that is what Blair clung to as he made his lawyerly case. It was the only case available to him in order to bring in the United Nations. Once Bush had agreed to this, on the basis that Blair would back him anyway – 'I'll be with you come what may,' Blair wrote in a famous memo – Bush too had to focus on WMD in a way that he probably was not planning to do beforehand. That is the sequence that led to the publication of dossiers and the presentations to the UN on Saddam's WMD – weapons that were subsequently discovered not to exist.

The thorny road to a disastrous war was not about leaders lying, but about leaders trying to make a case for war. When Churchill was prime minister, as the Second World War started to become incredibly hazardous, he made his famous public broadcast about the need to 'fight them on the beaches'. Churchill was not being truthful. There were real dangers at the time, but he knew he had to sound wholly confident about victory, when he could not have been. Was that a lie? Was it an act of persuasion to keep up people's spirits?

The terminology of 'lying', 'trust' and 'mendacity' is inadequate to explain what happened in relation to Iraq, and in many other policy areas that challenge elected leaders. In a way, what happened was much more serious. The intelligence was wrong. Weak politicians made the wrong calls for different reasons – ones that were explained by their characters and their political backgrounds. But what happened was more multi-layered and nuanced than a couple of national figures simply becoming reckless liars to the point of criminality.

———

Trust and mistrust have become so central to the perception of virtually every mainstream political leader that it is increasingly difficult sometimes to disentangle actual corruption – criminal acts that, understandably, lead voters to turn away from democratic politics and to loathe those they have elected. Genuine corruption, worthy of contemptuous mistrust, continues – as it has always done in politics. There is no reason why elected politicians, who are after all human beings, should be any purer than the rest of the human race. At the same time, there is no reason why they should be more impure, not least given the intense level of scrutiny to which they are subjected.

Across quite large swathes of the European Union, various parties and politicians are mired in allegations of corruption that are worthy of scathing mistrust. Corruption is another explanation for the decline of the mainstream – its failure to be robust as outsiders made their moves.

In Spain, the government of Mariano Rajoy became immersed in political corruption scandals, darkening his prospects of hanging onto power. Rajoy's People's Party, a recently commanding party of the centre right, was buffeted by arrests, revelations and resignations linked to corruption. In Valencia – for decades a bastion of People's Party power – the party became the target of a judicial probe into allegations of bid-rigging and illegal commissions. The judge leading the investigation named nine out of ten PP councillors in the city as formal suspects in the case. The party was also in trouble in Madrid, where the local party headquarters was raided by police over suspicions that the branch received illegal payments from businesses. The case claimed a prominent scalp. Esperanza Aguirre, a local PP leader and a highly influential figure inside the ruling party, announced her resignation, saying that she had accepted 'political responsibility' for the scandal. She added, in a revealing and sweeping sentence, 'Corruption is killing us.'

For Rajoy, the latest eruption of cases could scarcely have come at a worse time – not that there is a good time for a party to be defined by corruption. His party had emerged as the biggest bloc in parliament, after an inconclusive close general-election result in December 2015, but he relied on the support of other parties to be re-elected as prime minister. With his party mired in authority-sapping corruption scandals, that task was impossibly daunting.

In much of the democratic world, political parties are accused of being too centralized, failing to empower local parties and party members. According to this romantic critique, local parties must be given more power, and in some cases autonomy, in order to avoid out-of-touch leaders ruling in a bubble, cocooned from the views and ideas of party members.

A lot of the outsiders have made a pitch to their own parties by pledging that they will listen more to local members. They will let local parties decide who represents them in the national parliament and what the policies of the party should be. Such a transfer of power was a fundamental objective of Jeremy Corbyn, following his hero Tony Benn. In Europe, many parties are based on the principle of localism. And at Westminster, the House of Commons has been transformed over the past two decades, as many MPs now place representing their constituencies above being loyal to their leadership. Yet the experience of the PP in Spain is one example of many which suggests that, when the centre lacks control of local parties, there is a danger of malfunction, including corruption.

At which point the centre becomes the victim of what happens locally. It is not only the centre of a national party that suffers, but potentially an entire country. If incompetent or corrupt local figures are elected to national parliaments, they become part of the raw material for a government. It is not uncommon for a prime minister to look at his or her parliamentary party and struggle to appoint from it a formidable administration.

The solution to national-versus-local control over a political party is complicated, but must include a degree of central control and scrutiny over local parties. But such an exertion of control from the centre goes completely against fashionable orthodoxy, which insists that parties have become too centralized, too much obsessed by 'control freakery', as it is sometimes laughingly called. As some so-called control freaks at the centre of government have had cause to reflect: 'I don't feel in control of anything.'

A lack of control applied, to some extent, in another scandal that fuelled levels of mistrust to boiling point in the United Kingdom. The expenses scandal, involving Members of Parliament, led to some MPs serving prison sentences for fraudulently claiming expenses. Others had to explain why they were putting down claims for a duck house, or dog biscuits, as an expense. They struggled to do so.

The errant MPs had a case, of sorts. In a more reasonable age they would still have been rightly condemned, but perhaps might have been listened to. In an age of unreason, no one listened. MPs were making their fatal claims as part of an insular, parochial system that was partly put in place at Westminster because it was politically impossible for governments to agree significant pay rises for Members of Parliament. So they got stealthy rises, in the form of expenses or allowances. Officials encouraged MPs to put in claims, and only when the official Freedom of Information Act was put in place did these expenses ultimately become public knowledge. They were not expenses but allowances, for which there was a limit. MPs were encouraged to reach the limit. This is not a justification for what happened, but it is an explanation. The UK had not elected a parliament of crooks by some wild act.

MPs were foolish enough, or stupid enough, to take risks. Arguably, if they were foolish enough to fiddle their expenses for financial gain, they should never have been selected as candidates in the first place. But party leaderships have lost control in many parts of the democratic world to local party memberships and, as a result, the level of scrutiny of individual MPs and their local parties is sometimes non-existent. Although voters were shocked by the expenses scandal, nobody drew the conclusion that local parties and MPs in the UK need more controlling from the centre. In some contexts 'control' is seen as sinister – as in the 'control freaks' at the top of a party. Yet 'taking back control' is the most fashionable slogan of the anti-politics era.

The MPs' expenses scandal ensured that a third British prime minister in a row become buried in issues to do with trust and mistrust. Gordon Brown replaced Tony Blair, making trust his fundamental crusade, given the raging mistrust of Blair. This became the main reason why he felt he could succeed as prime minister. Blair felt exactly the same when he was on the edge of power, until he fell into a sea of mistrust.

A whole series of events led to Brown suffering precisely the same fate. To his torment, mistrust soared under his premiership – partly because the MPs' expenses saga happened under his watch. Brown, too, was attacked and teased for claiming for services like Sky TV, although his leadership suffered even more when some Labour MPs were charged with various forms of fraud. Some of his Cabinet ministers also faced separate allegations of misconduct. For Brown, the collapse of trust in his leadership was as tormenting as any other issue, including the financial crisis and his indecision over an early election. He had planned to personify trustworthiness. Very quickly he was seen as untrustworthy. He knew he was doomed when he read his plummeting poll ratings in relation to trust.

MPs' expenses and Iraq were ingredients in the Brexit referendum campaign, even though they had absolutely nothing to do with the issue of the European Union. They were ingredients because they had fuelled such mistrust of the 'elite' that when former prime ministers put the case for staying in the EU, they helped the other side. Leading Brexit campaigners were delighted when Brown or Blair made a speech, for they were not trusted.

There are other ways in which corruption manifests itself. France is extraordinary, in that each president seems to leave office amidst some scandal or other. Nicolas Sarkozy was charged in 2014 with corruption, linked to allegations that he received up to €50 million in illegal campaign financing from the Libyan dictator, Gaddafi. Sarkozy denied it, but the impact of the allegations against him continued to intensify to the point where, when he stood to be the right's mainstream candidate in the 2017 French election, he was, surprisingly, defeated at the first hurdle.

Before him, the French president Jacques Chirac was handed a two-year suspended prison sentence after being found guilty of embezzling public funds to illegally finance the party he led. The court said it found Chirac guilty in two related cases involving fake jobs. This was during his 1977–95 tenure as Paris' mayor.

François Hollande became president appearing to be, and claiming to be, a new, purer kind of leader. He, too, suffered from accusations that could form part of the plot of a political thriller. The allegations centred on his campaign manager, and mysterious offshore accounts held by his budget minister. Hollande faced journalists' questions and, as they were asked, voters noted that here was another part of the elected elite under fair, or unfair, suspicion.

In the French presidential election in 2017 a full judicial inquiry was launched after allegations that the leading centre-right candidate, François Fillon, had abused public funds. In the autumn of 2016 Fillon's Thatcherite economic views were being debated and analysed. By the start of 2017 his embryonic campaign was focused entirely on questions over whether his wife did the work that she was paid for.

Always, it seems, these elected insiders are under suspicion. In such a contest, the outsiders seem innocent of wrongdoing.

In Italy, the former prime minister Silvio Berlusconi started a year of community service at a care home near Milan, following a tax-fraud conviction, and that was not by any means the only court case in which he was embroiled. He was at one point banned from holding public office for five years. Up pops an innocent comedian – Beppe Grillo – to form a new political party, and that innocence is in many ways the essence of his appeal.

These serious allegations of criminality and corruption fuel mistrust about democratic politics. Voters elect various figures to power, and they leave office with allegations whirling around them. But even in these cases there is a degree to which the reaction is not fully justified. The elected politicians are not immune from the justice system in their various countries. There were consequences for the elected insiders. If they were accused, they had to answer those accusations. That is not to underplay the degree to which voters are legitimately angered by such revelations, but it does show that on the whole there is no place to hide, for democratically elected politicians.

This perception that leaders cannot be trusted has led to a paralysis of the mainstream. Step back and reflect on what intense mistrust means to a mainstream leader, and it is easy to see why they are fearful of acting in ways that are radical and meet the challenges of the times. If you are not trusted, it is not easy to announce and implement decisions that might benefit a country in the longer term while making short-term demands on the electorate. In such circumstances, leaders and voters must dance together. Investment in public spending and capital spending, the policy focus of outsiders on the left and the right, is much harder for mainstream leaders to implement if they are regarded as criminals. This is true even when the mainstream leaders are convinced of their innocence, and justifiably so. They read the focus groups, the opinion polls and the newspaper columnists; they know how they are perceived, and it saps their confidence. Yet in most cases the loathing of an electorate that once paid homage makes them determined to stay in power, in a pathetic, doomed attempt to persuade voters to like them again.

———

There are so many ironies and complexities in relation to this issue. The mainstream left parties, which rarely feel they are natural parties of government, go out of their way to win the trust of voters, media and the wider establishment. The main objective of Bill Clinton's New Democrats was to secure the trust of Middle America – the Washington establishment. In spite of his neurotic desire to please and to be seen as trustworthy and worthy of presidential power, or perhaps because of that desire, Clinton ended up being impeached. Blair went out of his way to be trusted by Middle England, the media that Middle England reads, watches and listens to, and he ended up as the subject of a police investigation and later almost in exile from his own country, because many voters believed he lied in order to take the country into what they regarded as an illegal war. Brown, who came to power determined to restore trust, is in similar exile, rarely seen or heard in the UK. Major was relieved to give up power; a test match at Lord's was an immediately more attractive alternative to politics. Yet for all their flaws, none of them were criminals and, as public figures, all were well intentioned.

Meanwhile, outsiders who have not been contaminated by power may be the subject of endless investigations and face a range of allegations, but they do not suffer the same electoral repercussions. The US presidential election in 2016 was emblematic of this: Hillary Clinton, stifled by allegations and perceptions of criminality that were without definitive proof, versus Donald Trump: the subject of several investigations – indeed, so many investigations about his financial affairs that some newspaper columnists predicted, or perhaps hoped, that he would face impeachment.

But Trump was the one who was on the offensive during much of the campaign, certainly in terms of allegations of wrongdoing and criminality. He was on the defensive about his attitudes towards women, but it was Hillary Clinton who, in matters to do with trust, was much more on the defensive. The reason is not a bias to the right or against the left, but a bias in favour of those who are outside politics. And Trump was trusted by some voters, when he was talking nonsense at times, in ways that he implicitly acknowledged after his victory by dumping quite a few of the absurd pledges made during the campaign. Hillary Clinton, more cautious and incremental in some of her policies, was not believed. That was because she had been immersed in democratic politics for decades and Trump had not.

The insiders – those we elect – are not believed. They become liars or are liars; they are spinners and they are criminals. The non-elected outsiders are those who speak for the people. As long as this prism is in place, democratic politics is in danger. It is, after all, we, the voters, who elect the politicians; and once they are elected we, the voters, quickly conclude that not only do we disagree with them or are disappointed by them, but we begin to regard some of them as criminals.

Here is a difficult issue. Inevitably politicians are scrutinized around the clock and are, rightly, held to account around the clock. They are the ones elected, even if they are nowhere near as powerful as they are perceived to be. We, the voters, are allowed to criticize these politicians with indiscriminate venom at any time of the day or night, but they are not allowed to respond in kind.

There was a classic example of this in the 2010 UK election when a voter attacked the then prime minister, Gordon Brown, over the issue of immigration. Gillian Duffy subsequently became a heroic figure in that campaign, as a representative of ordinary voters. After the encounter, Brown got into his car and didn't realize that a microphone was still recording what he was saying to an adviser as they drove off. He described the woman as 'a bigot'. It was one of the most devastating moments in Brown's long career, because he had been caught committing the ultimate offence: a politician criticizing a voter. That is not allowed. The other way round, it is more than allowed. Voters wallow in their desire and appetite to attack politicians, as does the media; but the media does not accept it when politicians turn on them, and neither do the voters. Brown had been caught and was forced to apologize in the most humiliating way. He went to visit Gillian Duffy and was caught, looking shattered, in a radio studio shortly afterwards.

But sometimes there is a need to acknowledge that voters can be at fault, even if politicians are not allowed to do so. The disdain of some voters for politics is partly unjustified. Anger at politicians is, of course, legitimate and welcome, a sign that voters are engaged with politics. They make connections with politics, at least when it seems to fail them. But total disdain is a lazy response to politics and to elected politicians. It is not enough to say, 'They're all the same – they're all a load of bloody crooks, in it for themselves', because none of that is true. Politicians are not in it for themselves. A lot of them could earn much more money doing other jobs. Power is no doubt addictive, but very limited and complicated, and nightmarishly draining. Instead of exploring the dilemmas the so-called insiders face – an exploration that voters might find interesting and compelling, and that might lead them at least to have some sympathy with the complexities of power – voters are either contemptuously indifferent or disdainful, and sometimes both.

There is a depressing contrast to the informed passion with which so many voters engage smartly with the twists and turns of sport. That engagement is understandable: like politics, sport is another great human drama. But some people follow all the vagaries of team selection – who's up, who's down – and the implications for the fate of individual teams; but when it comes to politics, it is simple mistrust that distorts their reaction. This is a problem for society, but it can only be addressed if it is accepted that voters are partly culpable.

However, they are only partly so. No one watches, or could watch, politics around the clock, in the raw: watching speeches and press conferences live, awaiting the outcome of meetings in which senior figures have been making key decisions, watching debates in various elected chambers around the democratic world. Anyone who did so would go bonkers; and no one has the time to do so anyway.

Inevitably this means that the media frames voters' ideas and views. It is the media that, by definition, mediates. It is our guide to the world of democratic politics. In order to understand why trust has become such a corrosive issue, paralysing mainstream leaders, we do not have to look just at politicians (some of whom are untrustworthy), or conclude that it is solely the fault of voters failing to engage properly, although that is an issue. We must look at that powerful force – the media – which mediates politics in a way that can sometimes make elected leaders feel powerless.

8

─────

POWERLESSNESS AND THE MEDIA

Today the so-called mainstream media – the newspapers and the broadcasters – can seem like relatively innocent relics struggling to survive, in the face of an avalanche of social-media outlets. The relics are the good guys taking on the purveyors of 'fake news'.

There is some truth in the evocation of the battle between old and new. Even if Donald Trump thinks otherwise, there is no contest between *The New York Times* and a fantasist blogger. But more orthodox media outlets played a significant role in the rise of the outsiders and the undermining of the mainstream insiders, both in the UK and in the US.

Arguably it is in both of these countries that political change has been especially dramatic, with the election of Trump, Brexit and the rise of Scottish nationalism. While outsiders made hay, the mainstream leaders in these two countries suffered wild fluctuations of reputation long before social media erupted. The focus on 'fake news' and 'post-truth' politics, after Brexit, and the rise of Trump serve to create a false impression, if only by implication, that there was an era of reliable news and an age when 'truth' was a defining force in politics, especially during elections and referendums. This is not the case. In order to understand the various crises in mainstream parties in the UK and the US, and their failure to adapt to tumultuous change, it is necessary to assess the role of the so-called mainstream media, broadcasters and, in some cases, mighty newspapers.

Here is an emblematic episode from the UK. When Sky News was about to launch a new political programme on Sunday mornings, the head of the network, John Ryley, made a revealing comment. Speaking towards the end of 2016, he proclaimed, with trumpets blaring, 'This will not be a show that reports from the Westminster bubble, but will be investigating how decisions made by the political elite affect the public and their lives. We will offer a new perspective on the political week for our customers across the UK and beyond.'[1]

Ryley meant well. He envisaged a programme that got out of London to make sense of voters' lives, and made the lost connections between those who seek to rule and the rest. The subsequent programme was first-rate, joining a range of excellent political programmes on a Sunday in the UK. Even so, virtually every senior broadcasting editor in the country expresses the ambition to report politics from 'outside the bubble', as Ryley did, as if he had hit upon a new idea.

In the late 1990s the BBC decided it would be a good idea to report politics 'outside Westminster' by sending some of its political correspondents to tour the UK and file reports from each location. Correspondents disappeared for months, without appearing on any outlet, because politics with national implications tends to take shape where nationally elected politicians are based during the week: at Westminster. The touring correspondents worked assiduously hard at offering ideas from around the UK, but major stories of national significance were erupting at Westminster, and they could not get on TV bulletins, with space for around eight reports in about thirty minutes. One of the no-longer-seen-or-heard BBC correspondents finally filed a report from the Hebrides, looking tanned and relaxed as he delivered a piece to camera from a boat. He then left the BBC and moved into Number Ten to work for Tony Blair. This was politics on TV, away from the 'bubble'.

In his similar focus on the fantasy 'bubble', Ryley was unintentionally framing an approach to politics that echoed very precisely the arguments made by outsiders across the democratic world. He spoke of a Westminster bubble and a political elite taking decisions, with the implication that those decisions are made in the bubble by the elite, without them contemplating the consequences for the public and their lives. It was therefore the duty of the heroic broadcaster to make the connections, in the light of indifference from the bubbled elite.

The attitude reflected in this outlook is a dangerous one. There is an obligation in the UK for broadcasters to be impartial. When a broadcaster speaks, makes an assertion or offers analysis, there is an assumption that impartiality is written into it. A casual viewer or listener might assume, when hearing ambitions for a new Sunday political programme: 'Ah, yes, there is this cocooned elite, and it takes broadcasters – like the deified political outsiders – to expose them for what they are.'

The significance is that Ryley is not unique in this, but is very much the latest in a long line of editors who believe they are speaking on behalf of the people – again, rather like the outsiders – against the political elite. Indeed, there is an almost comic quality to his claims that his new programme would be innovative, because there have been many, many attempts to frame political programmes as he envisaged in the UK, on Channel 4 as well as the BBC sending correspondents from Westminster to a boat on the Hebrides.

In the late 1990s, when the framing of 'politics out of Westminster' became the fashion, Channel 4 approached a columnist to enquire whether he would be interested in presenting a new weekly political programme. One of the questions asked of him was whether he could ride a horse. This seemed an unlikely qualification for a political programme, but the executives wanted to take the programme, as they put it, 'out into the real world and interview the people'. The interviewer would travel around on horseback, to symbolize distance from the elites cocooned in their urban bubble. The proposition was like something out of *Monty Python's Flying Circus*, but in their assumptions, some broadcasting editors were previewing the pitch of the outsiders, who go on their metaphorical horses to speak for the people. They were not part of the insulated elite.

If an editor begins with an assumption that politics is defined by the gap between a distant elite and the people, the end result on TV screens and the radio is bound to reflect that attitude. There is no left or right bias in such an assumption. There is a bias against politics, or a misunderstanding of how politics works. The starting point is well intentioned. If senior editors genuinely believe there are cocooned elites making decisions that impact on audiences without knowing quite what the consequences might be, then broadcasters must perform the noble duty. But given that elected insiders are too neurotically in touch, it is a duty that has fuelled the possibilities for the outsiders, and it has made life extremely difficult for the mainstream.

The most senior broadcasting journalist to challenge forensically such assumptions in the UK was the former Director General of the BBC John Birt. In the mid-1970s he wrote a series of articles for *The Times* arguing that, amidst much political and economic turbulence, broadcasters had a 'mission to explain'.[2] In a series of programmes for ITV, and then in several senior roles for the BBC, Birt made sense of his theory, appointing specialists who sought to explain what was happening, rather than report over-excitedly one event after another. Birt understood that governing the country was difficult and that the complexities were interesting and it was important to highlight them. This is almost the opposite view of many senior editors, who are not as interested in the complexities as in exposing the supposedly fatal flaws of the elected insiders.

The mindset had a distinct impact on the output. Aggressive interviewers have become fashionable, with the viewers' representative taking on the mighty, arrogant politicians. Interviewers who showed curiosity about the dilemmas of modern leadership were regarded as 'soft'. In the UK the tone of some interviews gave the impression that a politician was lying, when the reality was that if he or she answered the question candidly, all hell would break loose, which is exactly why the question was asked.

Inadvertently some broadcasting outlets in the UK also fuel the false sense that the mainstream are 'all the same'. Before Jeremy Corbyn was elected leader of the UK Labour Party in 2015, the BBC's nightly current affairs programme, *Newsnight*, would often host a panel of journalists supposedly reflecting a range of views on the political spectrum – one being a Labour supporter, another a Tory and a third floating on the ill-defined centre ground. But in reality they were all on the same space – Blairite Labour, a supporter of Cameron, and the third panellist sympathetic to both. The discussion was framed in a very narrow way, with all of them agreeing that Labour was doomed unless it admitted that the previous Labour government had spent too much; that the current Labour leadership, under Ed Miliband and Ed Balls, would acquire credibility only when it accepted the spending plans of the then chancellor, George

Osborne; and that Cameron and Osborne had seized the centre ground. All these were highly contentious assumptions. One of the positive consequences of the political upheaval in the UK since 2015 is that in studio discussions broadcasters are forced to recognize a wider range of voices on the political spectrum. They are not 'all the bloody same', all agreeing that austerity is an enduring virtue and represents the centre ground across the UK.

In the UK broadcasters have to be impartial. Contrary to the belief of some on the right and left, they try to be so at all times. But newspapers are not obliged to be non-partisan or balanced. Part of their influence is the fear they arouse in supposedly mighty politicians in the UK. The fear makes them weaker still, and then the subject of more undermining mockery – or much worse – in the newspapers.

While promoting his autobiography, *Kind of Blue*, at the end of 2016, the former chancellor Ken Clarke reminded audiences that he had sometimes received phone calls from the then prime minister, John Major, about obscure stories on the inside pages of the newspapers. Clarke would tell Major that he had not noticed the story and, if he had not noticed it, then most voters would not have done so, either. Major had become neurotically obsessed with newspaper coverage of his precarious leadership.

After the UK left the Exchange Rate Mechanism in September 1992, when Major's world got much darker, his allies sought to hide from him the first edition of the London *Evening Standard*, fearing that it would ruin the rest of his day. They sought to do the same with the first editions of the following day's newspapers, which arrived at Number Ten the evening before publication. They wanted him to sleep, and feared that one bad story on page eight would prevent him doing so.

Gordon Brown did not sleep very much when he was prime minister. Stewart Wood, a senior adviser who worked with him in Number Ten, told a BBC series in 2007:

> Gordon would usually get up very early, often around 5, and the first thing he would do is read all the newspapers which meant he was miserable by 6... some of us told him that he was probably the only person in the country who had read all the attacks on him in the papers but that did not comfort him.

Tony Blair, the prime minister who ruled with landslide majorities, regarded the media as his main political opponent. Blair told me, at the height of his battles with the BBC and some newspapers in 2004, that 'dealing with the media is like living in a flat with a demented tenant. You don't know whether to calm it down or knock it over the head with a cosh.' Would Blair have supported the war in Iraq if Rupert Murdoch had been a passionate opponent? I doubt it. Blair had calculated that he might have to take on Murdoch and his newspapers in a Europe-related referendum. He would not want to take them on again over a highly charged war. The fact that Murdoch and his newspapers hailed him, in relation to Iraq, was a factor in Blair's calculations in advance of the war in Iraq. When *The Sun* endorsed Labour in the 2005 election, its editorial stated that it was doing so for one reason alone: Blair's foreign policy, and in particular his support for the war in Iraq. *The Sun*'s endorsement led some TV bulletins, just as it had done when the paper backed Labour in the 1997 and 2001 general elections.

Most other papers turned against Blair, partly because of the war in Iraq or the way the invasion turned out. One of his final speeches as prime minister was an attack on the media in June 2007. He used a simile that compared the media to a 'feral beast tearing people and reputations to bits'.[3] Blair had spent years trying to charm and woo the media, but in an uncharacteristic cathartic scream, he said what he really thought.

The BBC programme *Newsnight* reported in February 2017 that David Cameron had tried to persuade the owner of the *Daily Mail* to sack its editor, Paul Dacre, on the eve of his Brexit referendum. Cameron failed in his mission, and the *Mail* went for him in the campaign. And I was with Cameron on a train to Norwich shortly before he became prime minister following the 2010 election, when he got a call from a colleague telling him that the columnist Simon Heffer had been dropped by the newspaper that he was writing for at the time. Cameron let out a spontaneous whoop of delight that bemused nearby travellers. Heffer, an influential columnist on the right, had been a critic of Cameron, and he continued his onslaughts at another newspaper soon afterwards.

These fragile, insecure political figures should have been less obsessed by the UK media and far less wound up by new stories and new columnists. But there were two reasons why a large part of their neurosis was justified. First, they were human beings, reading, hearing or watching outlets that suggested they were useless, mad or corrupt. Few human beings are entirely relaxed at such verdicts on their behaviour, especially when they are reported to a wide readership. Second, and much more important, these political figures had plans for government and knew it would be harder for them to make sense of them to the electorate if they were viewed with suspicion, at best. Often they chose to be powerless rather than face further slaughters in the media.

All four recent prime ministers would have behaved very differently if it were not for the UK media, or their fear of the newspapers and the broadcasters on the eve of the social-media explosion. They would have been perceived differently, too. Perhaps the media's reporting of Major, Blair, Brown and Cameron, when they were prime minister, was not a factor when pro-Brexit voters dismissed their passionate arguments for staying in the EU. Perhaps the reporting of them made no impact, when they all put a passionate case for a United Kingdom rather than Scottish independence. But I suspect that voters' perceptions of Westminster leaders, as reported in parts of the UK media, help to explain the rise of Scottish nationalism.

———

Similarly in the United States, in a very different media environment, parts of the old orthodox media were distorting perceptions of some senior elected politicians long before the emergence of fake news. The arguments that proved to be potent for Donald Trump began with the 'shock jocks' who were allowed to broadcast their provocative views in the US. They were the embryonic Trumps. They set the scene for him, and made the unsayable more than sayable.

While UK broadcasters are not allowed to be biased or polemical in a manner that is overtly partisan, the shock jocks are polemical as their *raison d'être*. They were thriving long before Trump made his outrageous observations during the campaign. When Trump declared, of Mexican immigrants, 'they're bringing drugs, they're bringing crime, they're rapists, and some, I assume, are good people', he was echoing the language of the shock jocks.[4] He was a presidential shock jock. It was when shock jocks began to acquire a following that shameless populism became part of the debate.

Indeed, when Trump made those comments about immigrants, on the first day of his official presidential campaign, the conservative radio host Joe Walsh, a former Republican Congressman, noted the calls and supportive tweets rolling in. Walsh gave an interview in which he predicted, 'Trump's going to be leading in the polls within two weeks, and these comments are the kind of comments that will put him on the front pages during the campaign.' Walsh defended Trump's comments on his radio show: 'If you say that America's becoming a browner country, all of a sudden you're racist. Trump's right, Trump's right, we've opened up our border to third world immigrants.'[5]

There was a unique dance between Trump's provocative, attention-grabbing statements during the campaign and quite a lot of the radio talk-show hosts, with their big followings in the world of radio.

In August 1988 the most prominent of the shock jocks, Rush Limbaugh, began appearing on fifty-six stations across the country. His success, alongside the march of similar broadcasters through morning radio outlets, changed the way some voters heard the news and the nature of political conversation.

Limbaugh, with his use of parody songs and much-repeated Trump-like terms such as 'feminazi', secured a TV show that attracted a wider audience. In 1993 the cover story for the *National Review* dubbed Limbaugh the 'leader of the opposition', for Clinton-era conservatives.[6] According to the then Senate minority leader Bob Dole, 'when Rush Limbaugh talks you know you're listening to the real world'.[7] Dole went on to secure his party's presidential nomination.

Gabe Hobbs, a radio consultant who helped put Trump on the air in an early 2000 series of radio commentaries for Clear Channel noted this:

> When Limbaugh came onto the scene in late 1988, he was saying things that resonated with a huge group of people who thought their voices weren't heard any more. Limbaugh would not only capture that; he'd state opinions for them. Donald Trump appears to me to have something very similar going on.[8]

That phrase about Limbaugh being the leader of the opposition has echoes in the United Kingdom. Some BBC editors argued that they regarded it as their task to be the opposition – certainly after Labour won its landslide in 1997 and the Conservatives were in disarray. Again, they were not being overtly partisan in making that assertion. They thought they were being dutiful. But it should not be the job of the supposedly impartial media to be the opposition, in any shape or form.

The so-called shock jocks had the space to do so. They had the right to do so and, in wallowing in the space they were given, they not only made Trump seem like the logical end of a sequence that they began, but they constantly undermined the Clinton presidency and did, indeed, become the opposition. It was an opposition that implied Bill Clinton was a crook. It was that coarsening of the political debate – the projection of an elected figure as someone who could not be trusted – that fuelled the assumptions of corruption and criminality that tormented not only Clinton's eight years in the White House, but Hillary Clinton's campaign, too.

The shock jocks changed the way people expected to hear other people talking about politics. By the late 1990s it was no longer shocking to hear graphic talk about sex, or insults, on the radio. Conservative talk-show hosts tore at the same time into the details of Clinton's intimate record of alleged infidelities.

Both Obama and Hillary Clinton were cautious politicians in relation to economic policy in particular. But both were exuberant social liberals. Trump was not. He was the counter to perceived political correctness. Those least surprised by his rise were the ones next to the microphones taking calls from the public. The talk-show host and politician Joe Walsh noted:

> People all say to me, 'Joe, you were the local Trump before Trump.' I had spoken like Trump as a Congressman. The national media hated it and they went after me, but people found it refreshing. I knew there was a pent-up demand from people to hear someone talk like that. But obviously I didn't have Trump's microphone, I was just a Congressman.[9]

The elected mainstream insiders struggling to make sense of an increasingly complex global economy, reading opinion polls, fearing elections, faced a new challenge. Orthodox media outlets worked on the assumption that they were the ones who spoke for the people against the elites, but it was crusading shock jocks who set the scene for Trump. Meanwhile, quite separately, the proliferation of media outlets in countries across Europe – a pattern that followed the model in the United States – led in itself to a more feverish atmosphere in which politics was reported. There were rolling news stations, and more news and current-affairs programmes on the main TV channels and radio stations. They started to feed off each other, sometimes creating a heightened sense of frenzy.

An early sign of this US-influenced expansion of news outlets in the United Kingdom was the reporting of John Major's government as it tottered towards electoral slaughter in 1997. There were huge tensions within that government over Europe, but the very grammar of political reporting, at the time of expanding media outlets, heightened the sense of drama the media were meant to be merely reporting.

There was one illuminating sequence – an early sign of the direction in which politics was going to move – in the spring of 1994, long before Twitter, blogs and Facebook were even remotely in anyone's mind. The then Home Secretary, Michael Howard, gave an interview to the *Today* programme about a Home Office issue, but at the end he was asked about a possible referendum in the United Kingdom on the euro. Howard did not altogether rule out that possibility. The question at the time was the subject of great internal debate within the government. The next morning *The Sunday Times* ran a photo of John Major seemingly with his head down, almost towards his lap, at a dinner in Leeds. He was trying to get to a glass of water, but it looked as if he was beleaguered and depressed.

That image, combined with Howard's relatively innocent comments about a referendum, generated a sense of drama. The BBC's political lunchtime programme, *The World This Weekend*, felt it needed a response to *The Sunday Times*. Given the feverish reporting of Michael Howard's innocent comments and *The Sunday Times'* front-page portrayal of a beleaguered prime minister, the Conservative Party chairman, Norman Fowler, felt obliged to appear on *The World This Weekend* to defend John Major and insist the government was united.

That response – the fact that Fowler felt the need to respond – in itself led the morning newspapers, which suggested that the government was in disarray. Producers on the next morning's *Today* programme read those first editions on the Sunday evening and concluded that, as 'Tory disarray' was a major running story, they needed to get one of the Eurosceptic backbench MP rebels to make the case for a referendum on the euro. On the Monday lunchtime another Cabinet minister had to come onto one of the many broadcasting outlets to defend John Major again from the rebel MP, even though that rebel had made this point before and was well known to have held Eurosceptic views for most of her life.

The same dance continued, between broadcasting outlets and newspapers, for a few more days. Channel 4 News and BBC's *Newsnight* on the Monday had further interviews, with more MPs repeating what they had said for several years. The newspapers then had enough quotes to lead their front pages again with news of a government in crisis. On the Tuesday morning the broadcasters, noting that the newspapers were still leading with the Conservative Party being in crisis, went overboard with the story: people defending Major, and the regular Eurosceptics coming back on again, to put their case against Europe. By the Tuesday evening, *Newsnight* opened its sequence with a shot of Number Ten, with its presenter posing the question, 'Can John Major survive as prime minister until the end of the week?', before the dramatic signature tune kicked in.

Nothing had happened – apart from an interplay between the expanding number of media outlets – and yet the result of this process was a question over whether Major could survive as prime minister. Incidentally, he survived for another three years.[10]

The same has happened in the United States for a longer period of time. On the whole, apart from the whole shock-jock industry, the tone is calmer in the UK, but the impact is very similar. When viewers watch the news, perhaps superficially, they see breaking news headlines and clock the level of scrutiny on senior political figures. There is a tendency to assume that the dynamic implies a kind of culpability at the top.

Journalists face a difficult balancing act between much-needed forensic scrutiny and falsely conveying a sense that these elected figures are culpable of mendacious malevolence. Sometimes the grammar of expanding broadcasting outlets alone, and the noise that accompanies that expansion, can make mainstream leaders seem pathetically besieged. In response, they have become more fearful. There are various reasons why leaders in the era of expanding outlets – the pre-Twitter era – became so neurotically cautious.

The change in tone is measured clearly in UK programmes such as the BBC's *Question Time*. When the programme was launched in the early 1980s, it was a compelling weekly debate between four political figures, around some of the great issues of the time: the future of the centre left; the split between the Labour Party and the SDP; Thatcherism and those challenging Thatcherism from within the Conservative Party. The programme was intelligent political drama. The chair, Robin Day, was a political addict who had curiosity about politics and politicians, although he was known for his robust interrogation.

In the late 1990s the BBC decided that politics had become boring. It hadn't. It was interesting, but in different, perhaps less obviously dramatic ways than in the early 1980s. Some editors took it upon themselves to make politics 'entertaining'. *Question Time* expanded to a panel of five, which meant that any discussion became even more superficial than it had been with four guests. The audience was whipped up into a level of hysteria in advance, the panel was chosen to heighten that level of hysteria, and it became a wholly predictable shouting match between caricatures – and most of those watching went away disillusioned with politics and politicians.

The response from mainstream leaders to media hysteria – pre-Trump and the rise of other outsiders – was to become cautious to the point of robotic, fearful of making a 'mistake' that would trigger an even noisier media onslaught. One of the reasons Hillary Clinton was so secretive and cautious was that she was brought up in a media culture that encouraged a degree of paranoia, with some editors justifying intense, round-the-clock scrutiny of her, warily suspicious in tone, on the basis that she was part of the cocooned elite. And yet, as the coverage became more relentless, she chose to become more cocooned.

Of course there is a danger of the reverse: a compliant media fearful of the elected leaders, or in some cases owned by an elected leader. In Italy Berlusconi either controlled or influenced six of the seven main terrestrial channels when he was prime minister – the most powerful form of media in a country where barely 10 per cent of the adult population buys a newspaper.[11] But he was the freakish exception. There are some similarities between Berlusconi and Trump, but the US president does not own most media companies, as his near-daily outburst against journalists demonstrates. In the US and the UK the mainstream media can, and do, reduce elected leaders to a sense of neurotic powerlessness, whose self-imposed sense of impotence exaggerates the power of the orthodox media. Outsiders have flourished and mainstream leaders are quickly viewed with disdain, in countries where the media culture is relatively respectful to elected politicians.

The French journalist and author Agnès Poirier, who lives in London, is struck by the contrast between the UK and France, even though outsiders make their historic mark in both countries:

We have no tradition of tabloids and we tend to believe in the written/printed word. If our press tend to be partisan, as in giving views and not pretending to be impartial and balanced (don't forget we have a tradition of pamphlet writing), however there is not a culture of lying outwardly like some believe the *Daily Mail* has done over Europe and Brussels for the last forty years. This would be inconceivable in France.

In that sense, newspapers in France are more responsible. Also, French journalists would accept without any qualm to withhold information if asked by the Interior Ministry for, say, reasons of national security. There is a sense that even journalists are citizens first, and that we must be discerning and cautious with the information we let out there.

To understand this culture, one must look at the economics of newspapers, which are still subsidized by the state in France. There is no pressure of getting a scoop at all costs, for instance.[12]

Such a media environment might have made it easier for mainstream leaders to thrive. But this was not the case with Sarkozy and Hollande, both single-term presidents and, in the latter's case, breaking all records in terms of low personal ratings. Meanwhile, Marine Le Pen has plenty of space on the political stage in France, without a national media screaming loudly and on a daily basis against elected rulers, as they do in some UK and US outlets.

Similarly, the German journalist and writer, Thomas Kielinger, who is also based in London, is in some respects an admirer of the UK's media and its lack of deference to elected rulers. He points out that the:

German media reflects the largely consensual politics in Germany. Most of the time there are not big differences between the Christian Democrats and the Social Democrats in German politics. Politics in Germany can be quite dull and political reporting can be similarly dull. Both politics and the media are much noisier and less consensual in the UK.[13]

Again, the consensual and more subdued media in Germany did not prevent a steep decline in support for the social democrats from around the start of this century, which only began to be significantly reversed under the leadership of Martin Schulz in the spring of 2017. Nor did the media – relatively supportive of Angela Merkel's asylum policy, at least in the early phase – stop some senior figures among the Christian Democrats from panicking openly when it appeared that the far-right AfD was starting to make great electoral strides at their expense. As this book has explored, there are many factors bigger than the media to explain the fragility of the mainstream and the rise of outsiders, ranging from insecurities about the global economy to the constraints on democratically elected leaders at a time when voters' demands on them are intimidatingly daunting.

Evidently the media does not rule in a vacuum, manipulating the views of voters irrespective of other external circumstances. Nonetheless, the media mediates, and some of the most dramatic political changes have taken place in the US and the UK where, pre-social media, some outlets undermined elected leaders to a point where flawed, but well-intentioned rulers morphed into near-insane 'criminals'.

———

In the US, the UK and much of the democratic world the era before the eruption of social media is looked back on with dewy-eyed nostalgia. In reality, websites, Twitter, Facebook and fears about 'fake news' followed on from what was already quite a media battering for elected leaders. The battering has intensified in some respects, but the sources are now more obvious and less subtle.

Following the election of Trump, and Brexit in particular, there are three related worries about the impact of social media on politics. The first is that some powerful websites produce wholly inaccurate propaganda that reaches a wide audience, sometimes in the heat of an election campaign. The second is that candidates for high office can lie indiscriminately and get away with it, in this post-truth era. The third is that Twitter can distort the reporting of politics, allowing outsiders to reach wide audiences with simplistic assertions that are re-tweeted uncritically by like-minded followers. These three worries coalesce around the election of Trump.

If Trump's presidency has a house publication, it will not be *The New York Times*, which Trump attacks regularly on Twitter and in press conferences. It will be Breitbart, a right-wing opinion and news website formed in 2007, which one former editor has described as 'Trump Pravda'. Trump appointed the website's executive chairman, Steve Bannon, a former Goldman Sachs banker, as his White House strategy chief.

The fast-growing Breitbart opinion and news website has become a rallying point for Trump's nationalist, sometimes racist and often angry, 'alt-right' support base. It campaigned hard for Trump throughout the primaries, waging war against the candidacy of the Florida senator Marco Rubio, before becoming Trump's supportive voice during the presidential election. 'So much of the media mocked us, laughed at us, called us all sorts of names,' said the site's editor-in-chief, Alexander Marlow, on the Sunday following Bannon's appointment. 'And then for us to be seen as integral to the election of a president, despite all of that hatred, is something that we certainly enjoy and savour.'[14]

During the election campaign, Hillary Clinton warned her supporters of the alt-right's 'emerging racist ideology' and 'the de facto merger between Breitbart and the Trump campaign… [which] represents a landmark achievement for this group, a fringe element that has effectively taken over the Republican party'.[15]

By the time Clinton highlighted the 'merger' in August 2016, Breitbart's US audience had more than doubled from 7.4 million users in September 2014 to 15.8 million.[16] That was still much smaller than those of *The Washington Post* and *The New York Times*, which recorded 83 million and 88 million respectively, but the growth was speedily upwards.

The wider proliferation of fake news during the campaign caused serious political writers in the US to despair. David Remnick, editor of *The New Yorker*, noted in the immediate aftermath of Trump's victory in 2016:

> The information loop has been shattered. On Facebook articles in the traditional fact-based press look the same as articles from the conspiratorial alternative Right media. Spokesmen for the unspeakable now have access to huge audiences. This was the cauldron, with so much misogynistic language, that helped to demean and destroy Clinton. The alt-right press was the purveyor of constant lies, propaganda and conspiracy theories that Trump used as the oxygen of his campaign.[17]

While Facebook can be an indiscriminate host, Twitter is a wild one. Anyone can be there, tweeting away. Across the democratic world the impact of Twitter has sped up politics again. The proliferation of broadcasting outlets, and their dance with the newspapers, made politics noisier and more short-term in the 1990s. Twitter has multiplied by 100 the pressures on elected leaders. There is instant and eternal commentary – informed or uninformed. And a leader would not be human if he or she did not seek the instant verdict available to them. If that verdict of the Greek chorus, as it appears on Twitter, is positive, the leader feels fleetingly more hopeful. If the tweets are derisory, he or she can lapse into paranoid gloom. Pre-Twitter and the rolling news, leaders would wait until the following day to read the verdict of the commentators on a speech, policy, interview or press conference. They could get on with leading, in the long spaces between the commentators' verdicts. Now they are stifled by instant judgements. They know, too, that their colleagues are reading the same tweets and blogs, forming judgements on the level of their vulnerability accordingly.

At Prime Minister's Questions in the UK – the weekly joust in the House of Commons – most MPs are reading the tweets on their phones as the exchanges unfold. They observe the battle between prime minister and leader of the Opposition and simultaneously read the verdicts of a thousand commentators. The various press secretaries do the same, in order to tell their leaders immediately afterwards how they have done. There is no rest in politics now. The insiders are not detached, but they are quickly exhausted.

Trump was the beneficiary of social-media battles during the 2016 election, partly because he tweeted with the instinct of an over-excited tabloid editor. He knew how to make waves and attract attention. There was no message discipline – the fashion in politics in the 1990s, as the centre left made its nervy recovery. But there was a constancy, and a shameless capacity to shock.

Trump's use of Twitter was highly effective during the campaign. Simple messages were carefully timed, replicating the old-fashioned news cycle. He quite often tweeted a provocative assertion late at night or in the early hours of the morning. His words would then dominate the morning news bulletins. As such, he got his simple messages across to large audiences. Twitter is self-feeding: if you have many millions of followers, those followers can re-tweet, and soon you are reaching a huge audience of target voters. Twitter is something of a gift for political outsiders, as momentum can be generated speedily and without costs. Target audiences are reached with ease. Trump's favourite form of communication becomes unavoidably linked with his relationship to truth. Is he tweeting fake news? Was his campaign more widely built around fake news?

Some newspaper and magazine editors in America are in agonies about whether they should have done more to expose Trump's mendacities during the campaign. Fact-checking journalists – the assiduous journalists who were seeking out the precise degree to which Trump was telling the truth – could often still be working in the early hours of every morning during the campaign, comparing the truth with the claims from the campaign. One journalist, the Toronto *Star*'s Washington bureau chief, Daniel Dale, who monitored Trump from 15 September until 8 November 2016, recorded a total of 560 false statements, an average of about twenty a day.[18]

The sense that the media allowed itself to be taken for a ride by the Trump campaign came to a crunch in September 2016 in Washington. By now enshrined as the Republican nominee, Trump invited political reporters to a press conference by promising to make a statement – an apology, it was assumed – about his long-held absurd allegation that President Obama was born outside the US. The location for the event happened to be the old post office on Pennsylvania Avenue, which Trump had just renovated into a luxury hotel.

Instead of apologizing, for nearly half an hour Trump subjected the media, and through them the American people, to a succession of speeches by retired military leaders singing his praises. Then, when Trump finally got round to issuing a short rebuttal of his theory about Obama, he prefaced it with yet another allegation that Hillary Clinton was responsible for having started the rumour in the first place. This was a sillier allegation than his original claim that Obama was born outside the US, and potentially more damaging as Clinton was his opponent, whereas Obama was about to leave the fray.

This was classic Trump: half an hour of free advertising, not only for his presidential campaign, but also for his new hotel – all handed to him on a plate by the cable networks, in exchange for a thirty-second non-apology and making further false allegations against his opponent.

What was new was the response of the media who had been forced to sit through this performance, cameras rolling, as though they were, arguably, Trump's dutiful playthings. Again, thoughtful journalists despaired at their gullibility. 'It was a political rick-roll,' observed CNN's Jake Tapper. Another said, 'We got played again.' And Jay Rosen, who teaches journalism at New York University, described this as a seminal moment: 'That's when people in the campaign press corps got disgusted, not just with Trump's mendacity and manipulation, but at themselves for playing along with it.'[19]

And yet there is too much wringing of hands, too much retrospective angst. If Trump was a candidate inviting journalists to attend a press conference to report on an apparent apology, and he did not make that apology, then it is for journalists to report the crude evasiveness – to make that sequence clear. And then, in the end, voters must decide. This is what happened. And if voters decide they are still willing to back the blatantly scheming candidate, it is in spite of (or perhaps because of) the swagger displayed at such moments.

These are not events about which the media need to feel guilty. It would have been odd for journalists not to attend the press conference of an eccentric presidential candidate, however contrived. Most press conferences in a presidential campaign are contrived. A lot of the coverage of the Trump press conference was highly sceptical. Many columns were written about the mendacity of Trump. The reality was that he still found a way to break through.

In terms of media culpability, Hillary Clinton was already bracketed as someone who could not be trusted, and that was as much to do with mainstream media coverage of politics, over many decades, as it was to do with Trump, Twitter and his manipulation of the TV networks.

There are times – and political campaigns are one of them – when the media's role is to report the battle and let the voters decide. In the same way that some noble journalists in the US are agonizing about whether they could have done more to expose Trump, and in some cases about the false reporting of Trump on social media, the BBC wonders whether it managed to get the notion of 'balance' correct during the Brexit referendum campaign. Those who argue that it failed to do so include the former Director General of the BBC, who now is chief executive of *The New York Times*, Mark Thompson. He and others argue that the BBC mistook balance to mean there must be a precise balance, even when one side had much greater obvious weight compared with the other.

One example often cited is when President Obama warned at a London press conference that if the UK left the European Union, it would be at the back of the queue for any trade agreement. In subsequent BBC bulletins, clips of Obama were juxtaposed with a relatively minor figure in the Brexit campaign, as if the two were of equal authority and weight: the President of the United States and a relatively unknown Brexiteer. Similarly, when a large number of authoritative economists put the case for staying in the EU, they were balanced in terms of time and apparent significance with a single response from somebody from the Brexit campaign – implying perhaps that there was an equal divide between economists, when most were opposed to Brexit.

Again, this is the wrong issue for the BBC to agonize about. There is only one way of resolving the dilemma of balance in referendums, and that is not to hold referendums. That is for a leader to decide, not the media. Referendums over complex, multi-layered issues are bound to become a political battle of exaggerated claims and counter-claims. The broadcasters have a responsibility to report the battle, and not to decide which side is more outlandish than the other, even if one side has many more weighty experts putting their case. The BBC reported the referendum as it should have done, discussing the claims and arguments of both sides. The fact that some Brexit-supporting voters chose to believe claims that, once outside the EU, the UK would have a spare £350 million a month to spend on the NHS is a matter for the voters, and reflects the failure of the 'Remain' campaign effectively to expose the lie.

In the United States, while journalists reflect on whether they could have done more to expose Trump, Trump has turned on journalists who are critical of him. Again, this is seen as alarming. There are many causes for alarm in relation to Trump, but his attitude towards the media is not one of them. Journalists criticize politicians. Elected politicians have the right to criticize journalists – even a US president spraying insults at a press conference like a bullying teenager in a playground. Journalists have the power of the last word when they file their reports and commentaries. It is up to the elected Trump, not the non-elected journalists, what he does at his rallies or his press conferences. A few critical journalists were ejected from his press conferences; one was turned away from a rally, having written a critical profile; and there is a long list of media outlets that have been banned from his campaign events. He has also been targeting *The New York Times*, but showed the degree to which he cared about the newspaper by paying its offices a visit in the immediate aftermath of his victory, even as he continued his attack on the media.

How alarming are all these developments, in the new era of social media? Do they undermine elected leaders and further boost irresponsible, untested outsiders? Compared with the reporting of politics in the supposedly far more authoritative mainstream media of the 1990s and the first decade of this century, I do not believe they are as significant.

All the potential advantages of social media for outsiders apply to the mainstream politicians, too. Twitter gives all politicians the opportunity to take control of the message. In the case of the US presidential campaign in 2016, Hillary Clinton failed to do so. She was not a teacher-politician. That was not a problem connected to social media, but to her candidacy. She did not recognize that explaining and compressing arguments in ways that are accessibly appealing is an essential qualification for leadership, not a bonus for those with communication skills. Clinton used Twitter, too, and reached many millions of people; but Trump's ruthless use of the news cycle, and the crude provocations of his attention-seeking tweets, showed that an outsider with limited resources – even someone as rich as Trump has limited resources in the context of a US presidential campaign – can make an election-winning national impact through social media, which does not cost any money at all.

But Trump is the elected insider now, and he will become a victim of the new speeded-up reporting of politics, as other elected insiders have been before him. Indeed, his neurotic, insecure and transparent obsession with the media shows the degree to which it holds power over him. He might have manipulated all forms of media outlets in the presidential campaign, but the outlets are now in a position to manipulate and torment him as he faces the dilemmas of power.

However much he shouts at journalists, excludes them from press conferences and tweets about their failings, they will be the ones to provoke him, in their scrutiny and as part of a fast-changing industry conditioned to make politicians' lives hellish. Trump's endless onslaughts on respected outlets, which include CNN and the BBC, are a reflection of his sense of fragility. They continue to report as they wish. He continues to harangue fruitlessly. He can call them 'fake news', or exclude individuals and organizations from his press conferences, but the journalists have the last word.

In the immediate aftermath of Trump's victory he continued to tweet in ways that were astonishing and illuminating. Of his tweets in the days that followed his extraordinary triumph, he tweeted twelve attacks on the media, and four on a satirical Broadway musical called *Hamilton*, along with various Twitter feuds with the cast of the musical. This was after his authority-enhancing, confidence-boosting victory. He should have been celebrating, but already he was getting angry with the media. Most elected leaders take a few years before they become tormented to the point of madness by the media. No one can accuse Trump of letting victory go to his head. He behaved as if he was still the outsider on the campaign trail. There was almost a modesty in his ongoing tweets against media outlets.

In government, inevitably, politics will become much tougher for Trump. The transition from election victory to the White House is the blissfully easy part of the sequence. A candidate has won and has not yet faced the dilemmas of power. Nevertheless, in this euphoric phase Trump showed sensitivity to criticism that is unprecedented.

He has already faced the difficult challenge of undoing some of his absurd campaigning mendacities, in terms of what he will actually do in power. But the presidential campaign is a political battle. It was not the job of *The New York Times* and *The New Yorker* to definitively expose Trump. Their role was to report and analyse what he was saying, and to let the voters decide. It was for Hillary Clinton and Trump's opponents to expose the level of mendacity, as he managed to unfairly, but successfully, frame her with references to criminality and corruption.

These were intense battles between a presidential candidate, and then the presidential winner, and the media. But they are not that unusual. Elected politicians, or politicians seeking election, are often in a state of paranoid fury about the media, and the media gets into a state about the way that paranoia manifests itself. These outbreaks of mutual paranoia matter less, in the end, than the fundamental assumption of still-powerful forces in the media that politicians are in it for themselves and need to be viewed as near-criminals in interviews, or in the way they are scrutinized. This is how space first became available for the outsider to flourish in the modern media, while it constrained cautious insiders and mainstream elected politicians, at a juncture where they needed to be expansive and accessible to an electorate that was frightened and bewildered by the scale of change in their lives.

Such a media climate makes it very hard for mainstream insiders to be honest about the limits of what they can do. When a media works on the assumption that they are part of a cocooned elite, for that cocooned elite to say, 'Look, I know you are all struggling at the moment, but there's not a lot I can do about it' is bound to be a near-fatal utterance. Instead, it is safer for them to affect a mighty omnipotence at a time when they are less omnipotent than they have ever been. A lot of the seemingly odd, evasive behaviour of the so-called mainstream insiders is partly explained by the way the media has come to view them.

Social media provides a chance for the mainstream to explain, and to regain a degree of control about the message, task and context in which they seek to rule. If they fail to do so, that is a reflection on them. Fake news is often so preposterous, and its self-interested source so obvious, that much of it is far less sinister than it appears to be. To take a vivid example: Bannon's influence on Trump is now one of the best-known elements of the presidency. At the same time, Bannon's association with Breitbart is the best-known part of his ascendancy to the White House. Trump and Breitbart then become closely connected in the minds of voters. When Breitbart attacks Trump's opponents, most voters will increasingly recognize the bias of the source. More orthodox outlets – a newspaper, a radio station – have greater credibility, and their undermining of nervy elected leaders is much more subtle.

The reporting of politics does not excuse the politicians' choice to be powerless when voters need them to intervene more, but it is part of the explanation as to why the mainstream vacated a section of the political stage and allowed the outsiders to move in, at least in the US and the UK. They feared a slaughtering from the media and, in their fearful caution, became less popular. With nothing to lose, the outsiders said what they wanted to say and became more popular.

CONCLUSION

Given that most outsiders are politically inexperienced and therefore naïve, convey contradictory messages, are without a secure support base and are doomed to become constrained insiders if they win power, why have mainstream leaders on the right and on the left given them so much space on the political stage? In some whodunnits, authors deploy the clever device of making all the suspects guilty as their mystery is solved. 'Guilt' is the wrong term in seeking an explanation for the rise of the political outsiders, but we are all culpable.

As is often the case, mainstream leaders have acted in ways they assumed would please voters, only to discover they alienated significant sections of the electorate.

The centre left chose to be powerless in the face of globalization partly out of calculated expediency. Based on electoral setbacks in the 1980s, some centre-left leaders assumed they could not win elections by putting the case overtly for more active government. They feared such a case would be widely interpreted as a plea to waste voters' hard-earned money, and as a way of stifling entrepreneurial innovation. For ideological reasons, some leaders on the centre right believed passionately in inactive government or at least a smaller state and, unlike the centre left, they did have the confidence to act on their convictions.

With globalization generating deep insecurities, the outsiders were given considerable ideological space in which to act on behalf of those who felt 'left behind' – or to claim to act on their behalf. The outsiders claimed they would act to make voters feel more secure while, for different reasons, mainstream parties would not.

While most outsiders are incoherent in their objectives, they are quick to use social media in order to advance their cause. Some of them are instinctively good at making points accessible. President Trump managed to make a case on Twitter for big spending increases by the simple act of personifying the state. He – Donald Trump, the anti-state celebrity businessman – would build roads, bridges and walls, and protect jobs. Some of his doting fans would recoil if he tweeted that it was time for the state to do more. Trump would never make such a case. In his ideological confusion, he believes in himself, but not in the state.

Now, as president, Trump is discovering the constraints of democratic power. In February 2017 a federal judge James Robart halted Trump's executive order that aimed to block all refugees and citizens of seven Muslim-majority countries from entering the US. All Trump could do was fume impotently that a 'so-called judge' had intervened to prevent him from acting. In the same month his National Security Adviser, Michael Flynn, was forced to resign over contacts with Russia made before Trump's term had begun. Trump was adamant that Flynn had done nothing wrong, but was compelled to accept his resignation.

The following month, in March 2017, Trump was forced to drop his plans to scrap Obamacare – Barack Obama's attempt to make healthcare more freely available to those on lower incomes. Before his election victory, and in the immediate aftermath, Trump had proclaimed confidently that the scrapping of Obamacare would be 'easy' and 'immediate'. That was when he was an outsider, free to say what he wanted when he wanted.

By the spring of 2017 Trump was an insider discovering the powerlessness of power. As a mighty president, he was made powerless because of internal divisions amongst Republicans in Washington. Moderate Republicans feared that Trump's muddled plans to replace Obamacare would leave many of their constituents without health provision, while right-wing Republicans decided the repeal did not go far enough. Trump had projected himself as the deal-maker. He failed to get an agreement in his first significant attempt as president.

Suddenly Trump was on the inside, discovering that exercising power is more complex than tweeting a pledge. The outsider had won and yet was powerless to impose his travel ban, retain his security adviser and change Obama's health policy, which many Republicans in Washington had passionately opposed for years. Trump was discovering that politics is more complicated on the inside. Parties are often divided and must somehow or other be bound together. In addition, proclaiming an aspiration is much easier than putting together a detailed policy that will work, when implemented. Democratic politics is demanding.

As *The New York Times* columnist David Brooks noted in the aftermath of Trump's failure to secure support from Congress for scrapping Obamacare: 'The new elite is worse than the old elite – and certainly more vapid.'[1]

Brooks was not a supporter of Obamacare, but in suggesting that Trump and his entourage were part of the Washington 'elite', he has wounded Obama's successor with a near-fatal blow. Trump the outsider is condemned as being part of an elite that he views with an anti-politics disdain. As an added insult, the columnist suggested that Trump is seen as leading an incompetent elite. No wonder Trump loathes *The New York Times*.

In very different circumstances Alexis Tsipras soon recognized the powerlessness of power, from the left's perspective, when he became prime minister of Greece in January 2015. It was much easier for him, from the outside, to pledge that he would end austerity and keep Greece in the eurozone. From the inside, he faced the contradiction behind the pledge and was trapped, as many leaders often are. Tsipras was facing the dilemmas of power.

Those facing the dilemmas are trapped partly by constitutional constraints. Most days of the year political columnists ask of leaders, 'Why don't you follow my advice and do x, y or z?' Quite often the answer is that they cannot do x, y or z, even if they would like to. They are incarcerated in coalitions, or have small majorities in their parliaments, facing impossible conundrums with unreliable support. But in failing to respond to the demands of columnists and others, they appear to be useless, when in reality they are powerless.

In March 2017 the UK's chancellor, Philip Hammond, unveiled what he thought was a safely cautious budget. Within a few hours all hell was breaking loose, because Hammond had announced a tax rise on the self-employed. The Conservative manifesto at the 2015 election had ruled out such an increase, but without tax rises there is no way governments in the democratic world can meet the demands from a growing elderly population, as well as all the other needs, ranging from housing to a modern transport system. Yet most tax rises are politically impossible to implement. As the late Roy Jenkins once noted astutely of UK voters, but with wider application: 'UK voters want northern European standards of public services and US levels of taxation.'² Jenkins was writing as one who had been an elected insider – as a former chancellor, Home Secretary and leader of the SDP – facing the conundrums. He was also highlighting a thorny problem for leaders well beyond the UK. Voters in northern Europe do not always leap with joy at the prospect of higher taxes, while in the US there is a growing hunger for better public provision without an accompanying willingness to pay higher taxes.

As well as choosing to be powerless, and rendered powerless, by constitutional constraints, elected leaders rule in an era of extreme mistrust. If they do not do x, y or z, the instinct of some voters is to assume that those they elected are liars and, in some cases, criminals. At the very least some voters feel ignored and overlooked.

Such feelings are a gift to outsiders, who promise vaguely to take back control and to act on behalf of those who feel 'left behind'. The instinct to mistrust elected leaders is fuelled by some media outlets, which regard their main duty in relation to elected leaders as being to ask, as one interviewer put it, 'Why is this lying bastard lying to me?' It goes without saying that sometimes politicians fuel the mistrust because they do not deserve to be trusted. They can be indiscriminately greedy, self-serving and, in a few cases, corrupt. But on the whole there is a more interesting and reassuring set of explanations as to why leaders behave in the way they do. As they seek to resolve the conundrums and dilemmas, they cannot always be candid and sometimes have to go back on previous pledges or declarations. Such scheming is part of politics and is preferable to the alternative way of resolving disputes, which is the use of force.

Perversely, it takes the use of force to change the fashionably negative prism through which democratic politics is viewed. In the UK that prism changed fleetingly on Wednesday 22 March 2017, when a single individual, Khalid Masood, killed four people, including a policeman, close to the Westminster Parliament. Suddenly Parliament ceased to be the 'Westminster bubble' and was instead portrayed reverentially in news reports as lying at the heart of the UK's democracy.

MPs, normally regarded as being part of a cocooned elite, were portrayed as ordinary human beings – their valuable contribution to democratic activity now threatened by a knife-wielding terrorist. Those working in the parliamentary buildings became what they are: human beings with different responsibilities – police, office staff and, mainly, hard-working politicians. No one reported the attack as being an attack on the Westminster bubble. Briefly, those we elect were humanized and perceived as humans.

These are some of the reasons why mainstream parties have struggled against the backdrop of globalization and the 2008 financial crash. The explanations point to several counter-intuitive steps, if mainstream parties and leaders are to meet the challenge posed by the outsiders.

The most demanding is the need for more forensic ideological reflection from both the centre left and centre right. Such reflection is always difficult and often dangerous. Most of the time in politics it is easier for a party not to delve too deeply, as introspection risks leading to fatal division and greater incoherence. But after a seismic event on the scale of the 2008 financial crash and the sweeping challenges of globalization, a degree of revisionism is both desirable and unavoidable. Avoiding such debate is not the safe option, but the risky one.

After its election defeat in 2010 the UK's Labour Party was emblematic in opting for soporific unity, until the explosion of Jeremy Corbyn's candidacy in the leadership contest that followed a second successive election defeat in 2015. Perhaps it would have been healthier for Labour to have staged a more volcanic debate during the leadership contest that took place after its general-election defeat in 2010. Similarly, social democrats in much of Europe lost support after the financial crash, without much debate as to why they were becoming unpopular.

On the centre right there was also little ideological revisionism after the financial crash. Guiding assumptions about the role of government remained largely unchanged for decades. These assumptions were the dominant force in much of the Western world from the early 1980s, and were based around the virtues of the light-touch state. From the turn of the century, centre-right parties showed themselves to be fairly adaptable in terms of their support for social liberalism. But some of them continued to worship at the altar of the Reagan/Thatcher economic orthodoxies that took hold in the incomparably different circumstances of the early 1980s.

Democratic politics is always late to respond to underlying economic changes. This is partly because insecure leaders look to the past for guidance, as they navigate a foggy future. But the past is a fickle guide. In the UK during the 1970s one government after another clung to corporatist policies that were obviously failing. On one level each prime minister knew such policies were not working, and yet was drawn to them like characters in a film noir heading towards their doom. Edward Heath was elected in 1970 with pledges to change labour laws and not intervene to save 'lame-duck' industries. He was strongly opposed to an incomes policy as a way of controlling wages. By the time of his fall, Heath had imposed an incomes policy that was being challenged by the miners' strike. He had scrapped most of his plans to reform labour laws and, fearing the social and economic consequences of high unemployment, intervened to save failing industries. His Labour opponent, Harold Wilson, argued against an incomes policy in the February 1974 election, hailing as an alternative his vaguely defined 'Social Contract' with the unions. Soon he was in favour of an incomes policy similar to Heath's. And Wilson's successor, Jim Callaghan, had opposed an incomes policy in the early 1970s. Soon after becoming prime minister he imposed a series of incomes policies that led to his fall. Many years later Callaghan reflected in an interview with the *New Statesman* that leaders in the 1970s had been brought up in the 1930s and were determined never to tolerate similar levels of high unemployment.[3] Their objective was noble, but they all became trapped by corporatist policies that they knew were not working. They were seeking guidance from the past, without noticing fully what was happening in front of their eyes.

During the 1979 election Callaghan noted to his senior adviser, Bernard Donoughue, that a 'sea change' was taking place and there was nothing he could do to reverse the tides. A similar sea change took place with the financial crash in 2008, and leaders looked back for guidance, as Callaghan and others had done in the 1970s. After the crash, borrowing remained cheap. Growth was fuelled by consumer spending, a spree supported by high levels of borrowing. Economies remained dependent on fragile financial sectors. Public spending was cut to such an extent that some regions became poorer still. Regulatory frameworks remained light. Leaders knew of no other regime. Half knowingly they were repeating the mistakes of the past, but they were the only mistakes they knew.

In 2016 some leaders showed signs of tentatively responding to the tidal waves that followed the 2008 crash. In her language, though much less so in her policies, the UK prime minister, Theresa May, hints at an understanding of the dramatically changing circumstances in which she rules. From the start of her leadership she has recognized that if leaders do not put the case for government and the way it can connect with the lives of voters, then no one else will. If no leader highlights the connections, voters will inevitably feel disconnected.

May's party-conference speech in October 2016 included a section that marked a significant moving on from the small-state focus of her recent predecessors. With a revolutionary flourish, an entire section of her speech was entitled 'Believing in the good that government can do'. In this section May argued daringly that she envisaged her 'government stepping up':

> Righting wrongs. Challenging vested interests. Taking big decisions. Doing what we believe to be right. Getting the job done.
>
> Because that's the good that government can do. And it's what I'm in this for. To stand up for the weak and stand up to the strong.
>
> And to put the power of government squarely at the service of ordinary working-class people... It's time to remember the good that government can do.
>
> Time for a new approach that says while government does not have all the answers, government can and should be a force for good; that the state exists to provide what individual people, communities and markets cannot; and that we should employ the power of government for the good of the people.
>
> Time to reject the ideological templates provided by the socialist left and the libertarian right and to embrace a new centre ground in which government steps up – and not back – to act on behalf of us all.
>
> Providing security from crime, but from ill health and unemployment too.
>
> Supporting free markets, but stepping in to repair them when they aren't working as they should.
>
> Encouraging business and supporting free trade, but not accepting one set of rules for some and another for everyone else.[4]

May is in danger of becoming interesting, in spite of herself. She is a cautious leader and shows few signs of translating the argument into a set of radical policies. But in framing an argument about the good that government can do, she moves her party to a different, potentially more fertile place from where it was before.

On the centre left there are similar tentative moves. The leader of the SDP in Germany since March 2017, Martin Schulz, has re-energized his confused and demoralized party by choosing not to be an echo of Angela Merkel or moving opportunistically to the right of her, as some of his predecessors chose to do. Among his pledges, Schulz has pledged to invest some of the budget surplus in education and other public services, rather than using it all to pay down debt. The ecstatic response from audiences flocking to hear a moderate figure from the centre left arguing about the good that government can do suggests that voters were waiting for an ideological vacuum to be filled.

Even in the UK Labour Party – suffering from a crisis of identity and purpose since the New Labour era ended traumatically with the aftermath of Iraq and the financial crisis – shows some fresh life in its thinking. Some of the younger MPs reflect on how voters feel a sense of powerlessness, and how a small sense of empowerment can make them engage with highly charged policy areas. Here is the MP for Wigan, Lisa Nandy, speaking at the think tank, the Institute for Public Policy Research, in March 2017 on the most sensitive policy area of them all:

> Not long ago Serco [a private company that is responsible for the delivery of some public services] decided to use the Britannia hotel in a quiet village in my constituency to house asylum seekers. Overnight, more than 100 young men arrived without warning. Far right organizations mobilized, and locally, people wanted to

know who they were, how long they were staying, what support
and security was in place and whether vicious rumours spread
by fascist organizations were true. It took action from the police
and community leaders, with my support, to change this. Not
long afterwards, we launched a Syrian Refugee appeal. We had
36,000 bags of donations in two weeks. The challenge for politics
is to enable people's intrinsic compassion to prevail over the very
human sense of insecurity – to ensure that people have control
over the things that matter in their lives. Handing block contracts
to Serco who buy up cheap accommodation and care only about
the bottom line is a major cause of this sense of powerlessness.
And in the face of overwhelming anxiety it is no wonder that
borders have become a symbol of 'social order, family life and
common decency'.[5]

Nandy's example highlights another reason why voters can
feel powerless. With private companies becoming responsible for
the delivery of some essential services, the lines of accountability
become blurred. To whom do voters turn, in order to express their
concerns? They cannot vote out Serco, if they disapprove of what the
company is doing, as the company does not stand for election. But
Nandy was less clear about what her preferred mediating agencies
should be, if not a private company. Her Labour colleague Chuka
Umunna, in a *New Statesman* article on 6 March 2017, argued for
devolving greater power to the regions:

Wherever there is a case to devolve power and resources, we
should be required to have a very good reason to say 'no'.
Labour can use the authority of government to help enable
people's participation in reform. For example, the land market
needs reforming to give communities the power to tackle
our acute housing crisis. Immigration needs to be brought
under democratic control with decision making devolved to

287

regions. The decentralization of power to take decision making closer to people's lives requires a more democratic model of the state and a genuine redistribution of capital and funding. Whitehall departments need joining up and the Treasury needs a collaborative not autocratic approach to local government.[6]

There are dangers in focusing too heavily on the devolution of power as a solution to the sense of powerlessness felt by many voters. The focus can too easily become a debate about process alone, in the same way that calls for an independent Scotland or for leaving the EU are an alternative to deeper thinking about how to fund and structure a modern health service or adequate education provision. Nonetheless, a debate about where power should lie, and what form the power should take, begins to address questions about accountability and the relationship between government and voters. In the absence of such a debate, the outsiders make their simplistic pledges to bring back control.

The rise of the outsiders and their espousal of a populist nationalism lead to an important, embryonic debate about power and accountability – a fruitful consequence of their rise. A debate that becomes one about 'foreigners' and immigration is more dangerous.

One red herring is a fashionable focus on 'identity politics'. What does 'identity politics' mean, in policy terms, and where does it lead? In the UK some leading figures on the centre left argue that they need to have a greater understanding of what it means to be English or British. Do they? What are the policy consequences of such an understanding? What are the sweeping generalizations about national identity on which the policies are based?

The 'atomization' of individuals – who are no longer bound together to the same extent as they used to be by common workplaces, working clubs, parties with mass memberships, trade unions, church, strong families, shared routines and interests – is a more tangible issue. To suggest that vague forms of patriotism address that atomization does not get the mainstream much beyond waffle. The attachment to football clubs and the popularity of communal activities (from running clubs, to literary festivals and amateur theatre) show that there continues to be a hunger for wider communal activity. No sane individual would want to rely on Facebook or Twitter alone as a way of communicating with other human beings. But no current binding institutions have compensated for the decline of political parties, church, trade unions, clubs and the smaller, more fractured state in some countries. The renewed interest in where power should lie, and in what form, is partly a search for new binding agencies.

A focus on where power lies, and who is accountable to whom, is long overdue, at least in the European Union, where Brexit and tensions in parts of the eurozone fuel a sense in some countries that 'power' lies in distant places. The voters face the consequences of decisions made from a daunting distance, without having the means to do anything about them. 'Europe', 'London' and 'Washington' have become shorthand for the powerlessness of atomized voters.

Only in the UK has this led to voters backing departure from the EU in a referendum. Pro-European leaders in the UK failed to find the language and the arguments to show that, far from 'Europe' ruling the UK, the UK held considerable sway in Europe. If the UK did not want to comply with significant EU initiatives, it was not forced to do so. The UK was out of the single currency and yet was a full member of the single market, influencing the direction of economic policy as much as any other member. It was opting in and out of arrangements on a regular basis. It chose to invade Iraq, when France and Germany were opposed to this. It chose its own tax rates and often boasted rates that were more competitive than those in other parts of the EU. It chose its own labour laws, hailing the flexibility of its workforce, even if it was far less productive than those in most other EU countries.

Most mainstream leaders, especially on the centre left, have been hopeless at framing wider arguments about economic policy. Forming accessible arguments is an essential part of leadership, and the means by which leaders can connect with voters. The most enduring leaders are political teachers, making sense of their policies around the clock, even when those policies make little sense. It is no coincidence that the longest-serving prime ministers in the UK in recent decades were Thatcher and Blair – both of them instinctive teachers, seeking to explain *why* they were acting in the way they were. Their arguments were simplistic and some of the policies were deeply flawed, but they constantly sought to make sense of them and to explain why they were pursuing various courses. Thatcher reduced her espousal of monetarism to a homily about her father having never spent more than he earned. Blair gave endless interviews on his 'Third Way' politics and why the 'radical centre' helped the many, and not the few. Only Obama found language from the centre left to expose the madness of a rush to balance budgets after the 2008 crash, by warning that if an aircraft is too heavy, it makes matters worse to take out the engine. Mostly it was the right that found accessible ways of explaining their hunger for spending cuts in order to balance the books.

The manner in which Martin Schulz in Germany and Emmanuel Macron in France – both unapologetic supporters of the EU – brought back to life arguments about being open and internationalist highlights the importance of big figures in politics and leadership.

Parties only flourish when they have smart leaders. Mainstream parties have been short of big leaders in recent decades.

———

The qualifications for leadership are rarely discussed. Given the fragility of democratic politics, they should be discussed more. Most vacancies for senior positions come with details of the qualifications required for the post. When it comes to standing for the leadership of a potential party of government, there is no such list. The ideological position of candidates is key in leadership contests or presidential races, but not their qualifications to lead. Yet no party will acquire ideological verve and momentum if a leader cannot lead. The daunting qualifications that are required include a capacity to frame policies with wide appeal, consistent with a party's clearly defined values; the skill to communicate the policies via the media to voters; the ability to unite a party around those policies, and then implement the programme in government, while remaining responsive to unexpected events and ready to fight and win elections. These qualifications must be accompanied by command of policy detail. Without these qualifications, no one need apply. Too many have applied, and been appointed to the top of mainstream parties on the left and right, without leadership skills.

The need to be a leader-teacher is especially vital in an era when voters' demands are high and a leader's capacity to deliver is limited. The capacity is not as limited as many mainstream leaders have chosen to assume, but is not as great as voters expect. Only the political teachers can bridge the dangerous gap.

Constitutional constraints make governing difficult, but they will not change. Coalitions remain likely in much of Europe, with the inevitable compromises and pragmatism they demand from each of the parties involved. The US constitution, with all its checks and balances, is widely regarded with a biblical reverence. When Obama's policies were being blocked, he and his allies despaired of the paralysing deadlock. But probably they are grateful for all the checks and balances that are making Trump's leadership more constrained, although he has the advantage of Republican majorities in Congress.

But if they are to remain constitutionally constrained, mainstream leaders need to find a way of communicating excitement about what they are doing, while explaining that they are acting with the equivalent of a ball and chain attached to them. This is not an easy challenge, but better than pretending to be omnipotent when they can hardly move on a crowded political stage. They need to educate voters about the dilemmas of leadership. Once again, no one else will do it for them – not least the orthodox media outlets, which tend to accept the fashionable view of politicians as a lofty elite, unintentionally fuelling the outsiders' narrative.

Social media offers mainstream leaders the chance to promote their message, as much as it does outsiders. But in many cases leaders have been too unsure what their message should be, to make full use of the opportunities. Although the outsiders espouse a range of contradictory ideas, they do so with confidence, helped by the fact that a lot of them do not recognize the contradictions of their anti-government, big-government convictions. In contrast, racked by self-doubt, the insiders tweet inauthentic contrivances.

Some mainstream parties are well ahead of many large companies in the private sector, in their use of Facebook and Twitter to reach target audiences during election campaigns. Obama's two presidential campaigns were a model. The UK's Conservative Party won the 2015 election partly by hiring innovative social-media experts. But it could not have been the only reason the Conservatives won, as the same brilliant team was hired by the 'Remain' campaign in the 2016 referendum and its smart targeting did not in itself lead to victory. But mainstream leaders are less effective at the round-the-clock messaging that Trump and other outsiders have turned into the equivalent of a tabloid newsroom.

Social media intensifies the heat and pace of politics. This is an unhealthy development and makes governing even harder. Leaders already have enough justified cause for their nervy paranoia. Now they can, and do, check Twitter most hours of the day, to get the reaction of commentators to what they have been up to. A single tweet can lead to a leader behaving differently. On the day British MPs debated whether or not to back gay marriage, the then prime minister, David Cameron, was nowhere to be seen. The political editor of *The Spectator*, James Forsyth, tweeted that Cameron's absence on such a big day was inexcusable. His criticism generated other similar tweets. The Number Ten press team panicked, and Cameron was persuaded to cancel meetings in order to give media interviews saying how proud he was that gay marriage was about to become legal.

Democratic politics was already being reported breathlessly, as if it were the equivalent of a 100-metre race, even though its actual pace is very slow. The time it takes for an idea to become a policy, and for that policy to be implemented, can be years – if the policy ever gets close to implementation. Twitter ramps up the distorting breathlessness. But the impact applies across the board. Outsiders might be beneficiaries early in their political career, as they torment mainstream leaders who are struggling to cope with the demands of power. But they will struggle, too, if or when they come close to government. Trump has already faced several crises as president – the political temperature rising speedily with round-the-clock news and comment. As a campaigner, he used Twitter like a skilful tabloid editor. In power, he tweets as a form of cathartic therapy. The tweets are doing him no good politically. He needs to tweet for his own sake now. In terms of his new position as an elected Washington insider, he is the victim of the pace of a highly charged media, having to respond to crises that partly feed off the never-ending outlets.

With his feverish tweeting, Trump is a freakish example that proves a much wider point. All political activity in democracies is conducted with more than one eye on what voters think and want. The biggest and most dangerous myth of modern times is that elected politicians work and live in a cocooned bubble, indifferent to voters. Even if they wanted to be loftily indifferent, they cannot be because they need to win elections.

Their continuous dance with voters is complex. Leaders often get judgements wrong, in terms of specific policies and in their misreading of how to swim with deep social and economic tides. They are late to recognize a fundamental sea change. Quite often that is because they are trying too hard to please voters. Rulers on both the centre left and centre right did not let the bankers flourish recklessly, before the 2008 crash, because they were indifferent to the rest of the electorate. They supported the light touch, on the basis of their judgement that the rest of the electorate would benefit from the economic growth generated by the booming financial sector. Similarly, support for the free movement of labour is not based on indifference to the indigenous population, but on a calculation that the entire economy benefits from immigration, in ways that help the indigenous population.

If voters feel left behind or need a sense of control, it is not because elected politicians sought to leave them feeling detached. With some justification, the New Labour project in the UK was accused of focusing too obsessively on so-called Middle England and its newspapers. Yet, in policy terms, it tried to make connections with those left behind. The introduction of the 'Sure Start' initiative was aimed at coordinating a range of services for families on low incomes. Ministers agonized about how to extend Sure Start to reach those who had opted out altogether from local institutions. There were many discussions about how those who attended Sure Start centres were, by definition, making connections with the services available, as they had chosen to engage. How to get those who needed help, but did not attend? Where were they, and which agencies were most suited to encourage new forms of engagement? These questions consumed ministerial time. Ministers did not find all the answers, but indifference was not the reason for the initiative's failure. The complexity of the challenge was closer to the explanation.

However complex the task, governments on the centre left and centre right need to do more to mitigate the iniquities of globalization. It is within their power to do so. House-building, high-class education, health provision and modern transport are always the meaty demands of government, ones that are more effectively addressed in some countries than in others. Globalization also changes working patterns in ways that demand new forms of government intervention.

As mainstream leaders navigate the terrain, many of them exaggerate the significance of regional division. Some areas are poorer than others. Cosmopolitan cities are more liberal than small towns. But the challenges are the same in cities with supposedly booming economies as they are in areas dependent on declining industries. Inhabitants of New York, Washington, London, Berlin and Stockholm struggle with housing costs, job insecurities, unreliable transport and schools, just as those living in the US Rust Belt do. The challenge for governments is to decide how best to intervene in markets in order to ensure adequate affordable housing, secure jobs, reliable transport and schools.

There is, though, a very large generational divide. Younger people in a city, small town or rural area cannot assume they will have a secure job for life. They struggle to pay soaring housing costs. In contrast, the elderly tend to be better off than their equivalents in previous generations. Fractured work patterns mean it is much harder for younger people to secure mortgages, when they need to prove to a lender that they are in secure employment. How best can governments intervene to address the generational divide?

Democratic politics would benefit from a more robust debate between centre left and centre right, in the aftermath of the financial crash. The centre-left case for a Keynesian response to the 2008 financial crash was put much more confidently by a few newspaper columnists – Paul Krugman in *The New York Times*, Martin Wolf in the *Financial Times*, William Keegan in *The Observer* – than it was by politicians. The centre-left politicians, with their nervy eyes on the voters, could not find a way of explaining why a deficit could be addressed by more government borrowing. With the centre left in retreat, the centre right had much of the stage to itself and, in imposing an excess of spending cuts, made itself so unpopular that it gave space to those even further to the right, who put the case for government hyperactivity.

This is a saga where culpability is widespread. The rise of puny outsiders takes place because of misjudgements from mainstream politicians; the powerlessness of those in power, constrained by constitutional safeguards; the reporting of a media that tends to accept the 'out-of-touch elite' narrative; and, of course, the greed of the very wealthy, who seek ways of getting even richer, even if their methods attract public opprobrium. Some of the very rich, with more money than they will ever know what to do with, still prefer taking ever higher bonuses and salaries in some sectors, even if they risk being subjected to intense public and media hostility. Their greed is irrational; they do not need the money, and presumably they are uncomfortable with public opprobrium. But for some people, greed prevails. Widening inequality is part of the backdrop that explains the rise of the outsiders.

Voters make misjudgements too, although no elected politician can ever criticize them – part of the imbalance in the relationship. Voters can throw insults at politicians, but a politician is doomed if it happens the other way round.

The right to vote is a privilege and should carry with it some responsibility. That responsibility should include some awareness of what is happening, and the consequences of taking one course rather than another. At the very least, some voters in Sunderland, where Nissan is a major employer, took a risk in supporting Brexit; as did those in Cornwall, where there is suddenly a worry that projects to improve broadband speeds and build transport hubs – both dependent on EU funding – are now under threat. Insecure low-earners in the Rust Belt region of the US are not automatically going to benefit from Trump's plans to cut taxes for high-earners and spend vast amounts more on defence spending. The need for heroes and villains is understandable. But a misunderstanding of how democratic politics works – why leaders behave in the way they do, and the dilemmas of power – also explains why the mainstream tottered and how the outsiders rose.

In February 2017 the BBC's *Newsnight* editor, Ian Katz, reported on why voters no longer trusted experts. He went to the seaside resort of Bognor Regis and, over a cup of tea, voters told him:

> There's too much scaremongering from so-called experts... All they do is study graphs.
>
> I don't believe they know best...
>
> A lot of people have good common sense, so why do we need experts?
>
> They get stuck in a little bubble...

A constructive response to these observations is impossible. The debate becomes pointlessly circuitous. To suggest that policy should be based partly on the findings of experts – those who are well informed – invites the defiant response that voters' common sense is more important.

The narrowing of debate and such circuitous exchanges extends more widely. A supporter of Scottish nationalism can respond to any question about a specific policy by arguing that the answer is an independent Scotland. How to meet the demand for better health provision? Independence. How to build more homes? Independence.

Independence is the answer to every complex policy dilemma. 'No, it is not!' 'Yes, it is!' The pantomime exchange is the only one possible.

The same applies to the broader debate about outsiders. They claim to speak for the people, because they are not part of the elite. As most of them had never been close to government when they began their journey, their claim to be on the outside is true, but is not in itself a qualification to speak on behalf of the people.

The fall of the outsiders is inevitable, over time. Electoral success destroys the essence of their pitch. They become insiders if they secure power, facing all the draining, confidence-sapping dilemmas that arise in democratic politics. The fashionable misunderstanding of those dilemmas and of how politics works – the assumption that politics is an ignoble vocation, rather than a noble one – fuels the outsiders' rise towards power and influence.

Yet something had to give in democratic politics. There was bound to be a time limit on leaders from different parties all claiming to be 'liberal' and assuming they were on the 'centre ground' as they made that claim. The terms 'liberal' and 'centre ground' are two flexible friends in politics, but their flexibility can be dangerous, too. If the outsiders have made an inadvertently positive contribution, it is to trigger constructive questions from mainstream parties about what form the centre ground takes, and tentative questions about the role of government in a globalized economy.

The answers are not fully formed. While we are all to blame for an era of heightened danger, we must all take responsibility for finding a way through: mainstream leaders; the media that mediates elected leaders' ideas and personalities; and the voters, who have more power and influence than they realize. The route will be stressful and hazardous.

Elected leaders are used to contemplating thorny routes. Democratic politics is unavoidably stressful and hazardous, as some outsiders discover when they have the misfortune to win power and leave the safety of the outside to become the new insiders.

POLITICAL PARTIES AND
POLITICIANS/ADVISERS

Tony **Abbott**: former Australian PM
AfD Party: right-wing Alternative for
   Germany party
Esperanza **Aguirre**: Spanish politician
Jonathan **Aitken**: former
   Conservative MP
Austrian People's Party
David **Axelrod**: adviser to Barack
   Obama
Ed **Balls**: former Labour shadow
   chancellor
Steve **Bannon**: Trump's White House
   strategy chief
Tony **Benn**: left-wing Labour MP
Silvio **Berlusconi**: former Italian
   PM and leader of the Forza Italia
   party
John **Boehner**: former Speaker of the
   US House of Representatives
Willy **Brandt**: former German
   chancellor
Gordon **Brown**: former PM
George W. **Bush**: former US
   president
Jeb **Bush**: Republican presidential
   candidate
Jim **Callaghan**: former PM
David **Cameron**: former PM
Alastair **Campbell**: Tony Blair's press
   secretary
Gianroberto **Casaleggio**: co-founder
   of the Italian M5S party

Mário **Centeno**: Portugal's finance
   minister
Jacques **Chirac**: former French
   president
**Christian Democratic Union of
   Germany (CDU)**
Ken **Clarke**: former UK chancellor
Nick **Clegg**: former deputy PM and
   Lib-Dem leader
Bill **Clinton**: former US president
Hillary **Clinton**: US presidential
   candidate
Robin **Cook**: former Foreign
   Secretary
Jeremy **Corbyn**: Labour leader
António **Costa**: Portugal's socialist
   leader and PM
Jon **Cruddas**: Labour MP
Ted **Cruz**: Republican presidential
   candidate
Dominic **Cummings**: one of the
   architects of the victory in the
   Brexit referendum
Danish People's Party
Alistair **Darling**: former UK
   chancellor
David **Davis**: Brexit secretary
Democratic Party (PD): Italy
Democratic Party: US
Bob **Dole**: US presidential candidate
Bernard **Donoughue**: adviser to Jim
   Callaghan

Iain **Duncan Smith**: former Conservative leader

Recep **Erdogan**: president of Turkey

Íñigo **Errejón**: Podemos' political secretary

Nigel **Farage**: former leader of UKIP

Werner **Faymann**: former Austrian chancellor

François **Fillon**: former French PM

Five Star Movement (M5S): Italy

Forza Italia party: Italy

Norman **Fowler**: former Conservative minister

Free Democratic Party: Germany

Freedom Party (FPÖ): Austria

Front National: France

Colonel **Gaddafi**: former Libyan dictator

Alexander **Gauland**: AfD politician

Julia **Gillard**: former Australian PM

Philip **Gould**: Labour adviser and guru

Michael **Gove**: former Justice Secretary and leading 'Out' campaigner

Green Party: Austria

Beppe **Grillo**: founder of the Five Star Movement, Italy

William **Hague**: former Conservative leader

Joe **Haines**: press secretary for Harold Wilson

Philip **Hammond**: UK chancellor

Pauline **Hanson**: leader of the One Nation party in Australia

Ted **Heath**: former PM

Norbert **Hofer**: far-right-wing presidential candidate in Austria, Freedom Party

François **Hollande**: French president

Michael **Howard**: former Conservative leader and Home Secretary

Tristram **Hunt**: former Labour MP

Pablo **Iglesias** Turrión: leader of Podemos in Spain

Diane **James**: briefly UKIP leader

Roy **Jenkins**: former leader of the SDP

Jobbik party: Hungary

Boris **Johnson**: Foreign Secretary

Lyndon B. **Johnson**: former US president

Lionel **Jospin**: former French PM

Sir Mervyn **King**: former Governor of the Bank of England

Neil **Kinnock**: former Labour leader

Pia **Kjærsgaard**: founder of the Danish People's Party

Oskar **Lafontaine**: former German minister

Nigel **Lawson**: former UK chancellor

Left Bloc: part of a coalition in Portugal

Left Party: Germany

Jean-Marie **Le Pen**: Front National, France

Marine **Le Pen**: Front National

Enrico **Letta**: Italian PM

Damian **McBride**: Gordon Brown's press secretary

John **McDonnell**: Labour MP

Emmanuel **Macron**: French minister

John **Major**: former PM

Peter **Mandelson**: former Labour politician and adviser

Catarina **Martins**: leader of Portugal's Left Bloc

Theresa **May**: PM

Angela **Merkel**: German chancellor

David **Miliband**: former Foreign Secretary

Ed **Miliband**: former Labour leader

François **Mitterrand**: former French president

Walter **Mondale**: former US vice-president

Mario **Monti**: former Italian PM

Chantal **Mouffe**: Belgian political theorist

Lisa **Nandy**: MP for Wigan

National Democratic Party of Germany (NPD)

Northern League (Lega Nord): Italy

Paul **Nuttall**: current leader of UKIP

Barack **Obama**: former US President

Occupy movement: global movement against social inequality

One Nation party: Australia

George **Osborne**: former Chancellor of the Exchequer

Party for Freedom: Holland

Pasok: Greek socialist party

Mike **Pence**: US vice-president

People's Party (PP): Spain

Frauke **Petry**: chairwoman of the Alternative for Germany (AfD) party

Podemos: left-wing party in Spain

Virginia **Raggi**: Mayor of Rome

Mariano **Rajoy**: Spanish PM

Matteo **Renzi**: former Italian PM

Republican Party: US

Marco **Rubio**: Florida senator

Kevin **Rudd**: former PM of Australia

Mark **Rutte**: Dutch prime minister

Paul **Ryan**: Speaker of the US House of Representatives

Alex **Salmond**: former SNP leader

Matteo **Salvini**: leader of Italy's Northern League

Antonis **Samaras**: former PM of Greece

Pedro **Sánchez**: former leader of PSOE in Spain

Bernie **Sanders**: US presidential candidate

Nicolas **Sarkozy**: former French president

Anthony **Scaramucci**: Trump adviser

Gerhard **Schroeder**: former German chancellor

Martin **Schulz**: leader of Germany's SDP

Scottish National Party (SNP): UK

Peter **Skaarup**: leader of the Danish People's Party

Social Democratic Party of Austria (SPÖ): Austria

Social Democratic Party (SPD): Germany

Social Democratic Party (SDP): UK

Social Democrats: Denmark

Spanish Socialist Workers' Party (PSOE)

Heinz-Christian **Strache**: Freedom Party

Nicola **Sturgeon**: SNP leader

Larry **Summers**: former US Secretary of the Treasury and economist

Sweden Democrats party

Syriza: left-wing party in Greece

Tea Party: US

Margaret **Thatcher**: former PM

Justin **Trudeau**: Canadian prime minister

Donald **Trump**: US president

Alexis **Tsipras**: leader of Greece's Syriza party

Malcolm **Turnbull**: Australian PM

Alexander **Van der Bellen**: President of Austria

Yanis **Varoufakis**: former Greek finance minister

William **Waldegrave**: former Conservative minister

Geert **Wilders**: founder of the Dutch Party for Freedom

Harold **Wilson**: former PM

Stewart **Wood**: a senior adviser to Gordon Brown

Steven **Woolfe**: UKIP leadership candidate

NOTES

22 Interview with Geert Wilders, *The Guardian*, 16 February 2008

23 Radio Sweden, 2 August 2014

24 *The Guardian*, 13 December 2014

25 *Daily Mail*, 28 January 2016

CHAPTER TWO: The Rise of the Left-Wing Outsiders

1 BBC News website, 22 January 2015

2 Quote from Alexis Tsipras' victory speech in Athens, *The Times*, 26 January 2015

3 Jeremy Corbyn speech, itv.com, 3 August 2015

4 BBC Radio 4, 17 March 2014

5 *The Corbyn Story*, BBC Radio 4, 11 July 2016

6 Politico, 4 December 2015

7 *Financial Times*, 22 September 2016

8 *The Independent*, 21 December 2015

9 *The Observer*, 17 September 2016

10 Ibid.

11 *The Washington Post*, 4 December 2016

12 *The New York Times*, 9 June 2015

13 cnn.com, 21 January 2016

CHAPTER THREE: Choosing to Be Powerless: The Mainstream Left

1 Tony Blair, Labour Party conference, 27 September 2005

2 George W. Bush at the Republican National Convention, as he accepted the nomination on 18 August 1988

3 Bill Clinton campaign brochure, 1992

4 Tony Blair, Labour Party spring conference, 14 February 1995; and in many subsequent speeches from Blair and Gordon Brown

5 *The Corbyn Story*, BBC Radio 4, 11 July 2016

6 Tony Blair and Gerhard Schroeder, 'Europe: The Third Way / Die Neue Mitte', 1998

7 Politico, 7 March 2016

8 Ibid.

9 *The Daily Telegraph*, 31 March 2016

10 *The Guardian*, 9 May 2016

11 *The Independent*, 9 June 2015

12 Interview on *The World This Weekend*, BBC Radio 4, 16 May 2015

13 *The Observer*, 11 July 2015

14 Chantal Mouffe, *Podemos: In the Name of the People*, London, 2016

15 Ibid.

CHAPTER FOUR: Choosing to Be Powerless: The Mainstream Right

1 Barack Obama, 'State of the Union Address', 25 January 2011

2 Ryan Lizza, *The New Yorker*, 6 August 2012

3 Quoted in an article by Stan
   Tenenhaus, *The New Republic*,
   24 August 2011
4 *Financial Times*, 11 November
   2016

5 Tony Blair, *The New European*,
   28 October 2016
6 *Today* programme, BBC Radio 4,
   28 October 2016
7 Interview in the *New Statesman*,
   21 December 1996

CHAPTER FIVE: The Powerlessness of Power

1 *The Independent*, 2 April 2009
2 Reuters, 20 June 2012
3 Nick Clegg, *Politics: Between the
   Extremes*, London, 2016
4 *The Daily Telegraph*,
   15 September 2016
5 *Huffington Post*, 20 October,
   2016
6 Ibid.
7 *The Washington Post*,
   30 November 2012

8 *Financial Times*, 30 November
   2012
9 Obama White House archives,
   30 November 2012
10 *The Washington Post*, 9 May 2014
11 'Barack Obama and Doris
   Kearns Goodwin: The Ultimate
   Exit Interview', *Vanity Fair*,
   21 September 2016
12 Interview on *This Week, Next
   Week*, BBC 1, 5 June 1988

CHAPTER SIX: Taking Back Control

1 Dominic Cummings, 'How the
   Brexit referendum was won', *The
   Spectator*, 9 January 2017
2 J. D. Vance, *Hillbilly Elegy: A
   Memoir of a Family and Culture
   in Crisis*, London and New York,
   2016
3 Barack Obama, final press
   conference, 18 January 2017
4 Politico, 10 May 2016
5 *The New York Times*, 13
   November 2016

6 Ibid.
7 David Axelrod interview with
   Barack Obama, 'The Axe Files',
   University of Chicago Institute
   of Politics & CNN, podcast,
   26 December 2016
8 Theresa May, speech to the
   World Economic Forum, Davos,
   19 January 2017
9 Theresa May, 'Plan for Britain',
   17 January 2017

CHAPTER SEVEN: Trust

1 Lexington column, *The
   Economist*, 20 December 2016
2 Chris Cillizza, *The Washington
   Post*, 9 November 2016

3 Angela Merkel, speaking in
   China after the G20 Summit, 5
   September 2016
4 William Waldegrave, *A Different
   Kind of Weather*, London, 2015

5 *Time* magazine, 24 May 2016
6 John Humphrys' interview of Andrew Gilligan, *Today* programme, BBC Radio 4, 29 May 2003
7 *The Mail on Sunday*, 1 June 2003

CHAPTER EIGHT: Powerlessness and the Media

1 *The Guardian*, 6 January 2017
2 John Birt and Peter Jay, *The Times*, 28 February 1975
3 reuters.com, 13 June 2007
4 *The Washington Post*, 16 June 2015
5 Joe Walsh quoted in the *Illinois Review*, 28 December 2016
6 Cover story, *National Review*, 6 September 1993
7 *The Washington Post*, 23 December 2015
8 Gabe Hobbs, quoted in a *Washington Post* article, 23 December 2015
9 *The Washington Post*, 23 December 2015
10 Steve Richards, 'Soundbite Politics', Reuters Foundation Paper, July 1994
11 *The Guardian*, 8 November 2010
12 Agnès Poirier, interview with the author, 3 March 2017
13 Thomas Kielinger, interview with the author, 3 March 2017
14 *The New York Times*, 13 November 2016
15 NBC News, 25 August 2016
16 *The Guardian*, 14 November 2016
17 *The New Yorker* website, November 2016
18 Toronto *Star*, November 2016
19 Jay Rosen, *The Guardian*, 22 November 2016

CONCLUSION

1 *The New York Times*, 24 March 2017
2 Roy Jenkins, *Evening Standard*, 14 June 2001
3 Interview by the author with James Callaghan, *New Statesman*, December 1996
4 Theresa May, speech at the Conservative Party conference, 5 October 2016
5 Lisa Nandy, speech at the Institute for Public Policy Research, 7 March 2017
6 Chuka Umunna, *New Statesman*, 6 March 2017

ACKNOWLEDGEMENTS

My thanks to Mike Harpley at Atlantic, who had this idea long before Brexit and the election of Donald Trump. Mike was generous enough to allow me to interpret his idea in my own way, partly as a means to explore the constraints on democratic politics that are too easily overlooked. I am also grateful to all those at Atlantic who met such a tight deadline, namely Mandy Greenfield, Sally Sargeant and Chris Bell. Thanks also to my agent, Andrew Gordon, at David Higham Associates, who is brilliantly forensic and encouraging, qualities especially valued when writing speedily about fast moving events. I am also grateful to Professor Alasdair Blair who took the time to read the manuscript.

INDEX

INDEX

Bush, Jeb 89

Caffier, Lorenz 28
Callaghan, Jim 156, 157, 283–4
Camden Town, London 74, 75–6
Cameron, David 16, 17, 110, 172–3, 188, 253
  and 2010 general election 64
  and 2015 general election 25, 172
  and EU referendum 7, 164, 175–6, 234
  and George Osborne 147–54
  and the media 255, 256, 293
  as party leader 5, 73, 114
  as prime minister 116, 140
  resignation 38
Campbell, Alastair 162, 226–7, 232, 233
Canada 4, 64
Carney, Mark 188
Carter, Jimmy 104
Casaleggio, Gianroberto 49
Centeno, Mário 81
centralized control 238–40
'centre-ground' consensus 97–8
Channel 4 250–51, 261
Cheney, Dick 59
China 187, 192, 202–3
Chirac, Jacques 133, 241
Christian Democratic Union of Germany
  (CDU) 28, 122, 168–70, 177
Churchill, Winston 236
Civic Choice (Italy) 210
Clarke, Ken 253
Clegg, Nick 114, 155, 171–2, 179–80
climate change 15, 50, 198–9
Clinton, Bill 100–102, 103–4, 107, 113, 136,
  202–3, 223–5, 243, 258
  impeachment 223–4
Clinton, Hillary 3, 180, 211
  and 2016 presidential campaign 39, 47, 65,
    115–17, 119, 120–21, 130, 131–2, 135,
    192, 198, 203–4, 212–13, 266, 273
  and allegations of corruption 224–5, 244,
    258, 269–70
  and Democrat nomination 7, 86–7, 92
  and the media 262–3
coalitions 166–74, 179–80, 212, 291–2
'cocooned elite' 250–51, 275, 282
Commodities Futures Modernization Act 104
Common Market 42
Conservative Party (UK) 2, 7, 12, 62, 73, 107,
  123, 155
  coalition government 17
  conference (2016) 285–6
  general election (1992) 100–102

general election (2005) 25
media 16–17, 216, 220–21, 259–61
modernization 147–50
Cook, Robin 107, 231, 232
Corbyn, Jeremy 2, 8, 65, 72–8, 90, 91, 122,
  153, 238, 252, 282
Cornwall, England 117
corruption 236–8
Costa, António 79, 81
Cruddas, Jon 131
Cruz, Ted 90
Cummings, Dominic 37–8, 190

Dacre, Paul 255
Daily Mail 255
Dale, Daniel 269
Danish People's Party 43, 47, 52, 54–5
  policies 55
Darling, Alistair 117, 163–4
Davis, David 77
Day, Robin 262
Death of American Virtue: Clinton vs. Starr, The
  (Gormley) 224
defections 176
Democratic Party of Italy (PD) 48
Democratic Party (US) 2, 7, 8, 64, 86–8, 92,
  98–9, 107, 181–4, 186, 243
Denmark 30, 43, 54–5
Dole, Bob 257
Donoughue, Bernard 284
Duffy, Gillian 245
Duncan Smith, Iain 150

Ecclestone, Bernie 222
Economist, The 30, 209
education 197
Erdogan, Recep Tayyip 4
Errejón, Íñigo 85, 132, 134
European Central Bank 68, 81, 89, 187, 191
European Stability Mechanism 71
European Union (EU) 5, 40–2, 69–71, 81–2,
  167, 170, 289–90
  free movement 24–5, 120, 146, 206
  immigrants 31–2
  refugees 30, 127–8
  see also Brexit
eurosceptics 5, 127, 148
eurozone 68, 80, 82, 89, 91, 187
Evening Standard 253
Exchange Rate Mechanism 253
expenses scandal (UK) 239–40

Facebook 265, 267

310

INDEX

INDEX